Dedication

I dedicate this book to all adults that are just "hanging in there" and especially to Sandy who hangs with me every day.

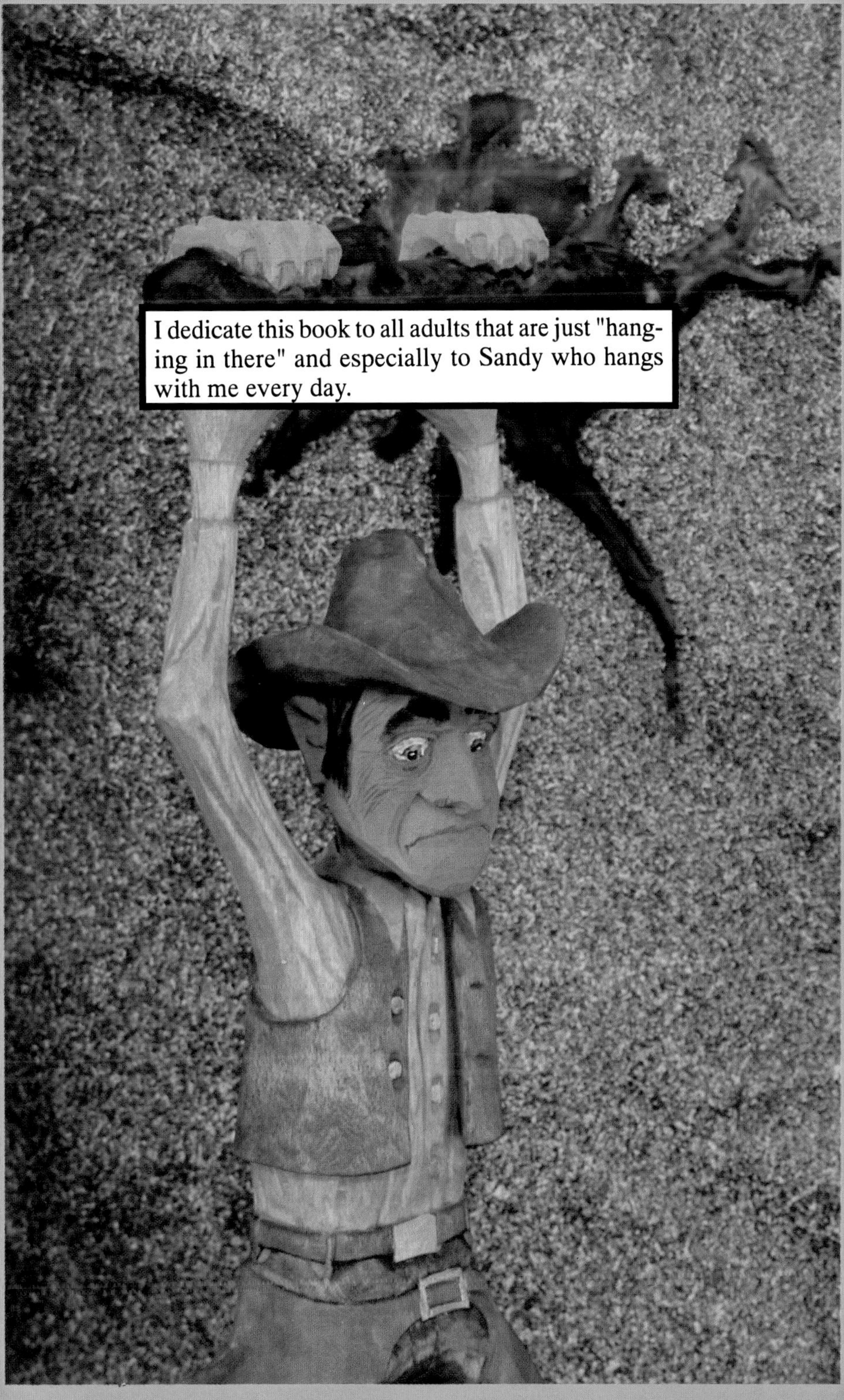

INTRODUCTION

I call the subject of this book "Hanging in There." I laughingly tell people that it represents my philosophy of life and to some extent that is true. With the hectic pace of today's world and the burden of responsibilities so characteristic of our adult population, I often do feel that I *am* just hanging in there.

This piece was first carved in response to a few of my doctoral students who were complaining about the multiple burdens of taking classes, writing dissertations, and standing a two day preliminary examination while attending to the daily loads of earning a living, parenting and spousing. When I shared the carving with the students and dedicated it to their plight, it brought a chuckle or two and did seem to relieve their anxieties.

The carving I completed for the photography in this book I left with Peter and Nancy Schiffer as an expression of my appreciation for their gracious hospitality during my stay in Atglen, Pennsylvania while putting this and other books together. It was also a special expression of thanks for their contributions to the art and craft of woodcarving through the publication of many excellent books.

Blanks for the project in this book may be ordered from the author whose address is, until at least the year 2005, 11052 Sandhurst Drive, Boise, Idaho 83709. If you are ever in Boise, give him a call at (208) 322-1463. He enjoys chewing the fat with other carvers. Just beware of the bull!

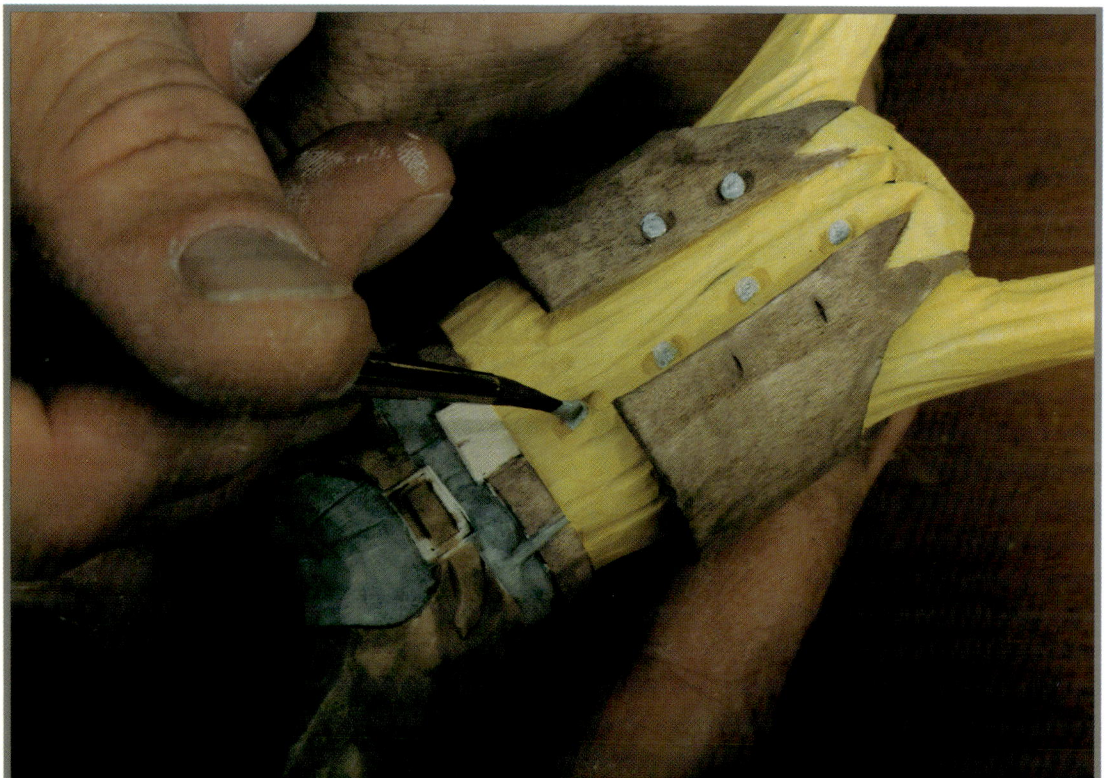

Patterns

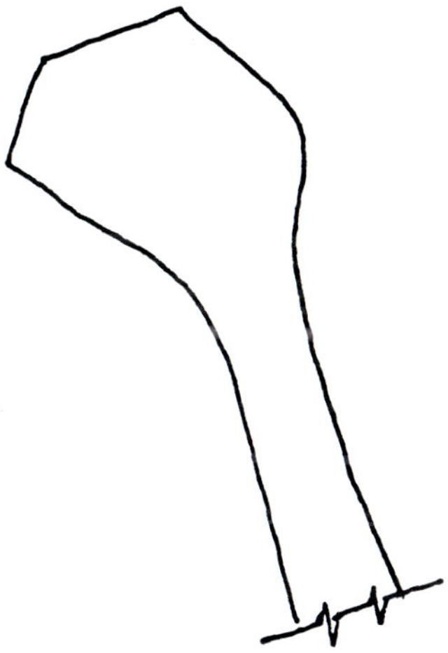

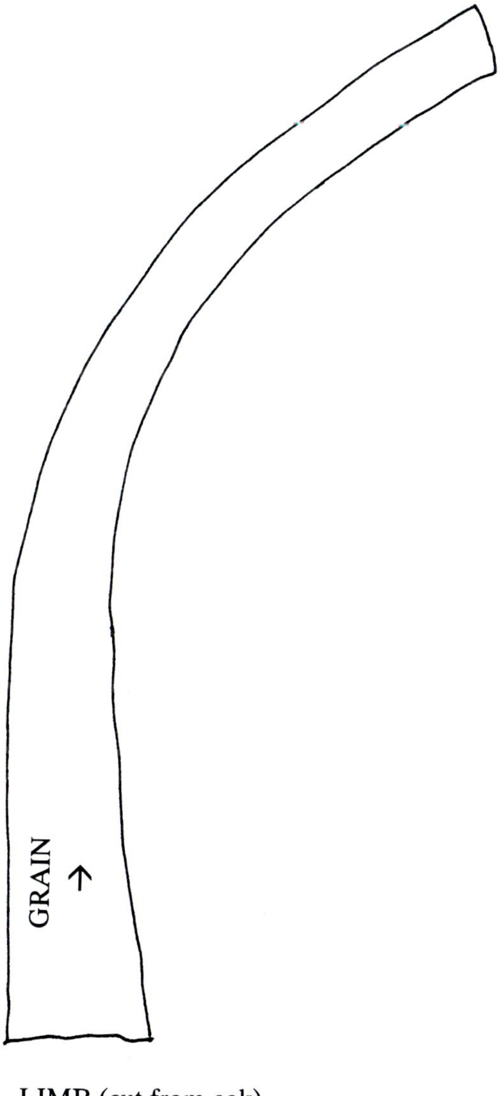

LIMB (cut from oak)

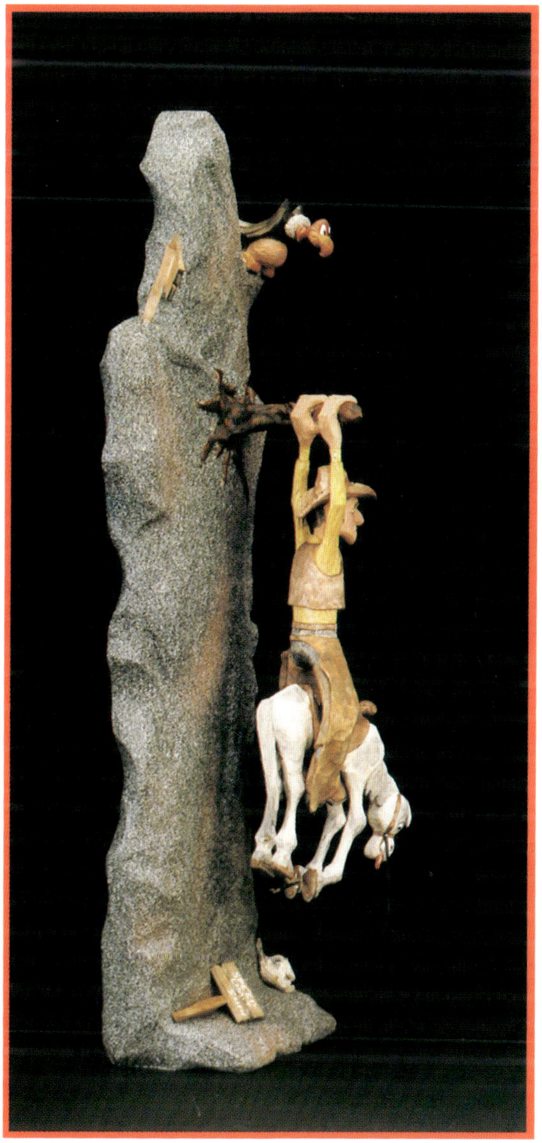

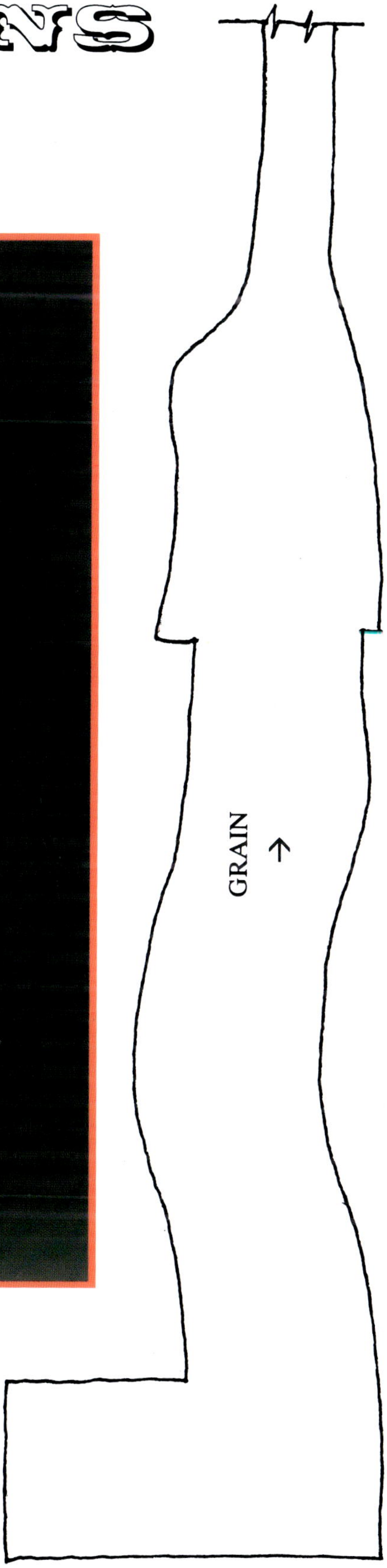

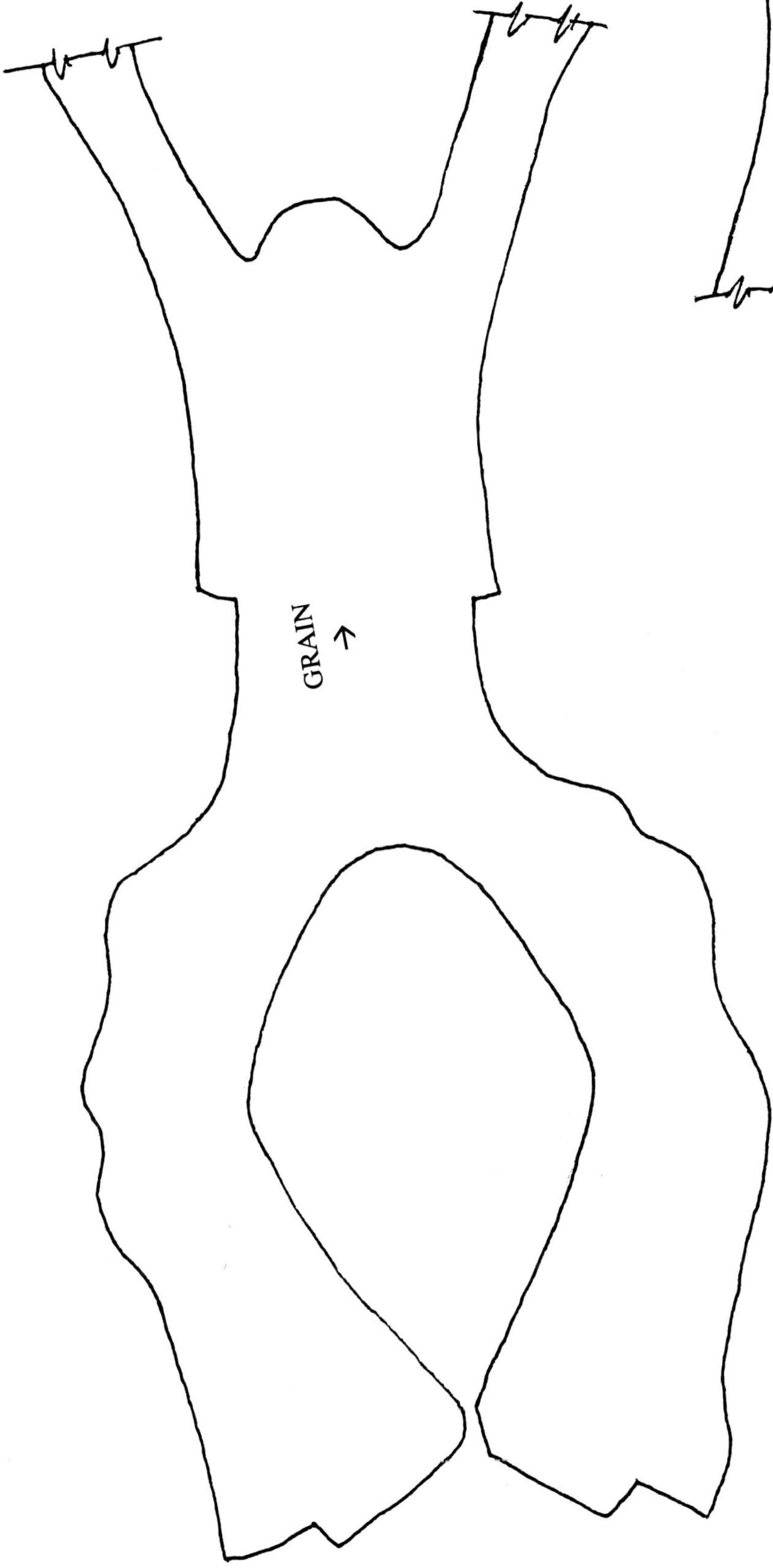
GRAIN

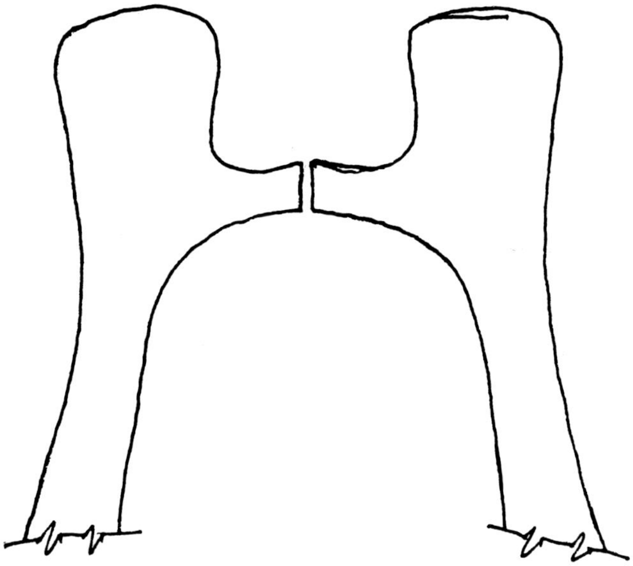

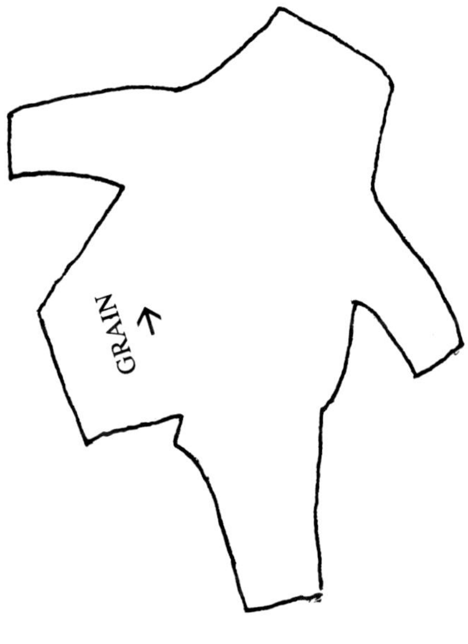
GRAIN

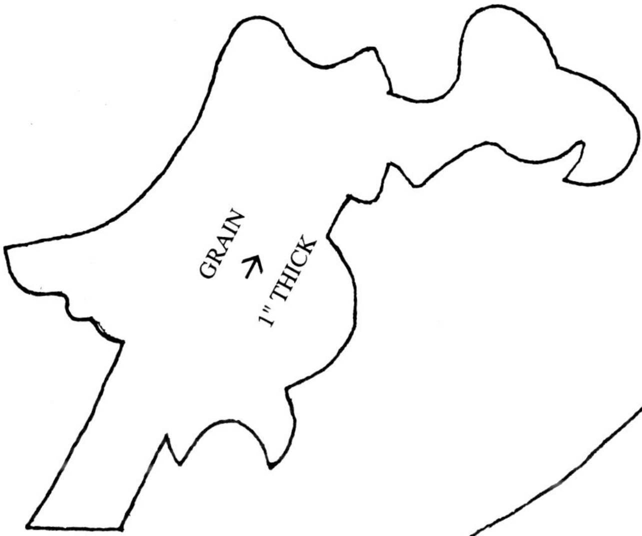

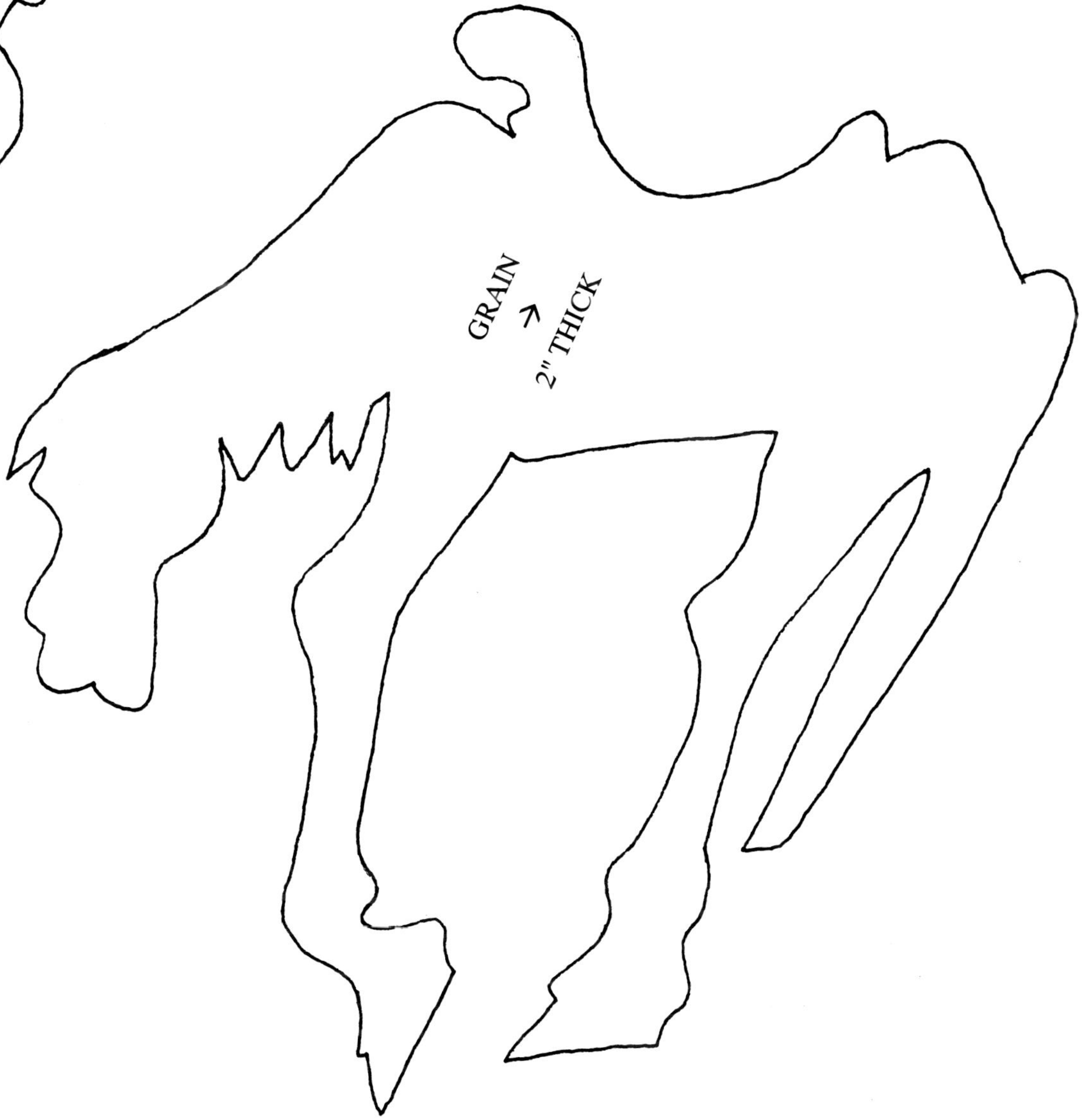

TOOLS

Here are the tools you will need for this project:

I use a Kevlar carving glove impervious to knife cuts, a series of bench knives, a Foredom or Dremel rotary power tool with a Kutzall burr, and a band saw. The gouges I use are a 1/4" #9 gouge, 1/2" #3 fishtail gouge, three different size V tools (1/4", 1/8", and a micro 2 mm or 1/16" V gouge), a 3/16" deep gouge, a 1/8" #5, and a 1/2" #7 gouge, 3/32" deep gouge (deep gouges are also called veiners).

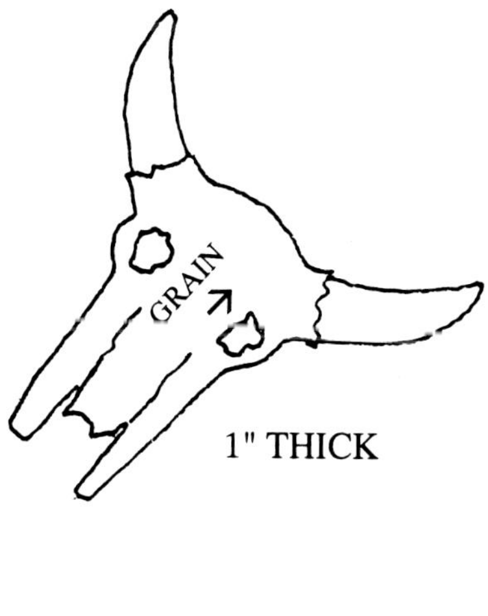

PROJECT CARVING

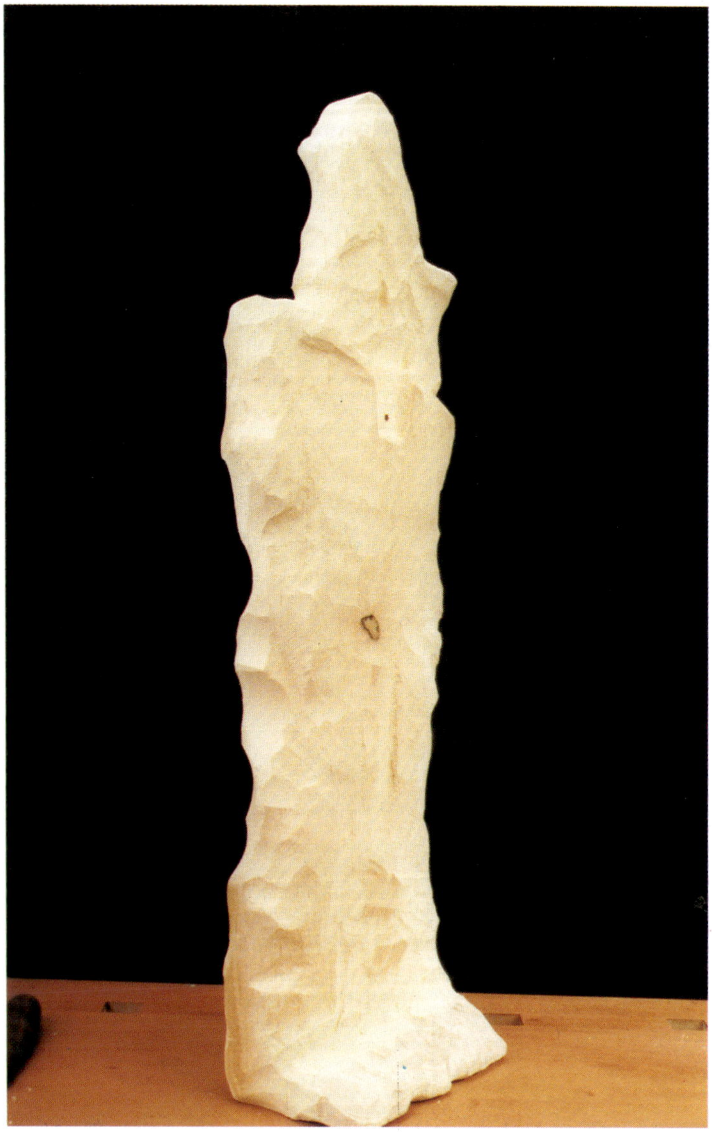

This hunk of rock was cut from 2" x 8" wide, 26" high sugar pine. You could use any kind of wood available. The important characteristic should be the ease with which you can form several features. The first feature that is important is the trail along the upper 25% of the rock.

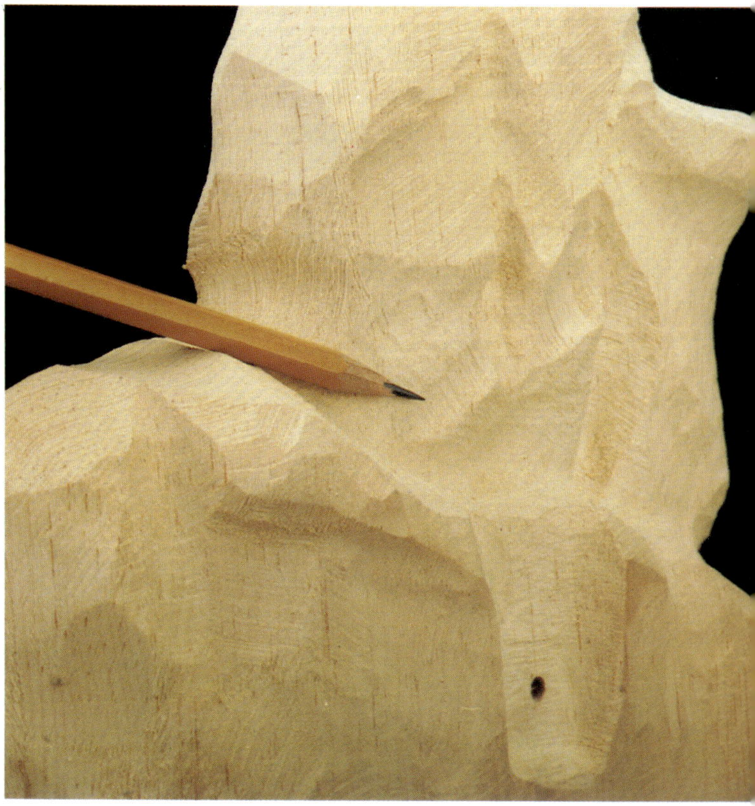

The trail is shown here.

Another feature that's important is the location on the rock of the limb from which the cowboy hangs. The limb should be 17" to 18" from the bottom of the rock.

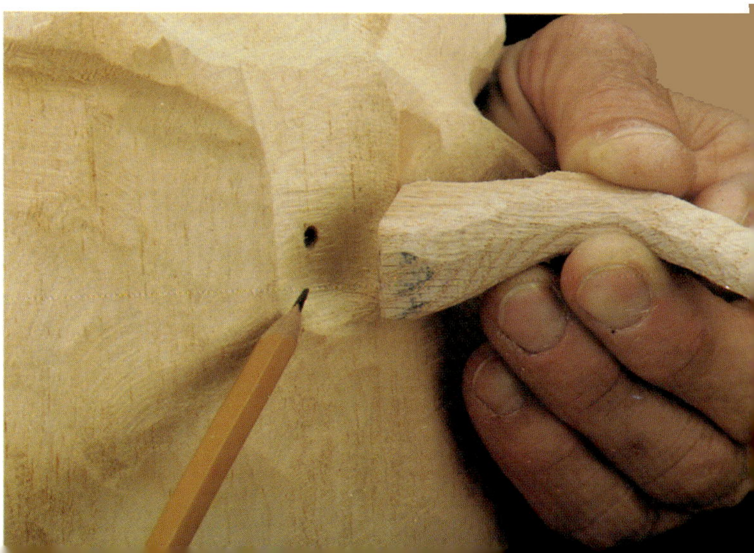

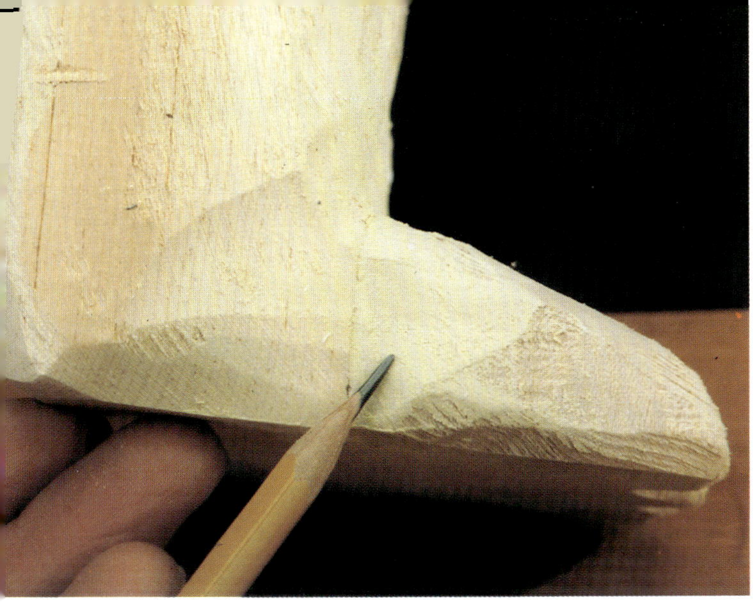

The ledge at the base of the rock was made from a short (3") piece of 2" thick wood and glued to the bottom of the cliff face. Cracks were filled with wood putty.

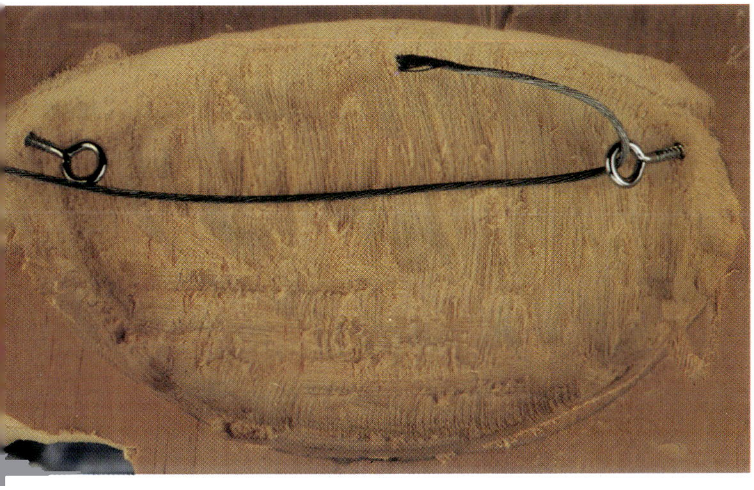

On the back of the cliff I have recessed an area about 1/2" deep that will allow the carving to hang flush with the wall after eyelets and hanging wire have been installed.

The cliff's finish can be left coarse because of the nature of the paint we'll use to give the wood a rocky appearance. These are the two paints we'll use. The darker Granite texture will be sprayed over the entire piece of wood. Allow to dry. Then the lighter Stone texture will be used to break the monotony of the darker paint.

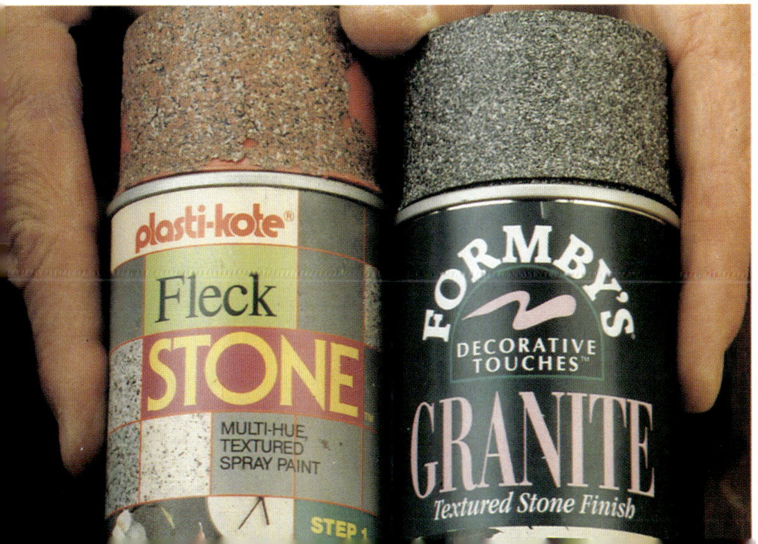

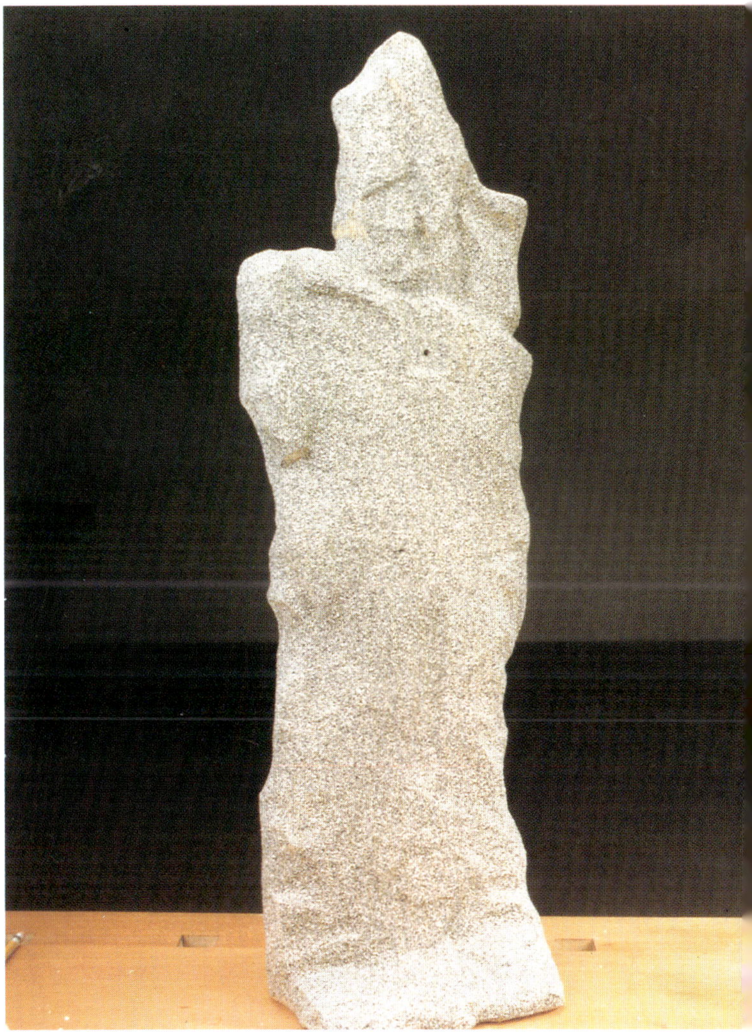

The first coat has been applied.

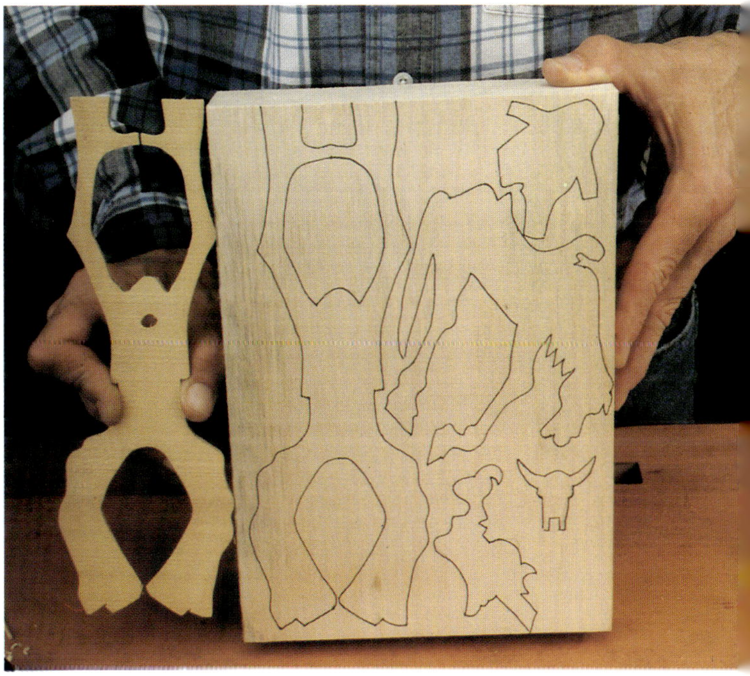

I have transfered the paper patterns—as drawn in this book—to my 2" thick basswood block. Here are the five principle pieces required for this carving.

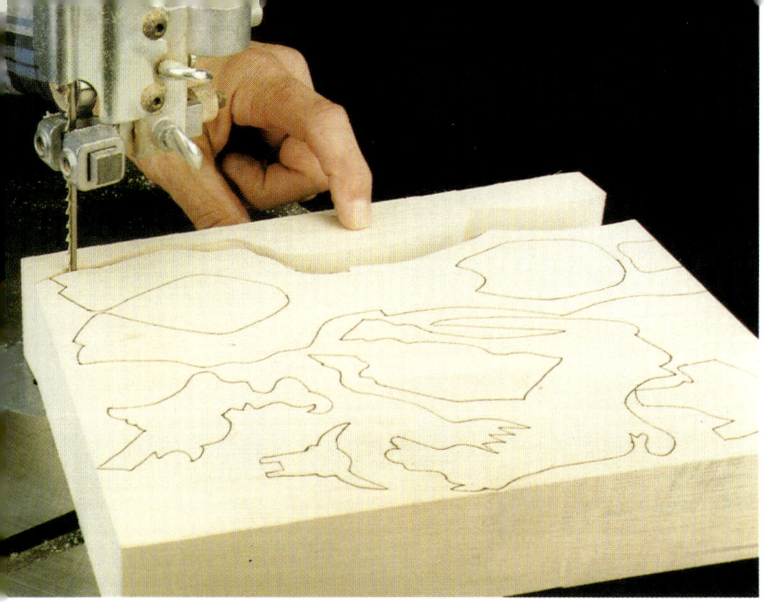

This wood scrap should be cut first and saved for later use in cutting the profile of the cowboy's body. Continue cutting out the front views with the band saw.

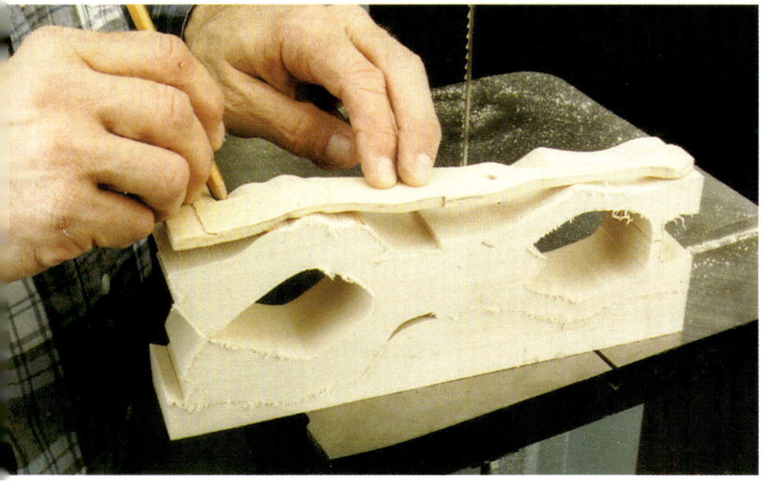

With the cowboy's body placed onto the block of wood that we saved, draw the profile of cowboy's body. This profile was created using Bojangles, the flexible pattern of a cowboy used in my first book "Carving Cowboys with Cleve Taylor."

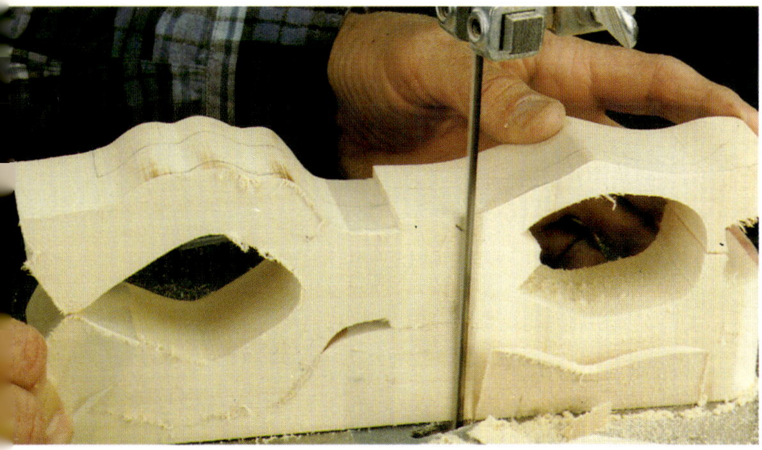

Cut the profile of cowboy's body. You may want to use tape to hold the two pieces of wood securely together.

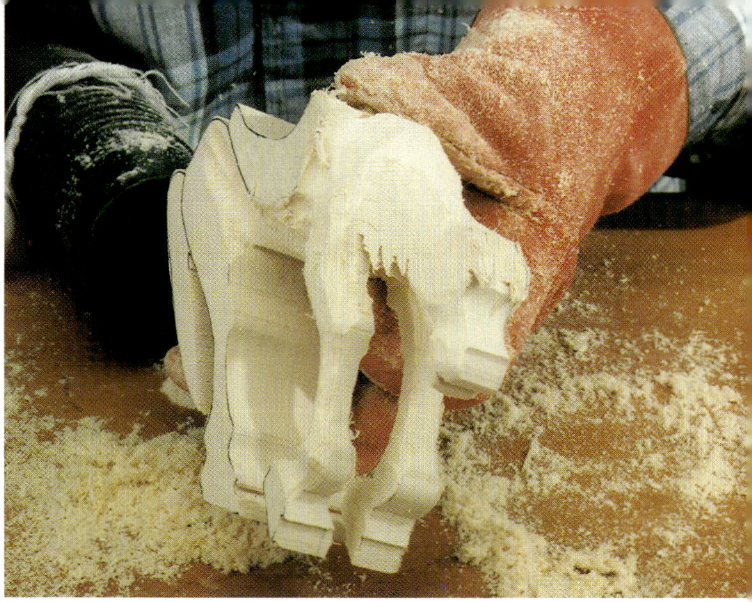

Lay out the front view of the horse and sketch in the saddle and legs on either side. Start removing unwanted wood with either a Foredom tool with a Kutzall burr or with gouges and knives. We are interested in removing excess wood from between the legs and along the neck and head. Generally shape the horse and saddle to a rough resemblance to the finished carving.

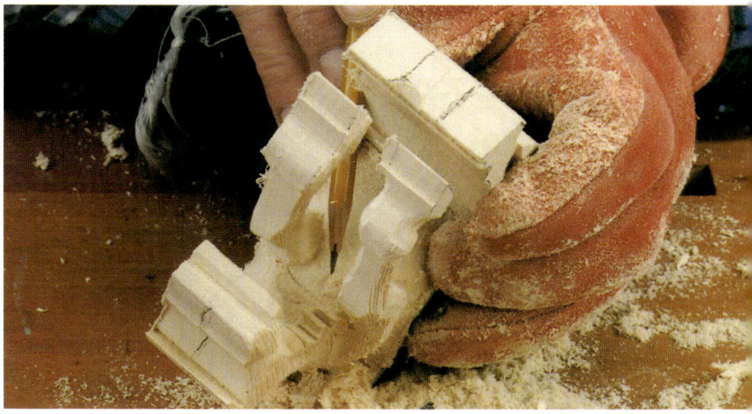

We want this area between the upper part of the front legs—where they join the body—to be as widely separated as possible. This is where the cowboy's boots will be placed after assembly.

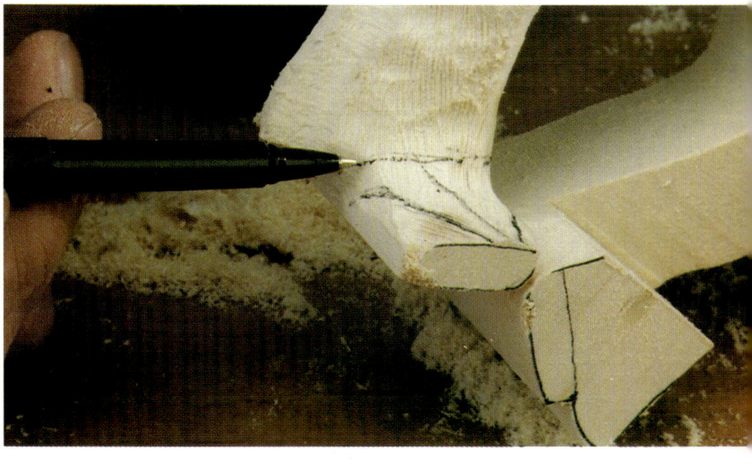

Moving to the cowboy, the first step in rough shaping the cowboy's body is to remove excess wood at the boot and chaps as shown. Sketch in the boot with the toe pointed in as much as possible.

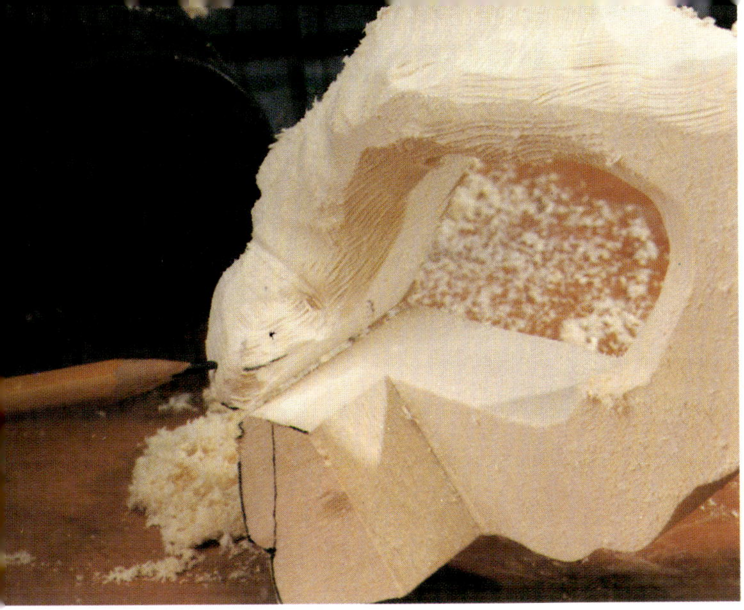

Continue to round the leg and remove wood from the front of the boot. The reason for getting the boots as slim as possible is that we must fit them between the horse's front legs.

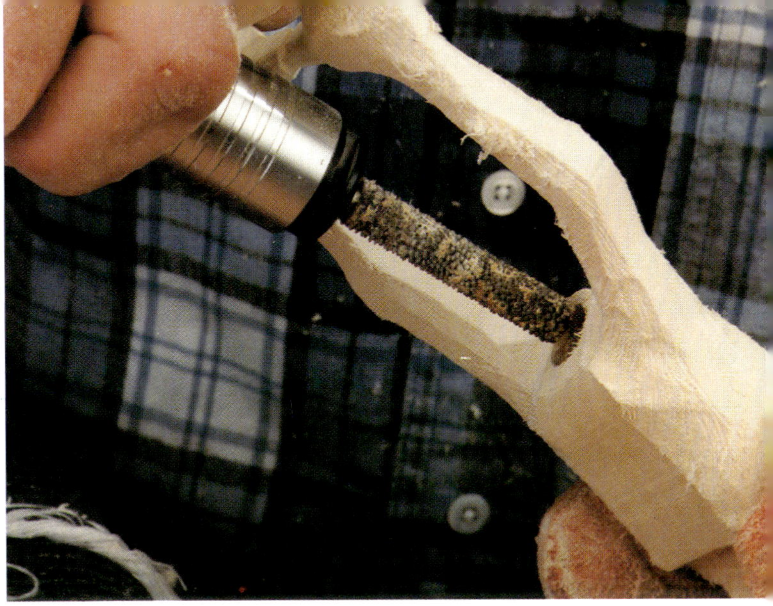

The final rough shaping step for the cowboy's body is to bore a hole into which the neck will fit, approximately 1/2" in diameter. The Foredom with the 1/4" Kutzall bit makes quick work of this.

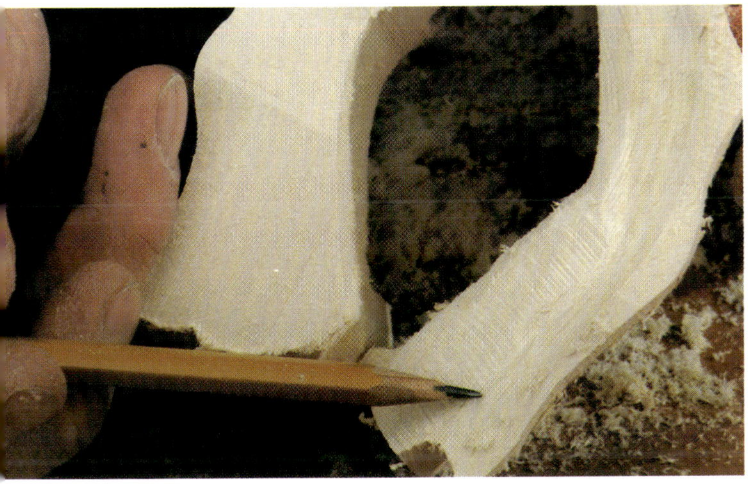

Along the back of the pant leg, accent the chaps and shape the back of the boot.

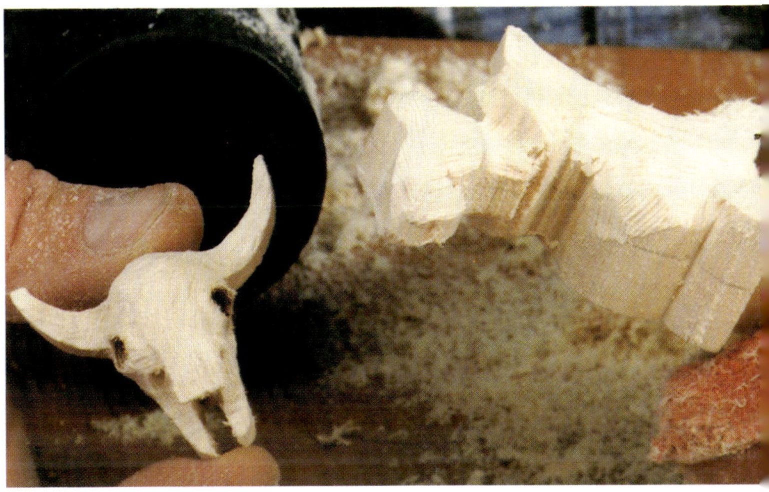

In a similar fashion, at this point draw in the front view and use the Foredom tool with the 1/4" Kutzall burr to remove unwanted wood from the buzzard and the bison's skull.

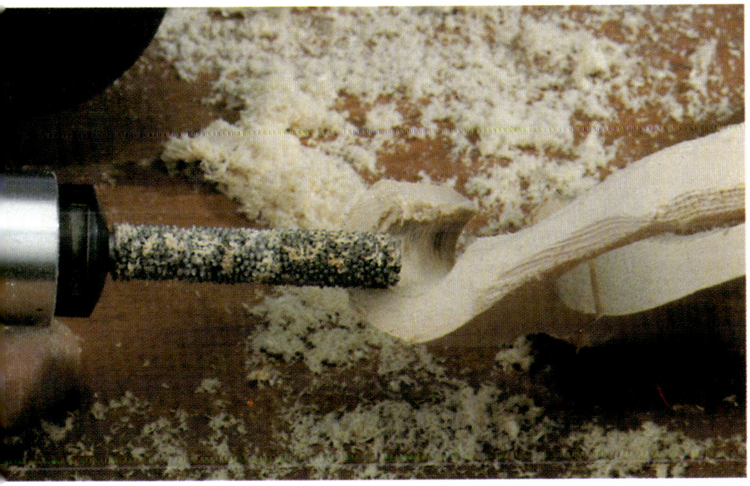

After rounding the arm, use a Foredom with a 1/4" Kutzall bit to shape the inside of the hand to fit the tree trunk from which the cowboy will hang.

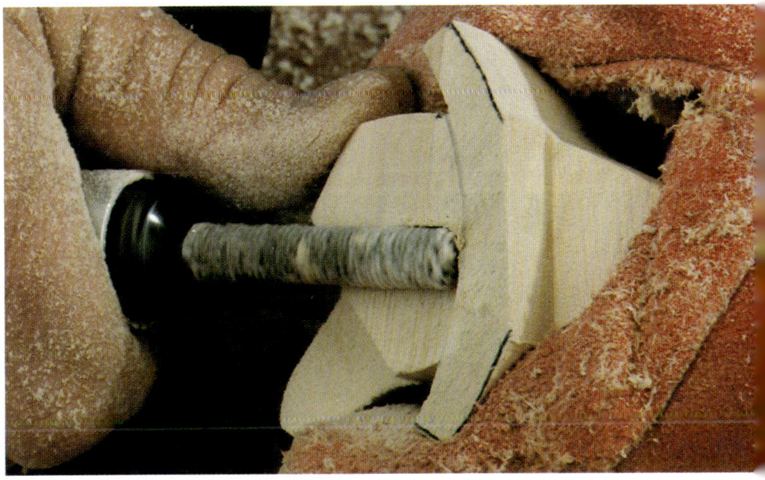

Moving on to the cowboy's head, draw in the bottom of the hat brim and remove wood below the brim on the cowboys head.

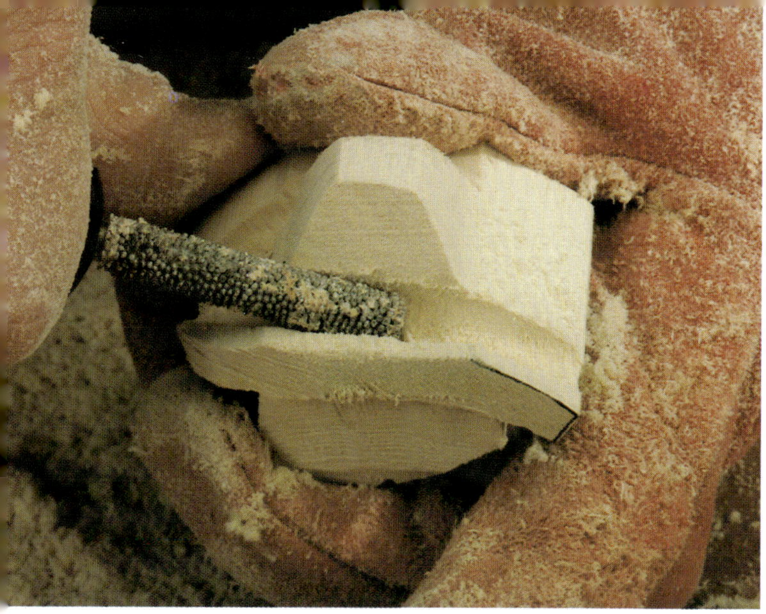

Shape the front of the hat brim with the 1/4" Kutzall bit and remove wood from between the crown of the hat and the brim.

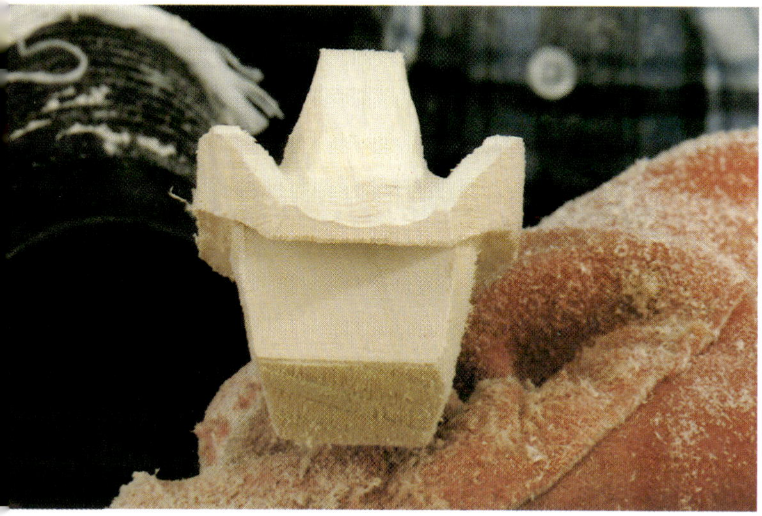

This is how the rough-cut head and rough-shaped hat should look at this point.

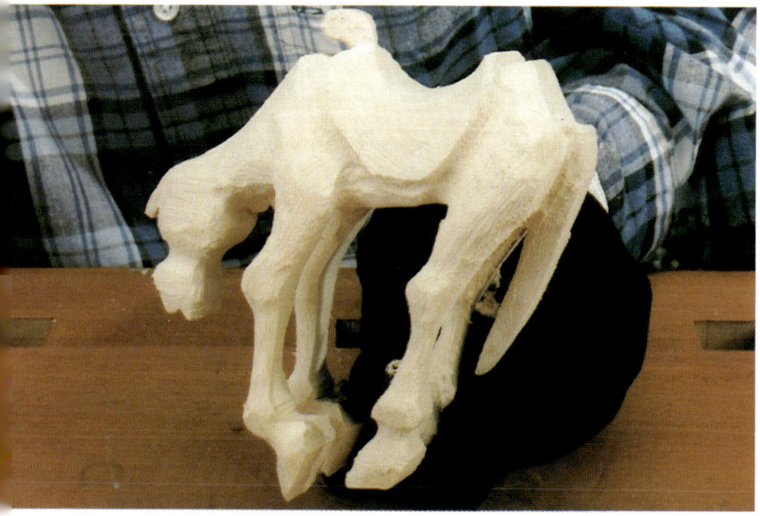

Returning to the horse, this is the roughly shaped blank we will begin to detail.

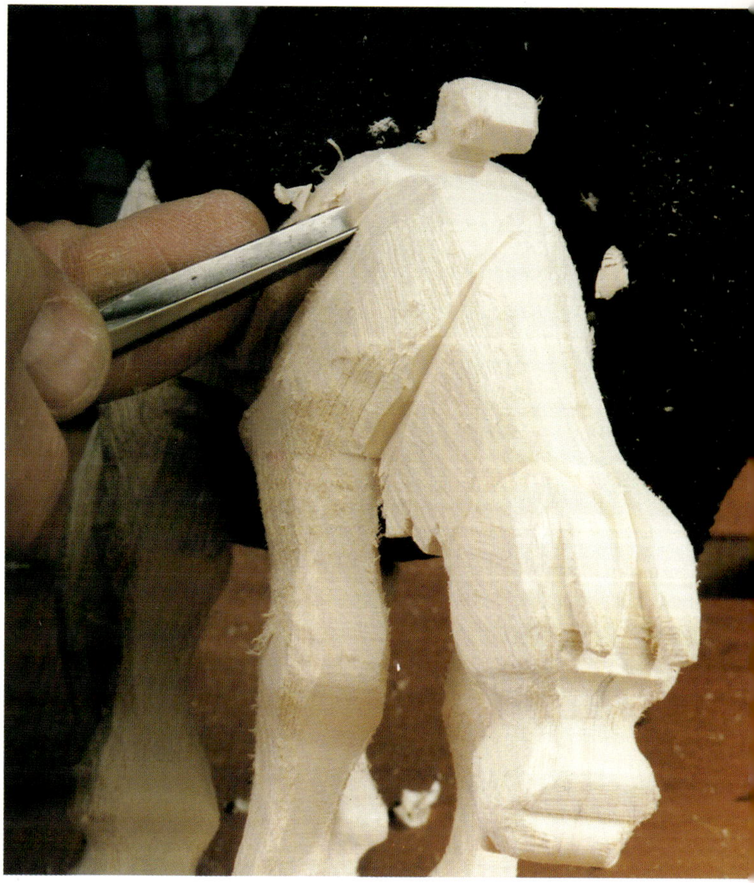

Outline the major features (the saddle, horse's mane, ears, and tail) with a large V tool.

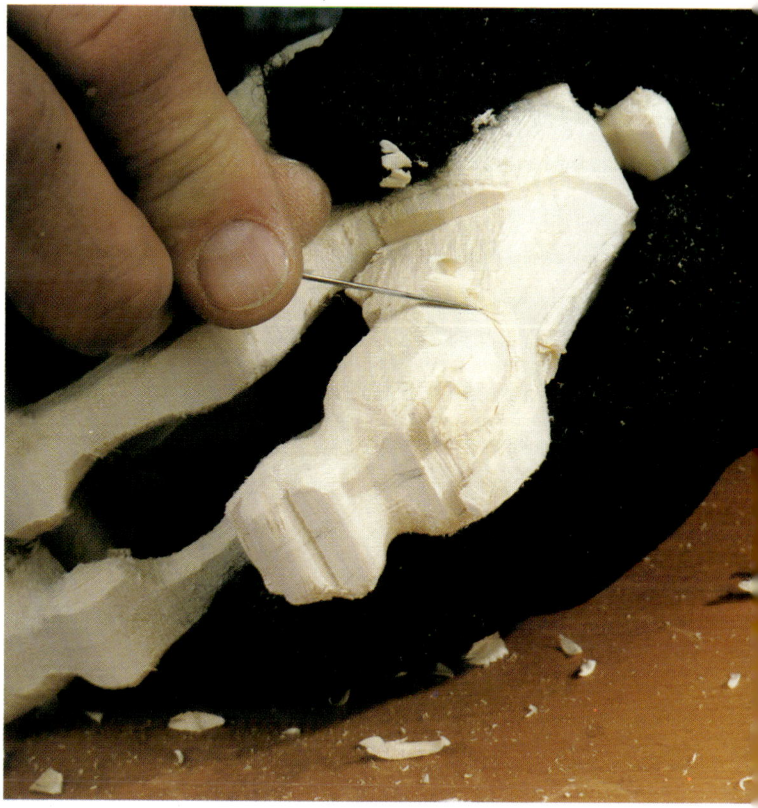

Begin cleaning off saw and burr marks and generally shaping the horse with a detail knife and gouges.

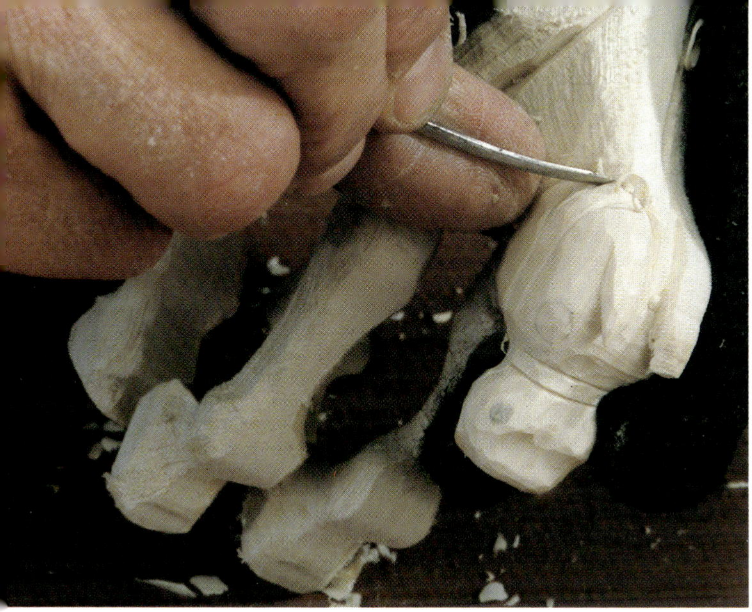

After cleaning the head of saw and burr marks, locate and pencil in the nostrils, eyes and bridle. Follow along either side of the bridle with a small 1/16" V tool and relieve the wood to the depth of the V tool cut.

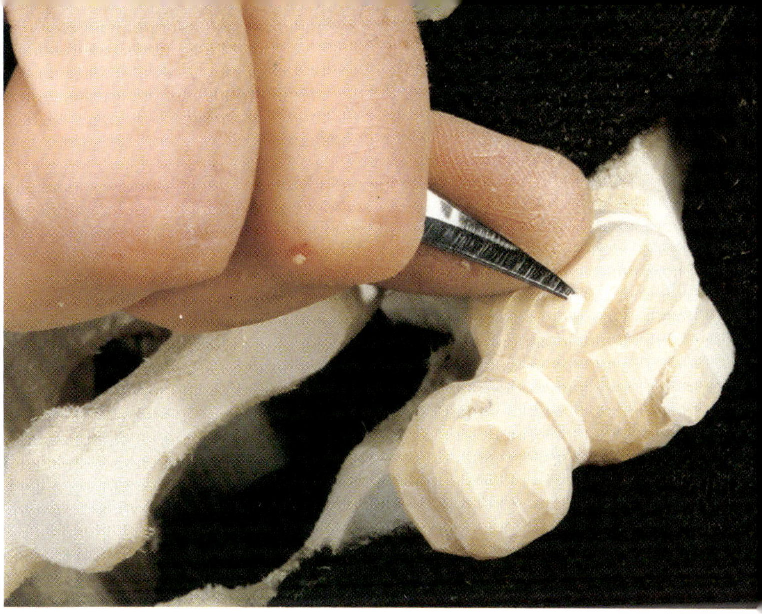

Round the eyeball with the tip of your detail knife.

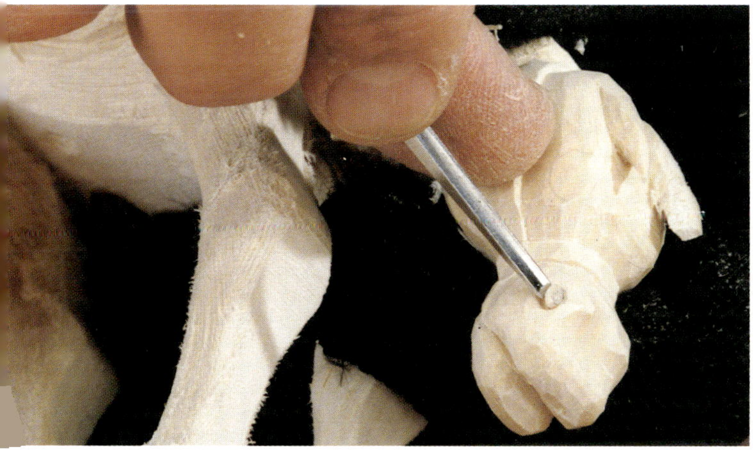

Using a small, shallow gouge, chip out a hole about 1/8" deep for the nostril.

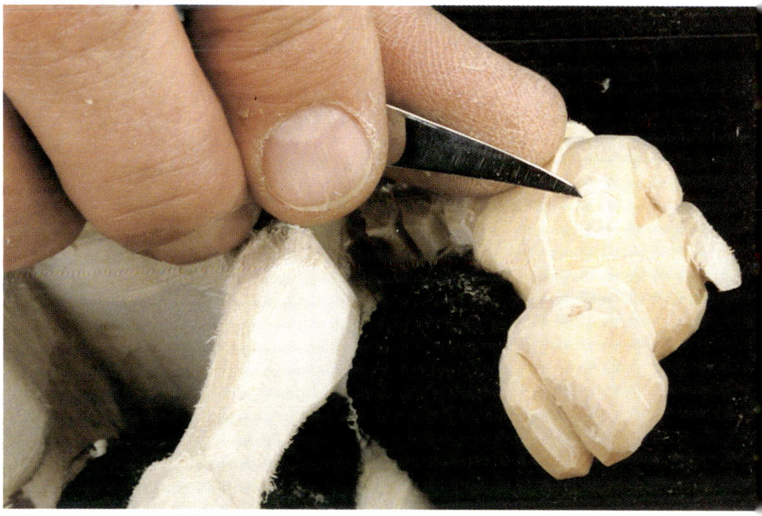

Sketch the upper eyelid and score them using the knife tip. Relieve the eyeball below the eyelid with the knife tip as well.

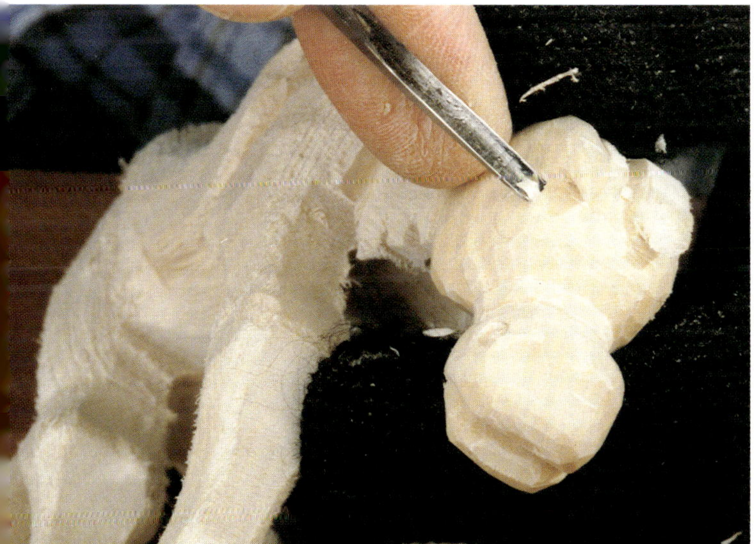

With a medium sized gouge cut in the eye.

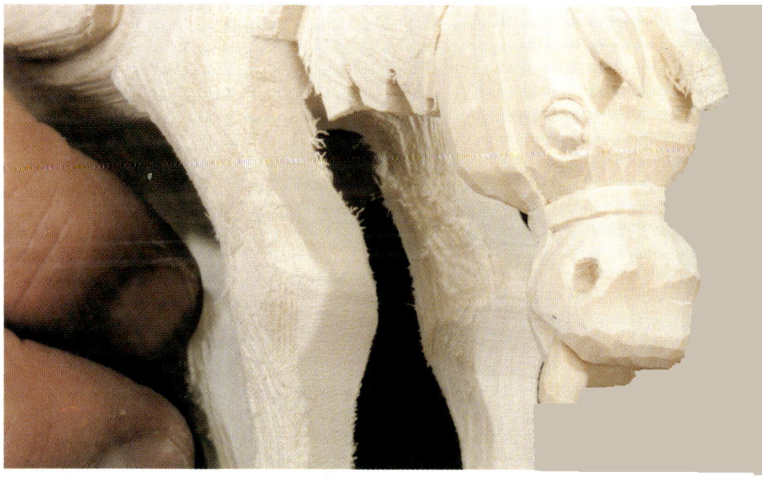

From a piece of scrap wood, carve yourself a tongue about 3/8" long x 3/16" wide. Prepare a small slot in the corner of the horse's mouth and, with Elmer's glue on the base of the tongue, insert the tongue into the slot.

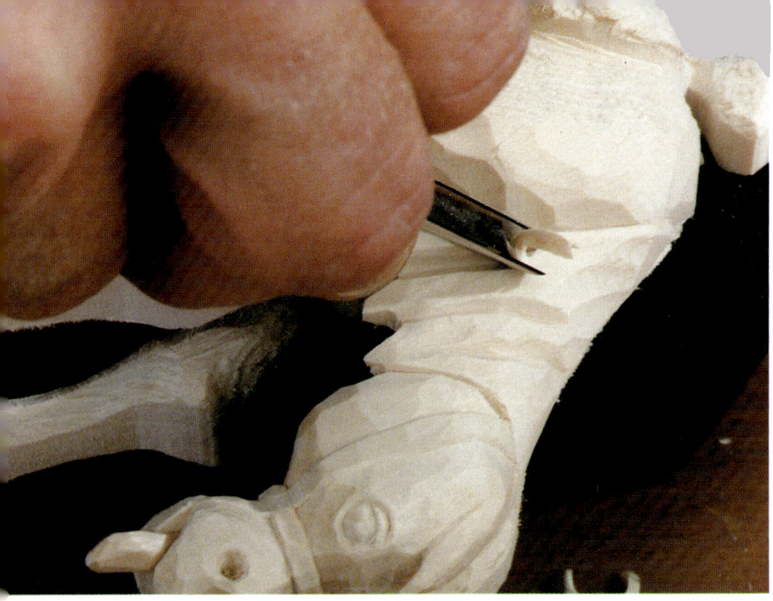

After cleaning and shaping the mane, use a large V tool and gouges to add deep cuts to the mane. This creates a flowing mane.

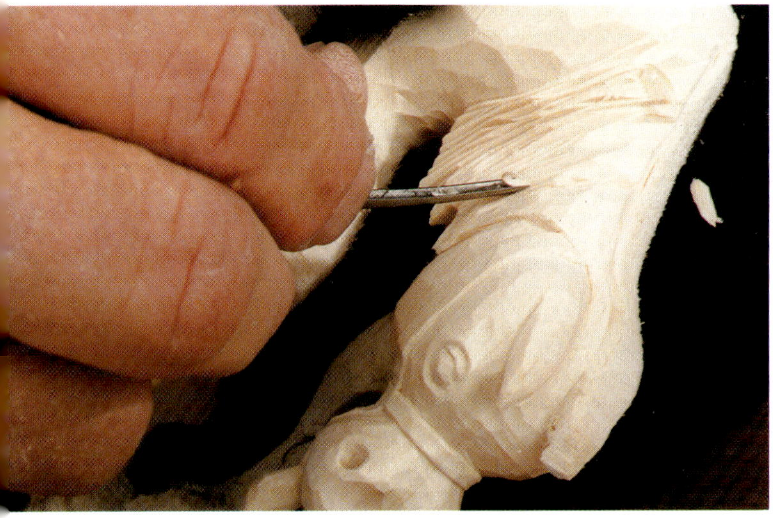

Follow the general direction of these rough cuts with a smaller V tool, cutting very irregular patterns in depth and direction, to give the mane an unkempt appearance.

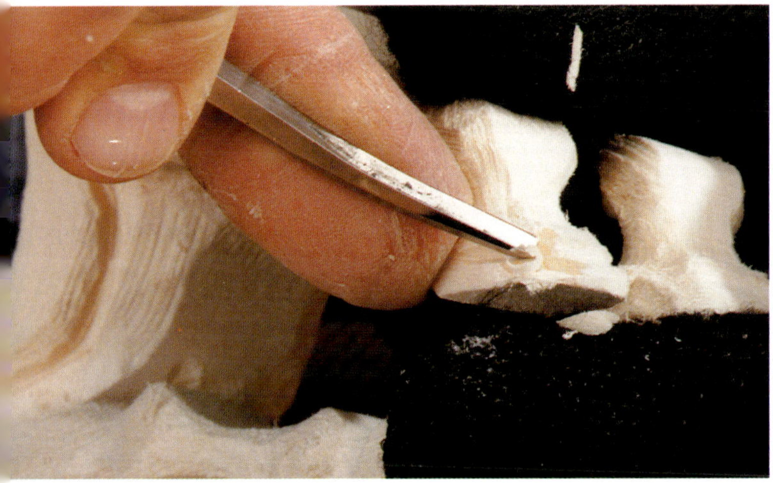

With a small V tool, outline the long hair that will extend over the horse's hoof.

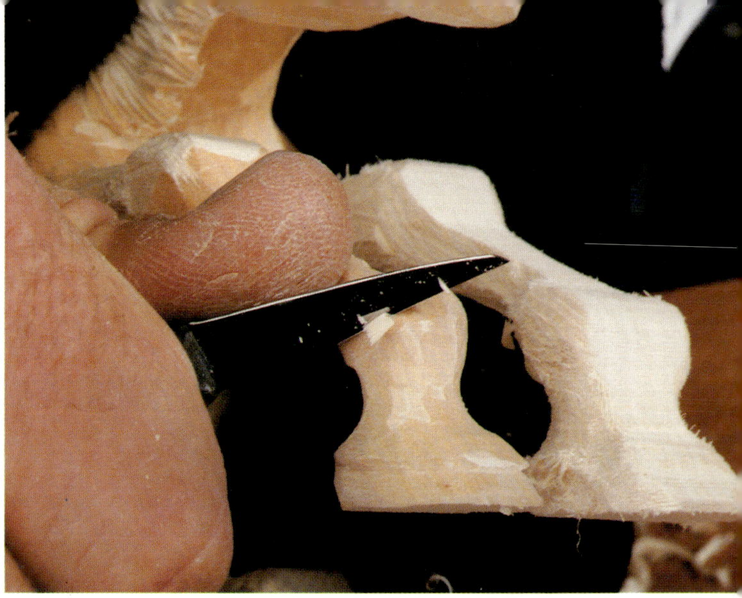

With detail knife and gouges, remove saw and burr marks and shape the hoof.

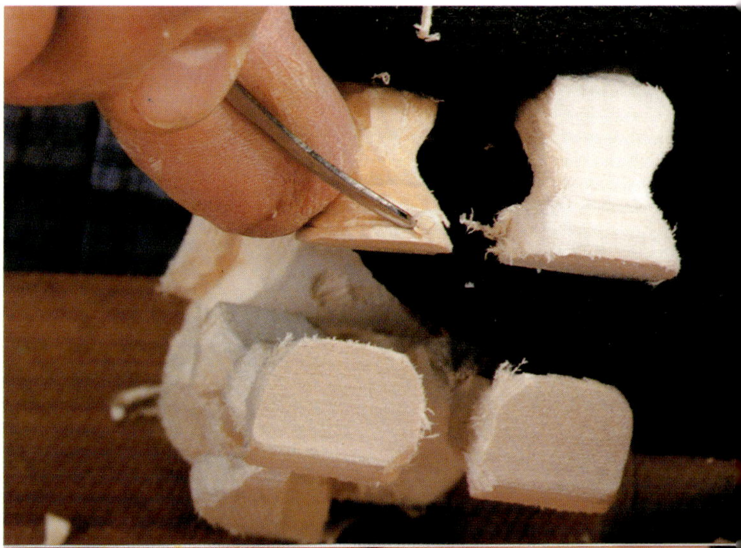

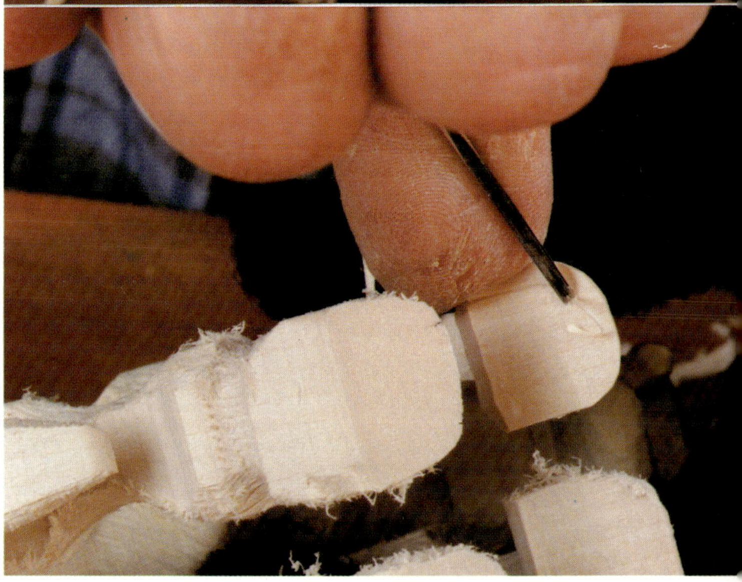

The hoof has been formed and the leg is starting to take shape. With your smallest V tool, etch around the perimeter of the hoof—both on the top and underneath—to outline the horse shoe.

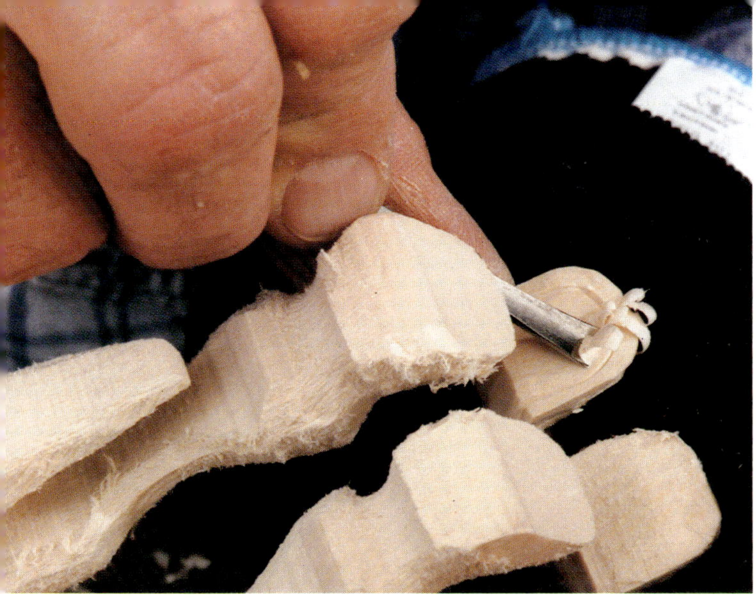

Relieve the wood at the base of the hoof on the inside of the horse shoe ...

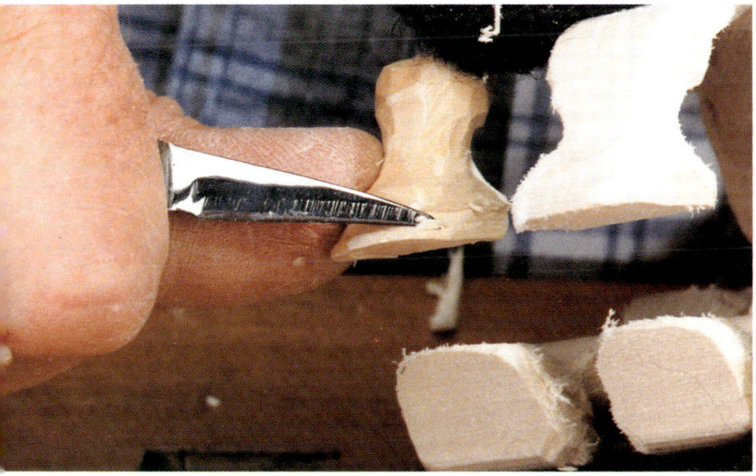

... and along the front and sides of the hoof.

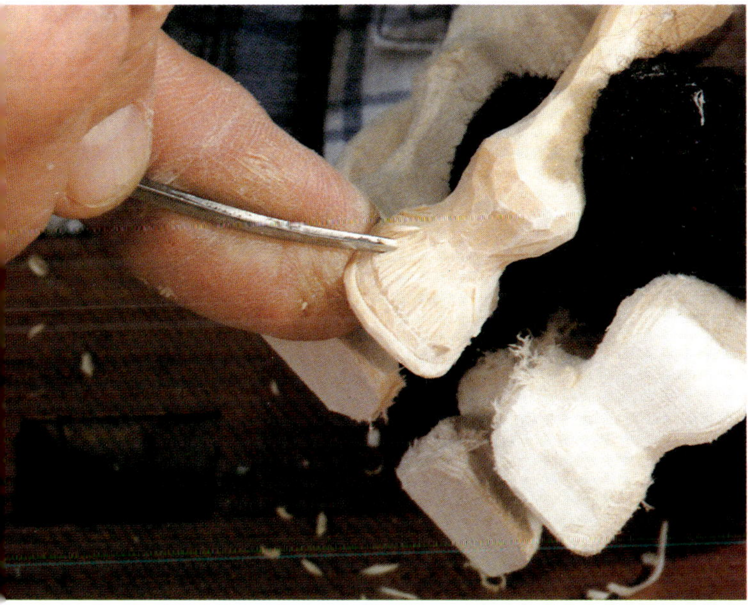

Use your small V tool to carve long hair overhanging the hoof.

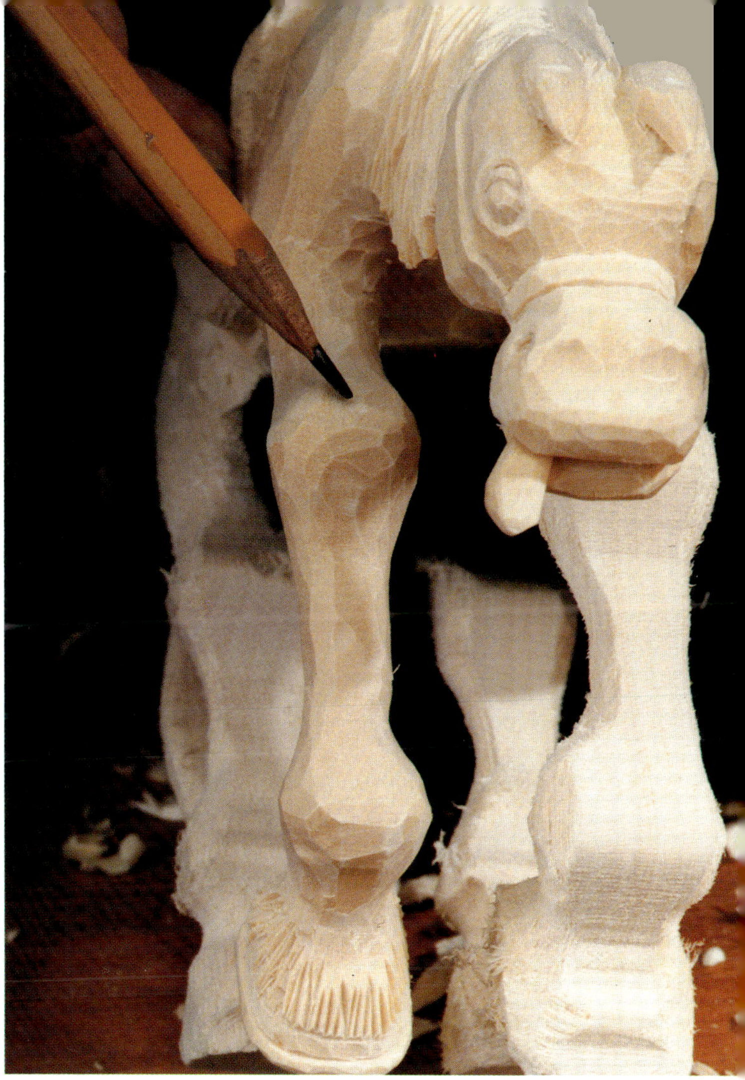

Here is a completed leg, hoof and horse shoe. Note the large joints at the knee and ankle. Carve the other three legs in a similar way. Do not carve a horse shoe on the right rear hoof.

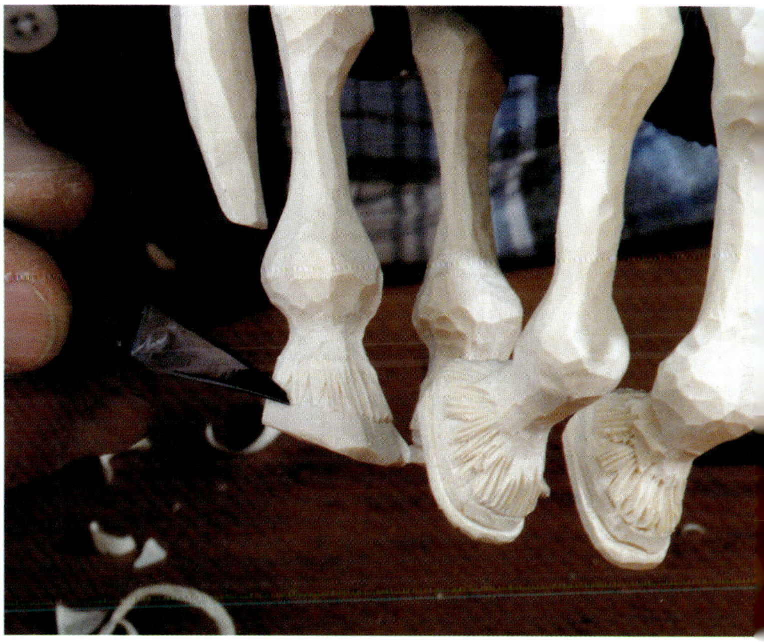

Note that we have horse shoes on all this but this right rear hoof. We will do something with this hoof later but for now let's clean up the tail.

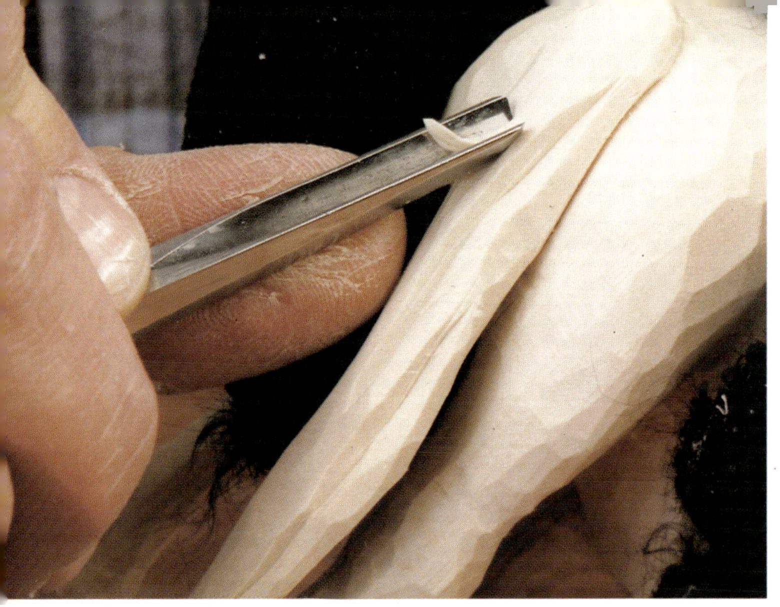

After cleaning the tail, use your large V tool and gouges to remove large sections of the tail, giving it multiple planes and depth. As with the mane, this will soften the tail, preventing a hard or stiff appearance.

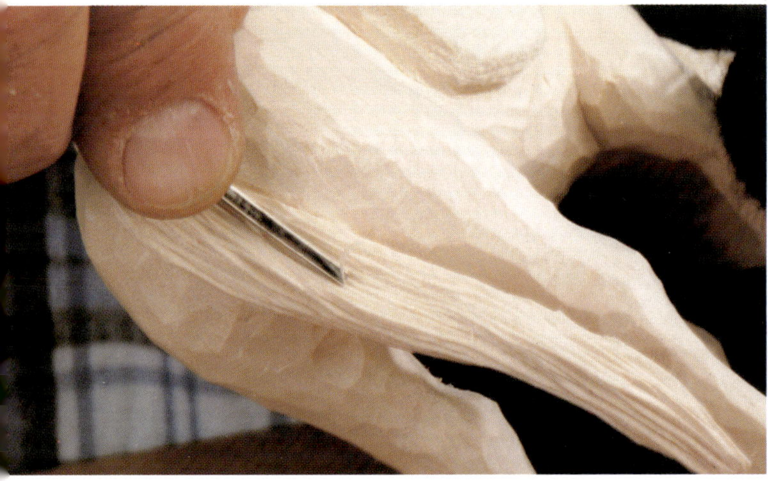

Use your small V tool and carve hair along the many facets of the tail. Make your cuts irregular in both depth and direction.

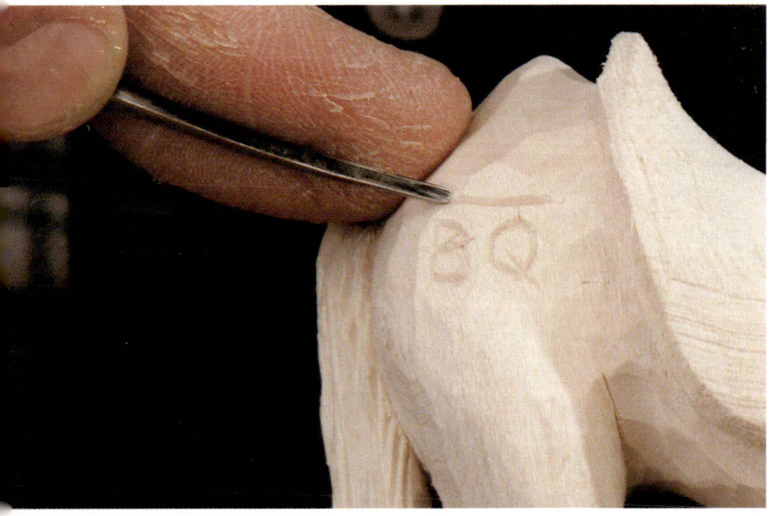

Let's put a brand on this horse. Use the V tool to trace around the letters as shown. In case you haven't figured it out, this is Barbecue.

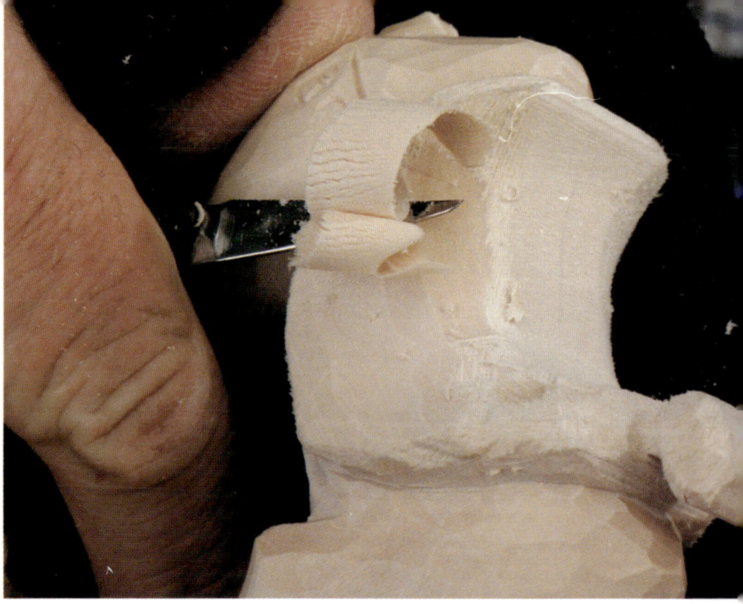

Using your detail knife and 1/2" fishtail gouge, clean saw marks from the saddle. Don't spend a lot of time forming the completed saddle at this time. As we begin to fit the horse and saddle between the cowboy's legs, we will spend considerable time working with the saddle until it fits snugly.

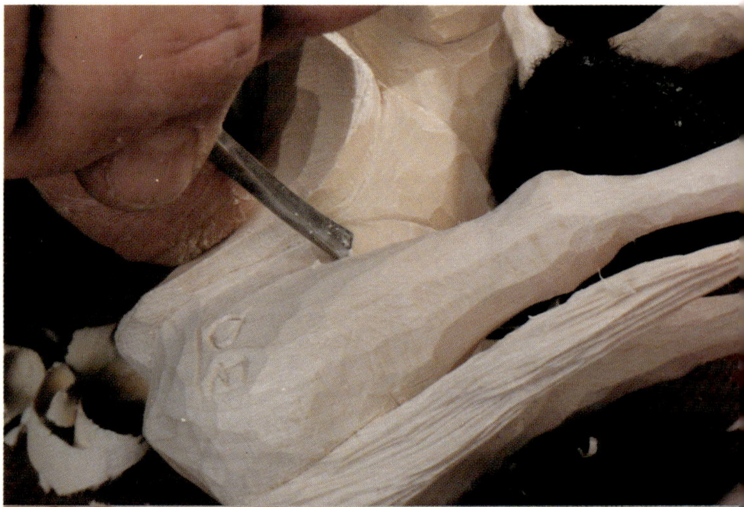

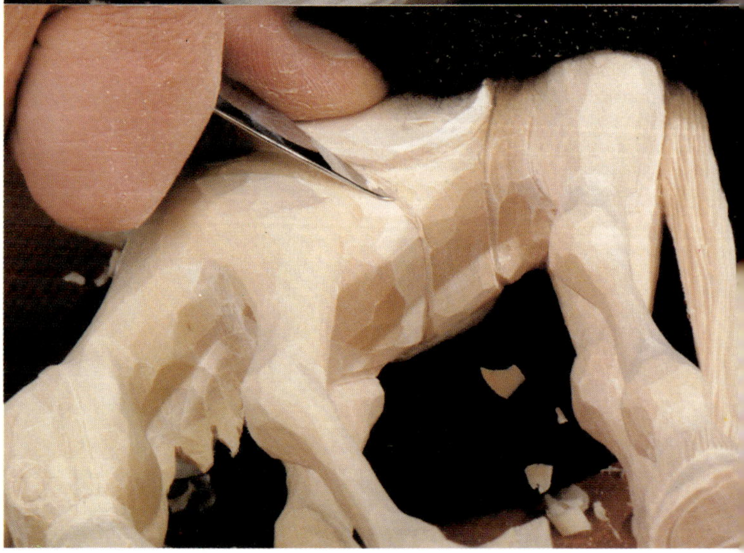

Draw in the saddle's belly band. Cut this belly band into the horse using a detail knife and a medium V tool. Use a 1/4" shallow gouge to relieve the wood on either side of this belly band.

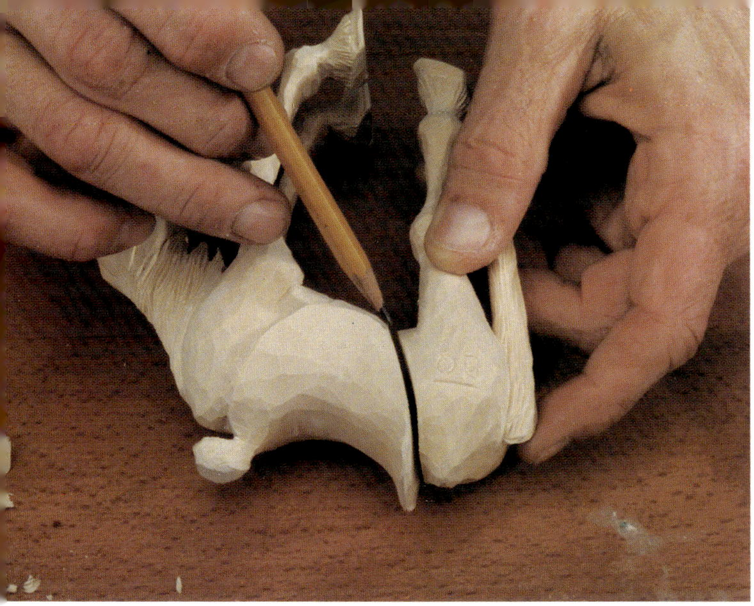

Take the horse to the band saw and carefully saw along the saddle and the back edge of the belly band. The finished cut should look like this.

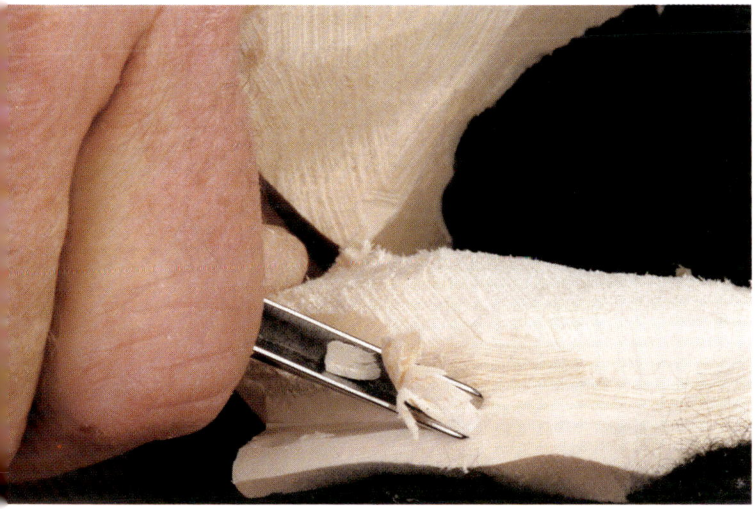

Lay the horse aside for a while. We'll work on the cowboy's legs, shaping them to fit between the front legs of the horse and around the saddle. Begin to shape the boots and the backs of the legs with the large V tool. Separate the chaps from the rear of the boots and jeans.

The shaped boot at this point.

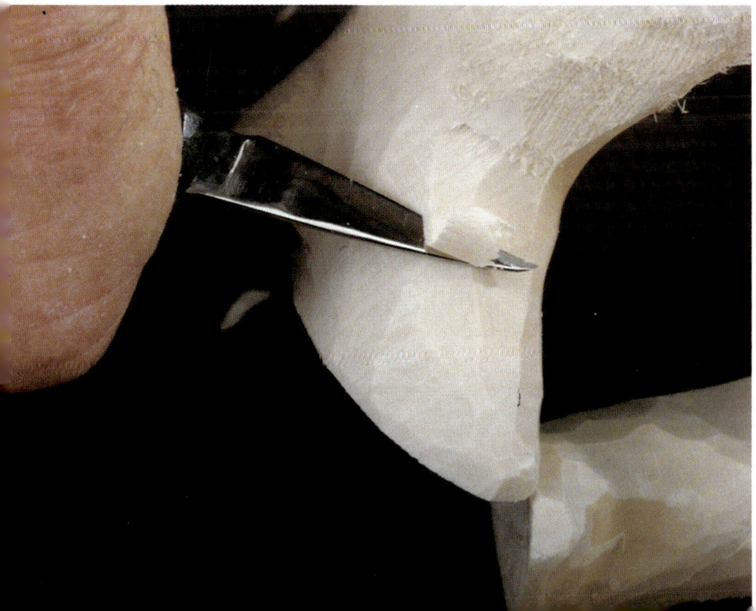

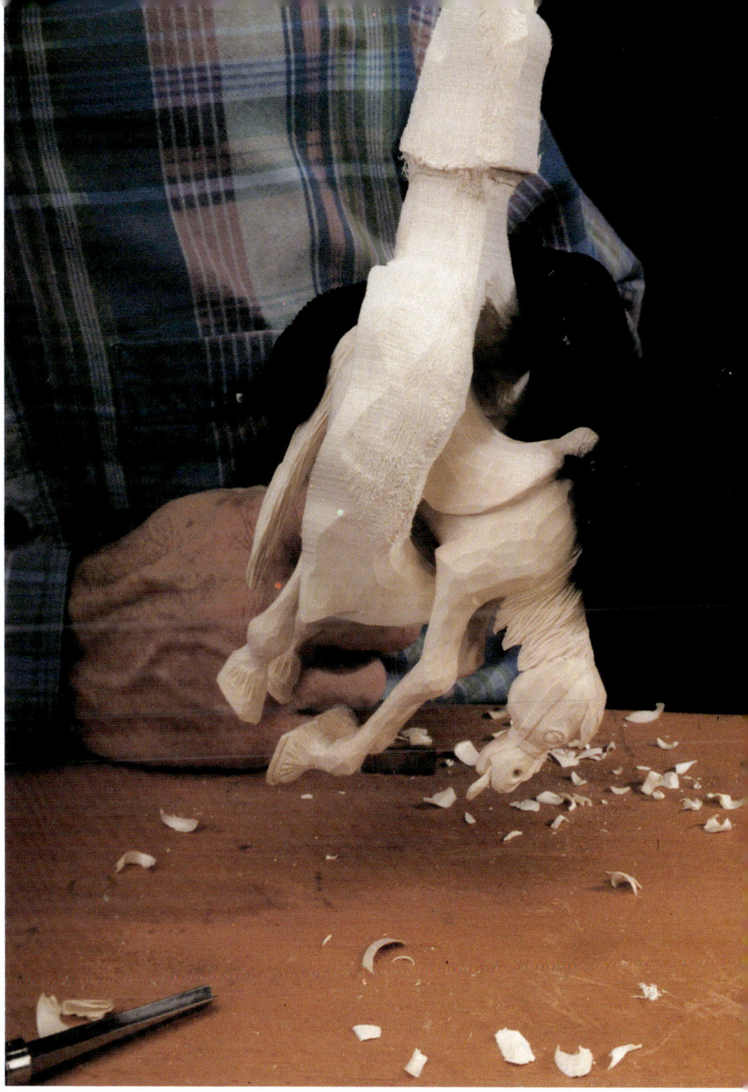

Fit the two pieces of horse together between the cowboy's legs. Place the toes of the boots between the two front legs of the horse. If the three pieces do not fit together, you might want to remove some wood from either side of the horse's saddle or along the inside of the cowboy's legs. If the boots do not fit between the horse's two front legs, remove more wood from the boots and/or the insides of the horse's legs.

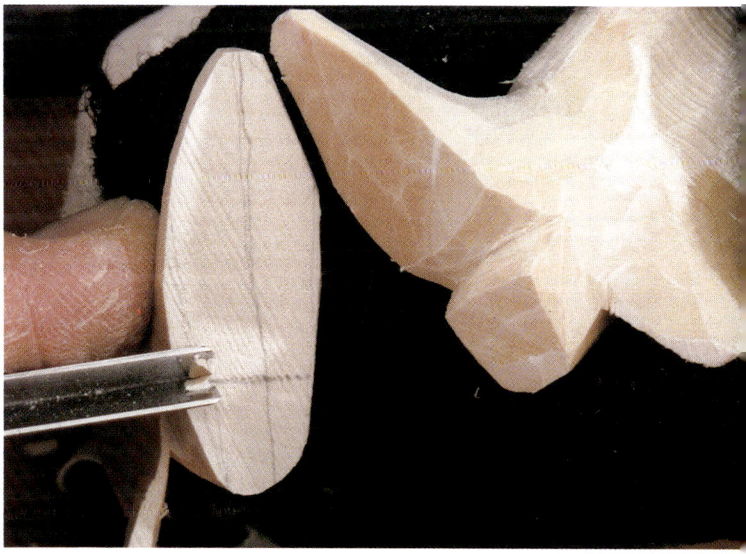

Shape the bottom of the boots and draw in the location of the heels. Use your large V tool to form the heels.

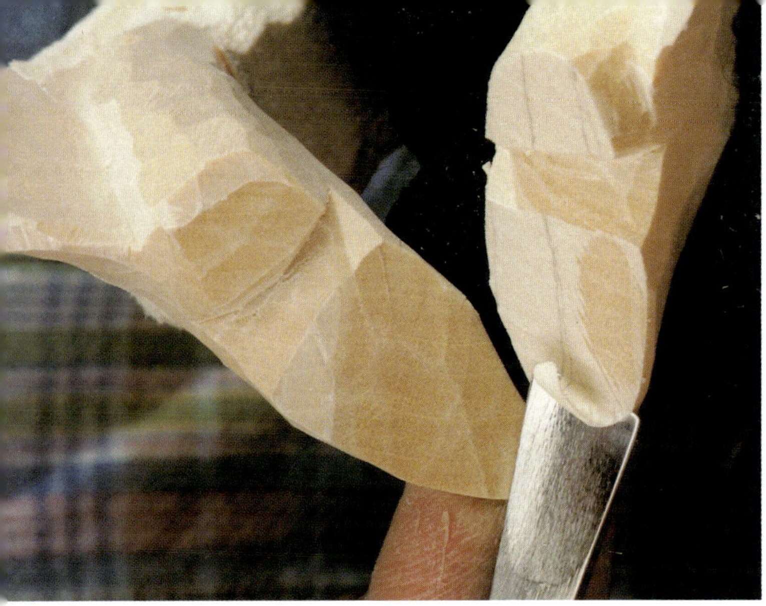

Remove saw marks from the bottom of the boots using your large fish-tail gouge.

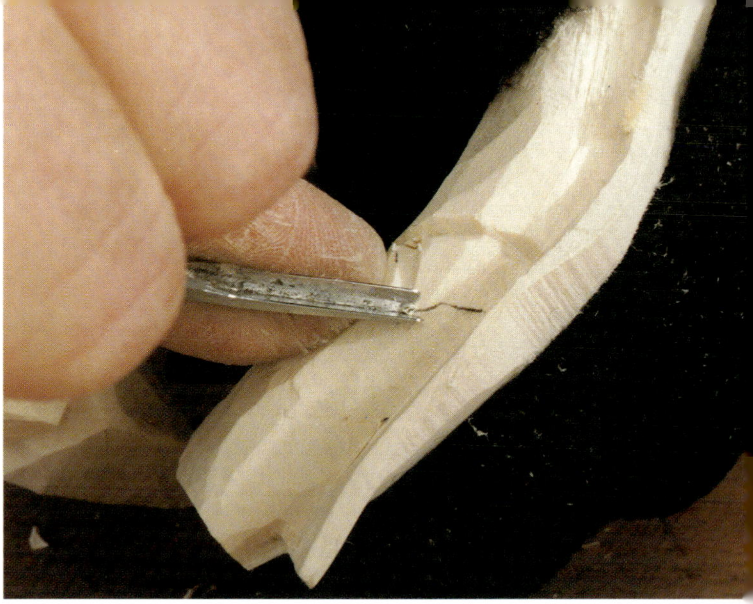

Use your 1/8" V tool to follow the chap and boot lines.

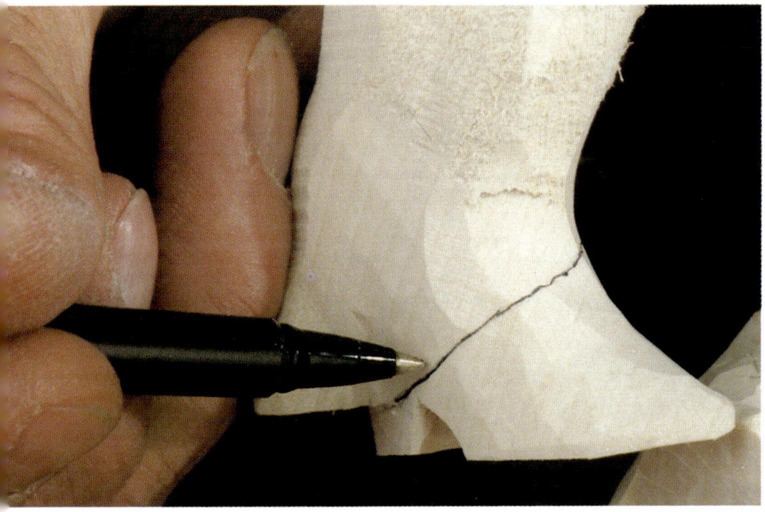

Sketch the chaps across the front of the boots.

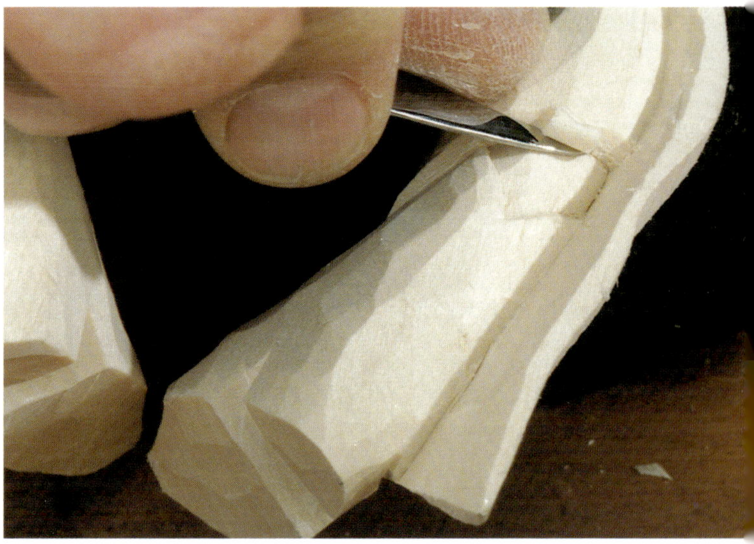

Relieve the wood between the V-shaped boot top and the bottom of the chap.

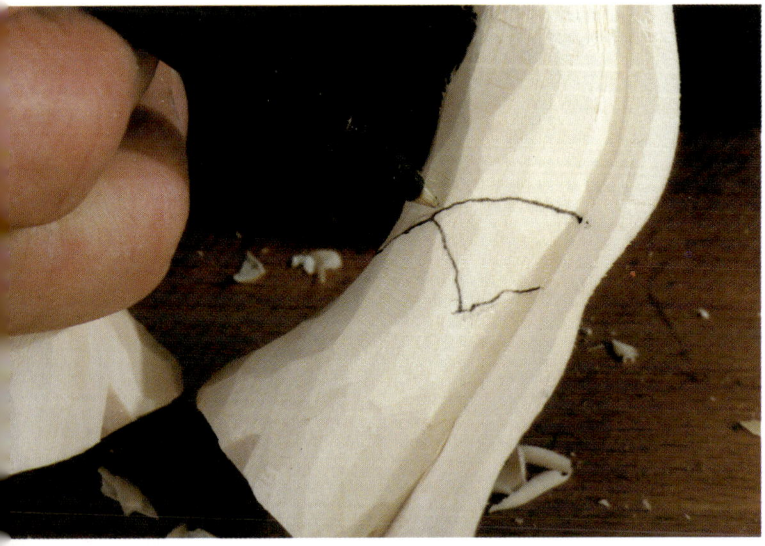

Continue sketching to the rear of the leg. Draw the back of the boot as it intersects with chap.

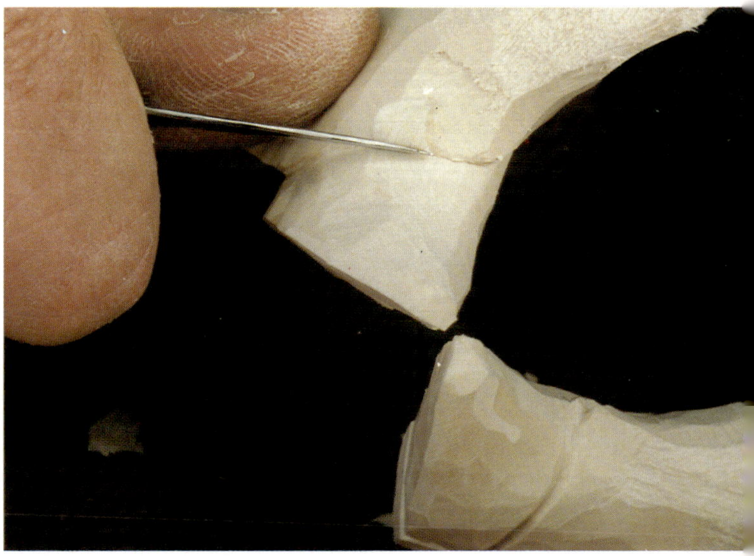

Relieve wood from the boot to the base of the chap.

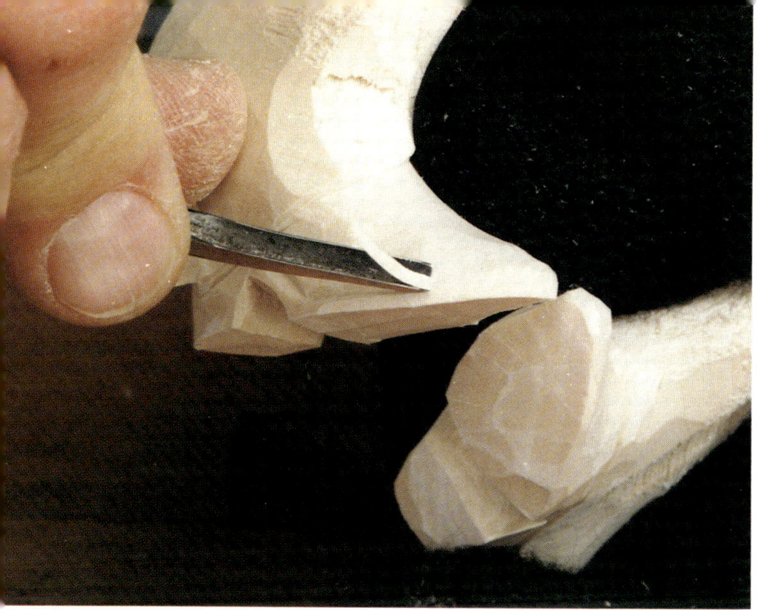

Using your medium V tool, carve in the separation between the boot's leather upper and the sole.

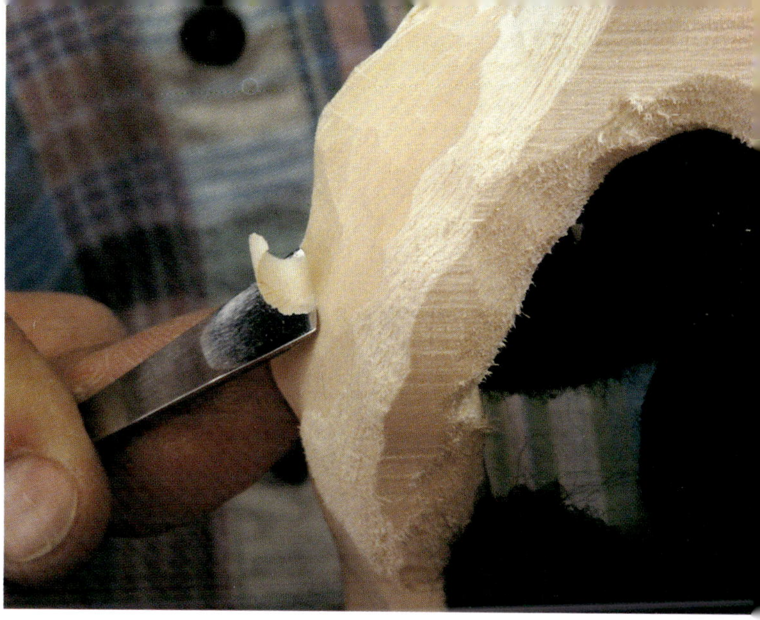

Use the 1/2" fishtail to remove wood from either side of the channel formed with your large, shallow gouge along the chaps.

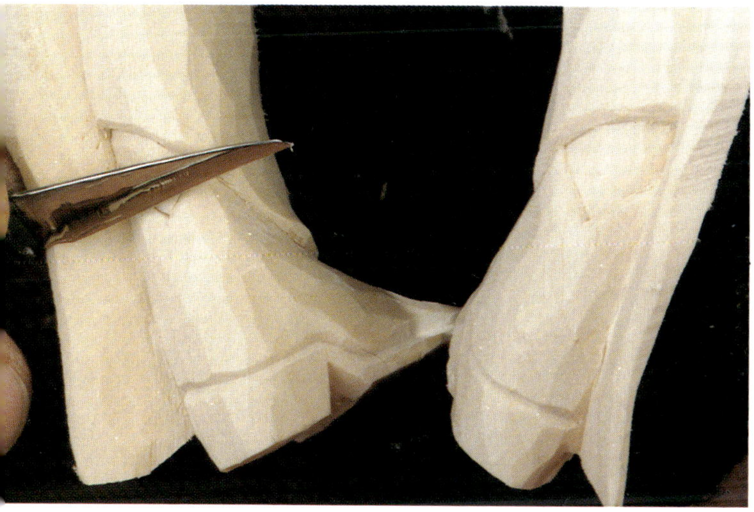

The backs of the cowboy's boots so far.

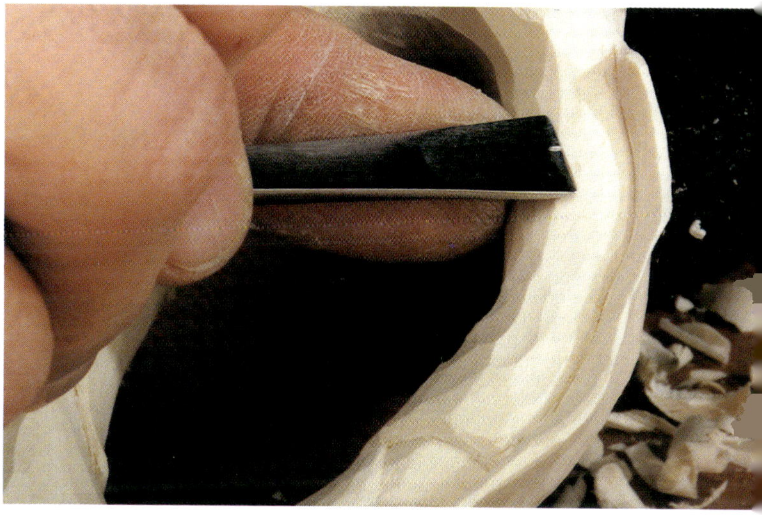

Using your fishtail gouge and detail knife, finish shaping the rear of each leg.

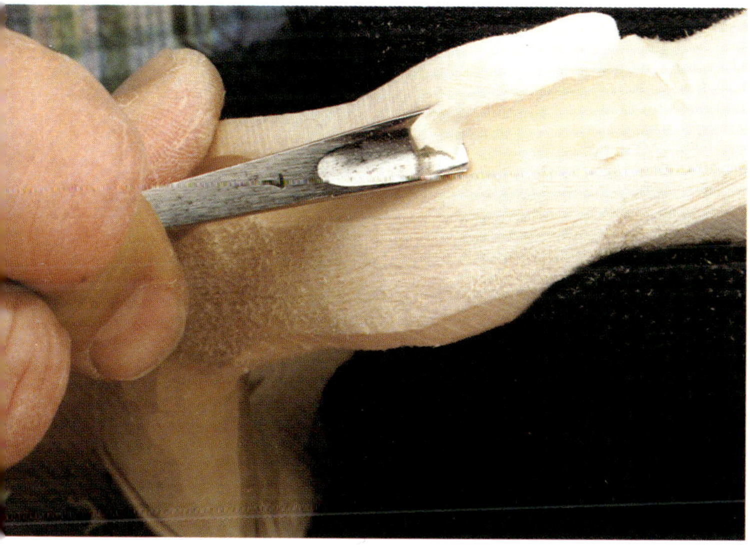

Use your large, shallow gouge to accent the flair of the chaps. These cuts will also serve to make the legs narrower.

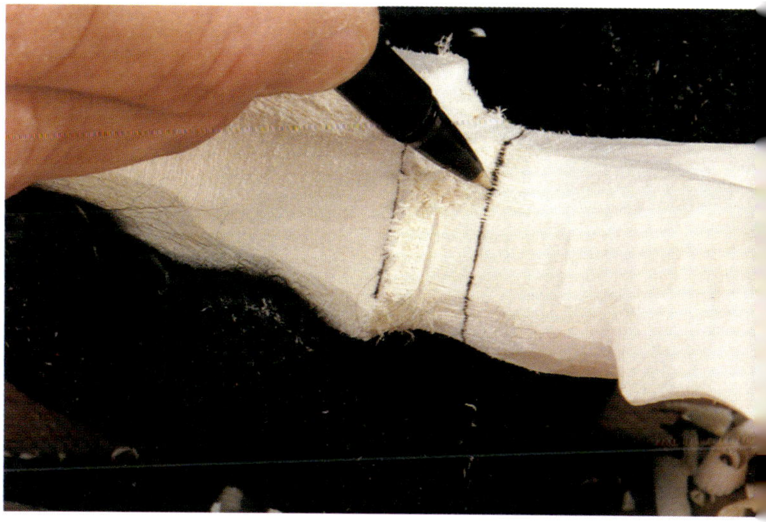

After you have finished cleaning the legs, locate the waistline and base of the vest.

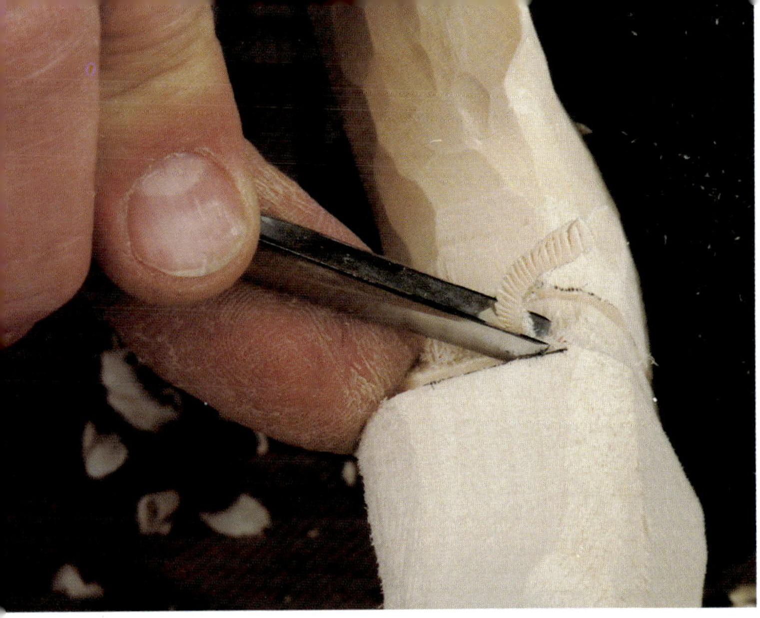

Now use your large V tool to score along the waistline and bottom of the vest.

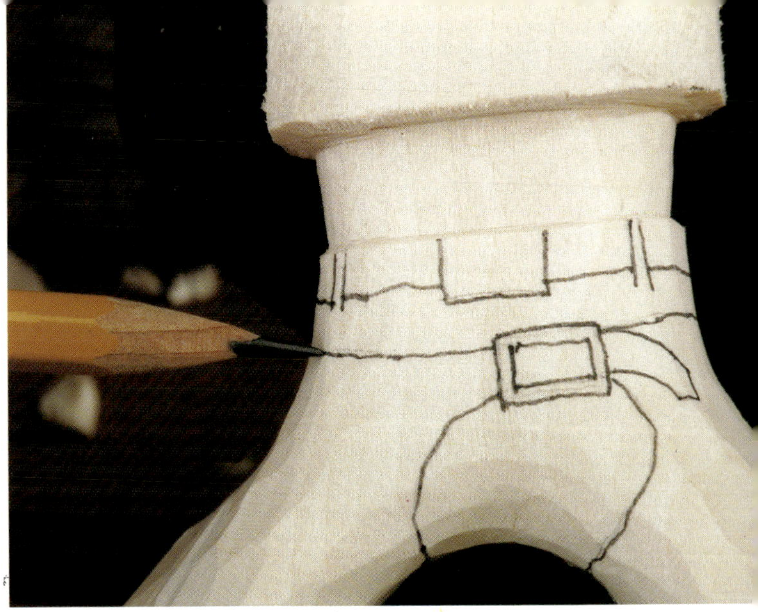

Draw the details of the belt loops, including buckles at the waistline and at the top of the chaps.

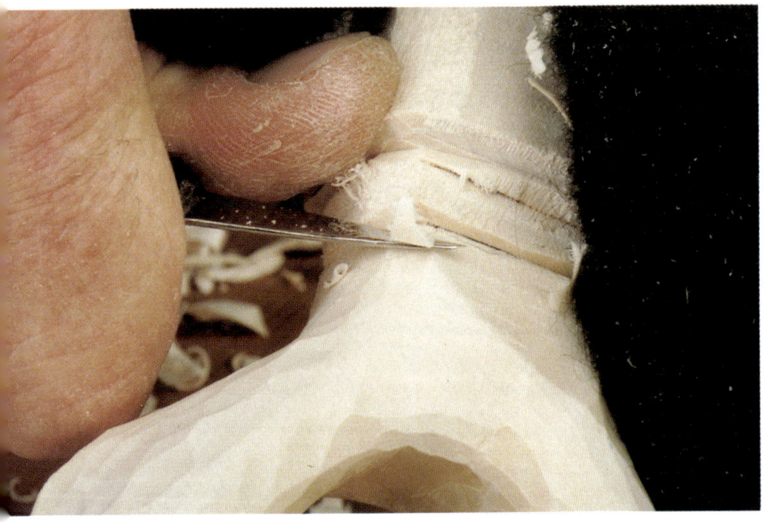

Use your detail knife to clean up to the waistline.

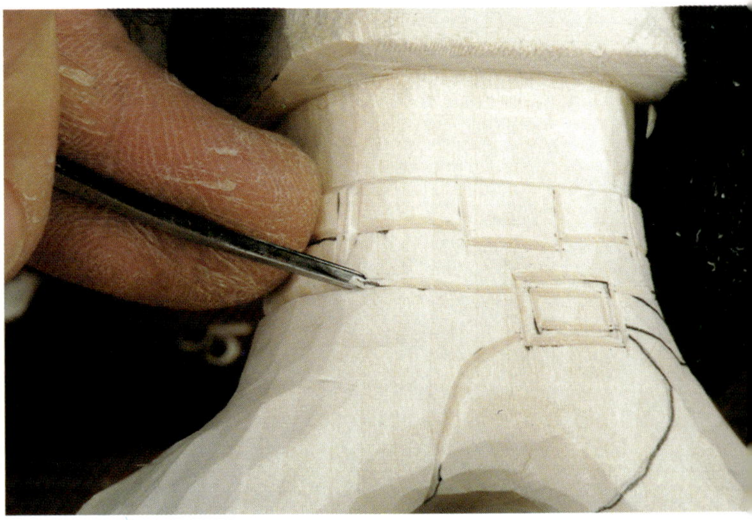

Using your small V tool, lightly cut these details in to the front ...

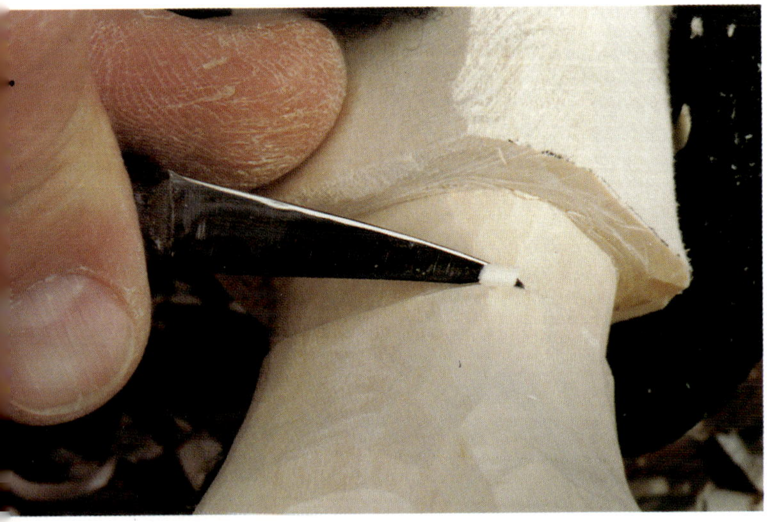

Relieve the wood between the waistline and the bottom of the vest. This area is the shirt and should be carved without any indication of a blouse effect at the waistline since this old guy is stretched to the limit by the weight of the horse between his legs.

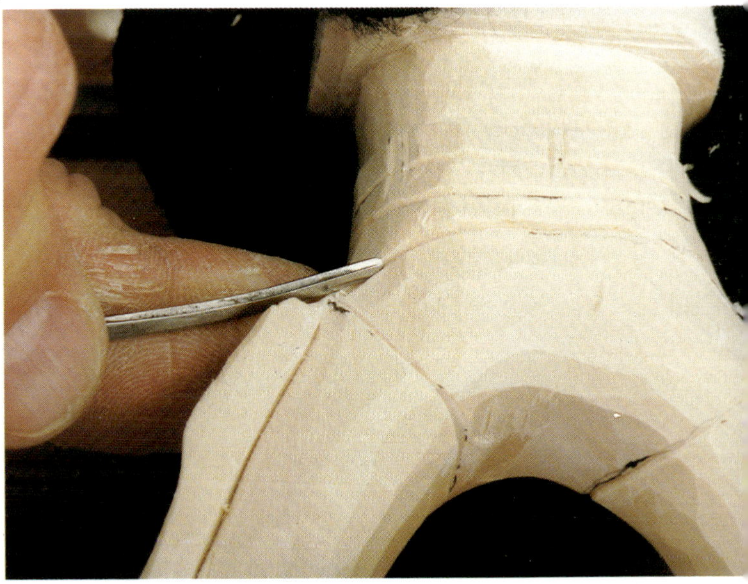

... and rear of the pants and chaps.

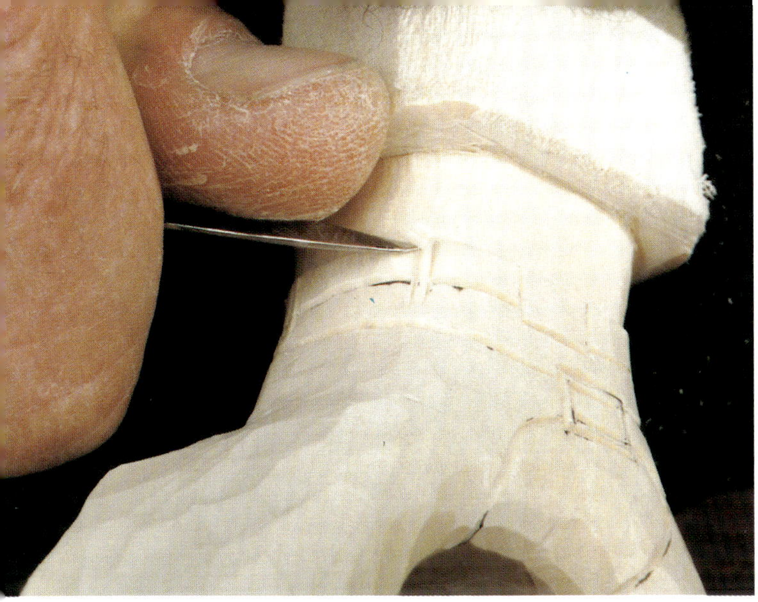

Using your detail knife, relieve the pants belt on either side of the belt loops and buckles.

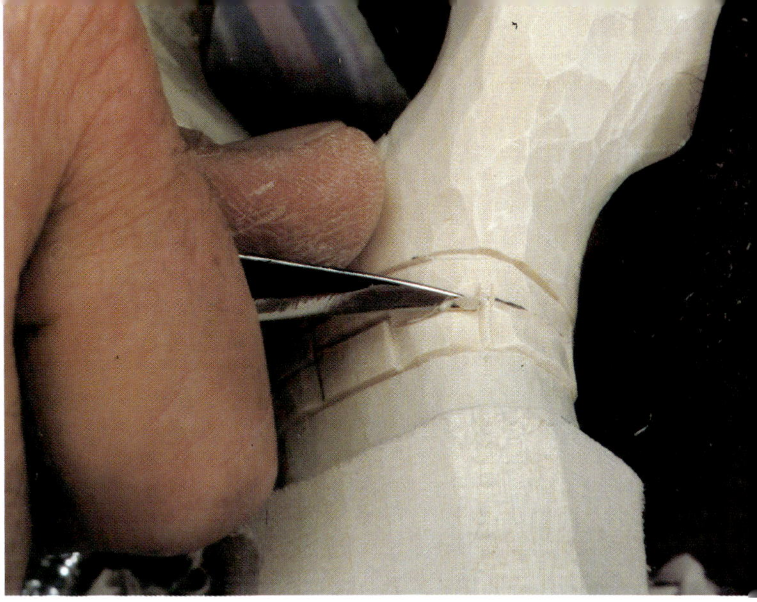

Chip out the resultant triangle. Repeat this on both sides of each belt loop and around the belt buckle.

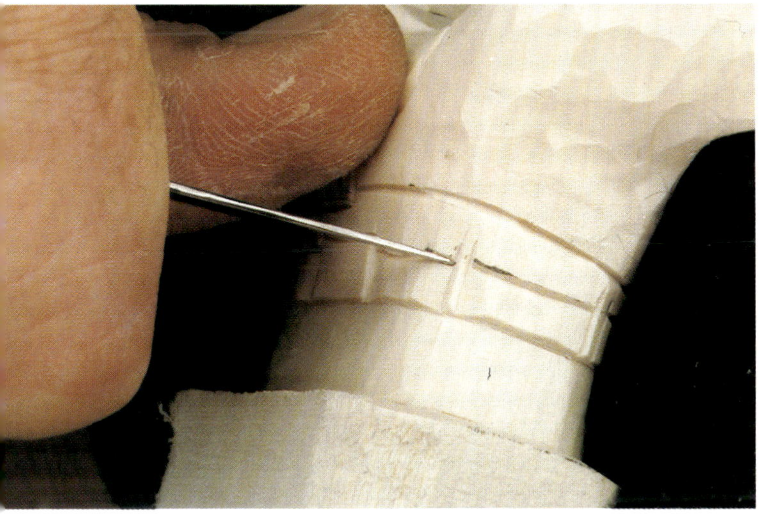

Along the bottom of the belt at each belt loop, and on either side of the belt buckle, remove a small chip to accent those intersections. Do this by slipping your knife tip along the bottom side of the belt next to the belt loop ...

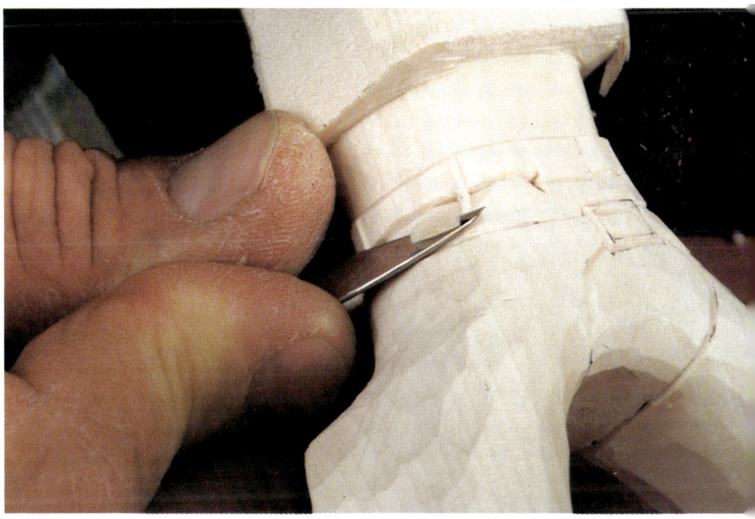

Relieve wood from below the belt to the top of chaps.

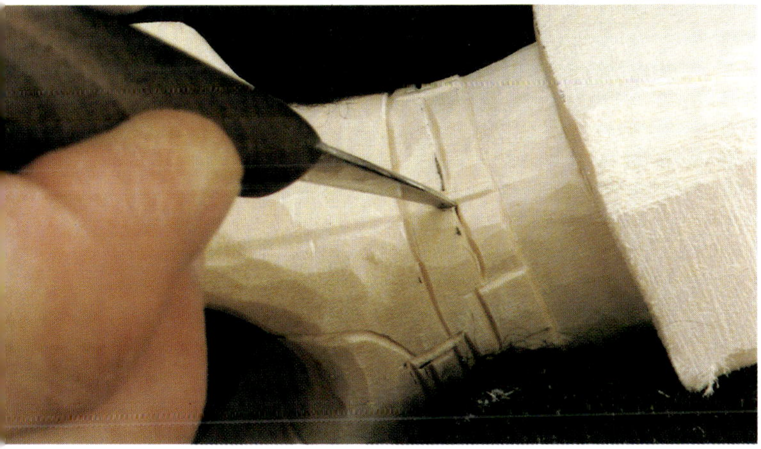

... and along the side the belt loop. Make sure this cut intersects with the previous cut.

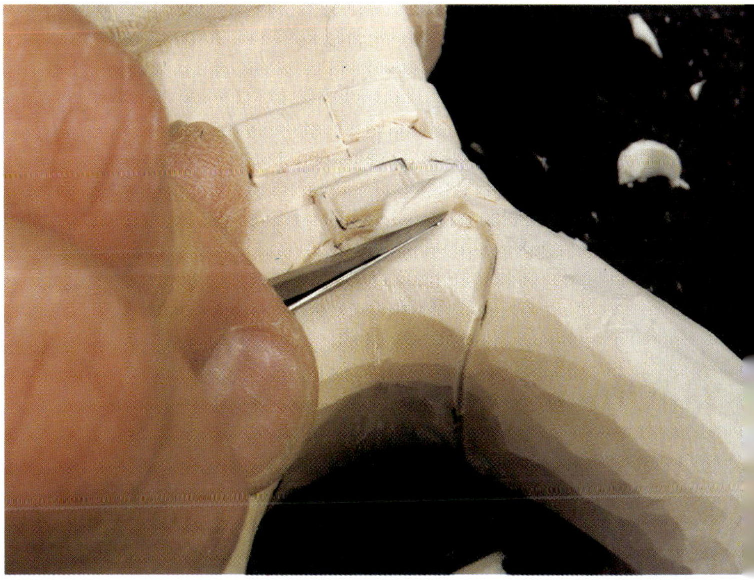

Relieving wood from beneath of chaps in the front ...

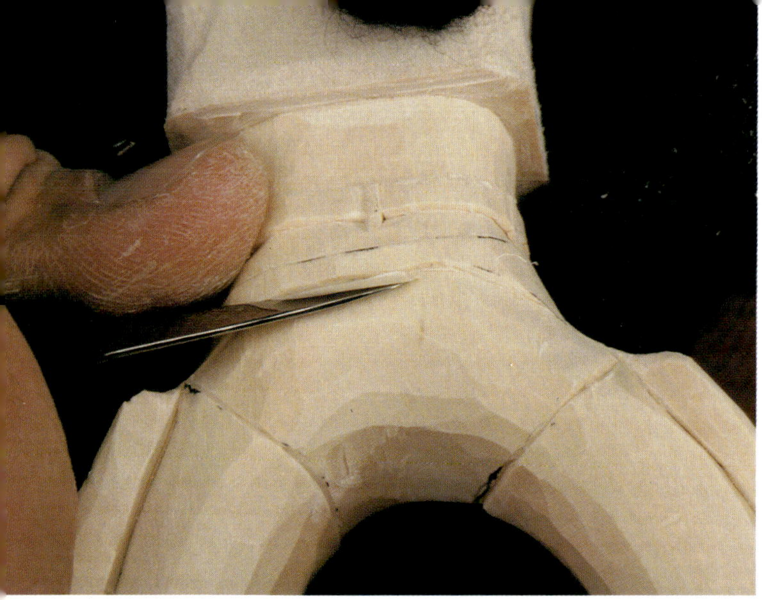

... and the rear.

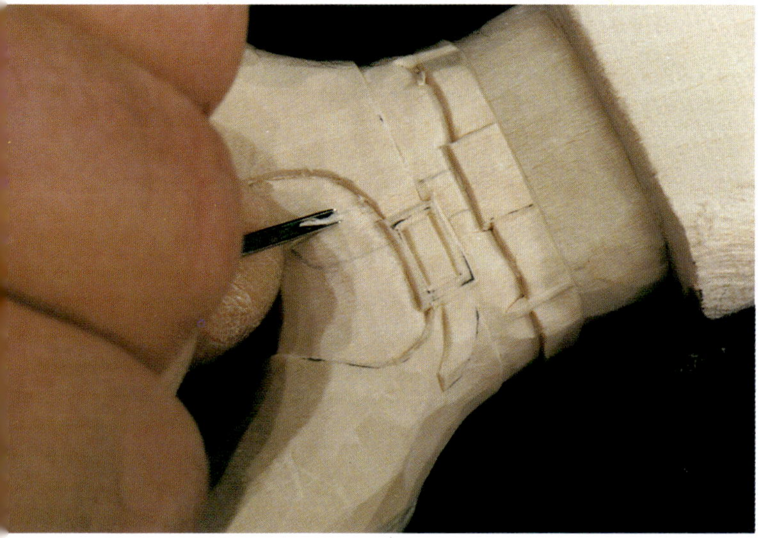

Use your smallest V tool to cut in a fly on the front of the pants.

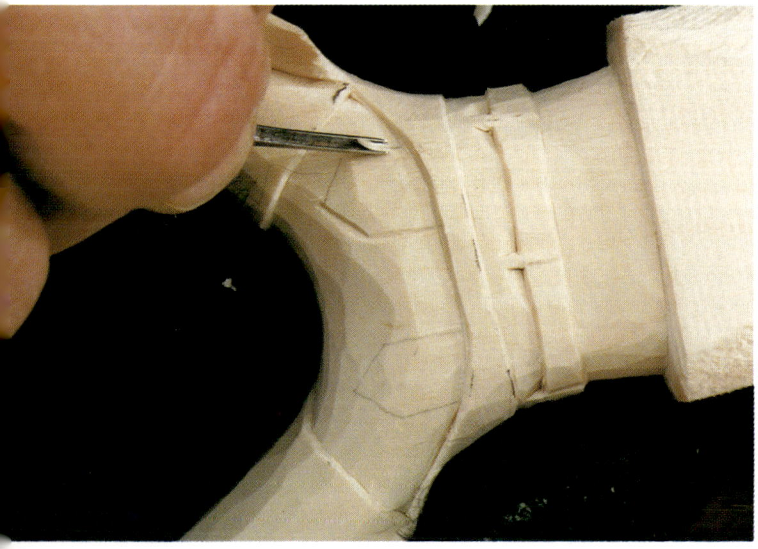

Sketch in and cut along the jeans pockets with the small V tool on the back of the pants.

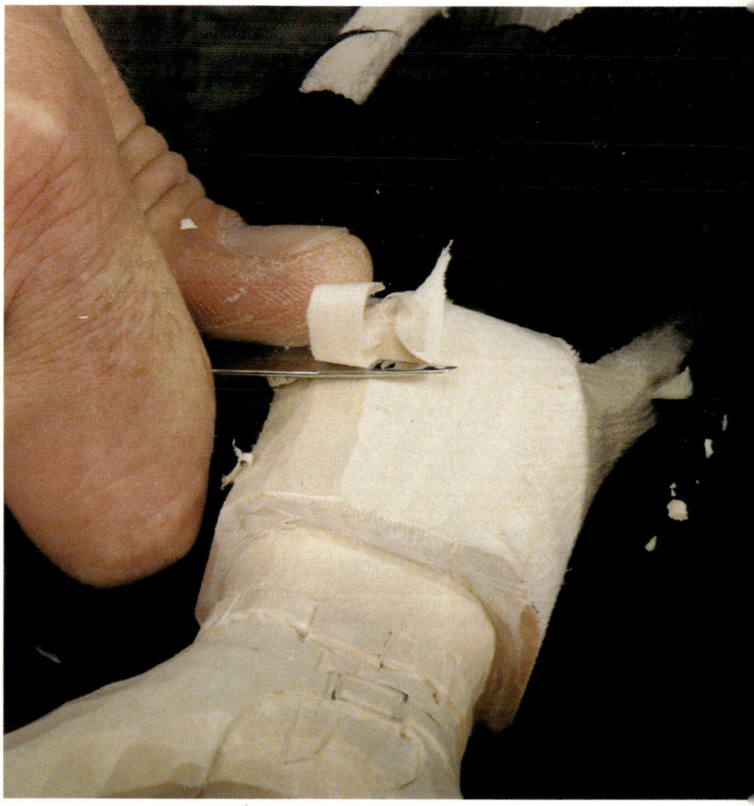

Using your detail knife, remove saw and burr marks from the vest.

Draw the shirt collar, front of the vest, and vest's arm holes as shown.

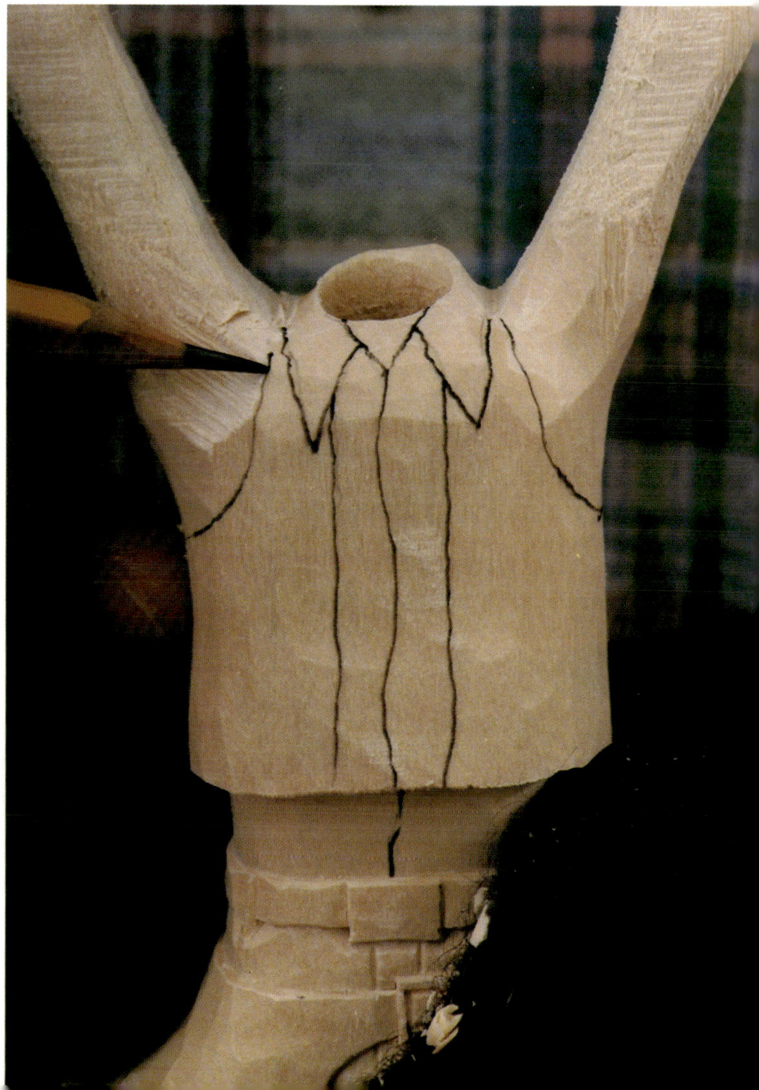

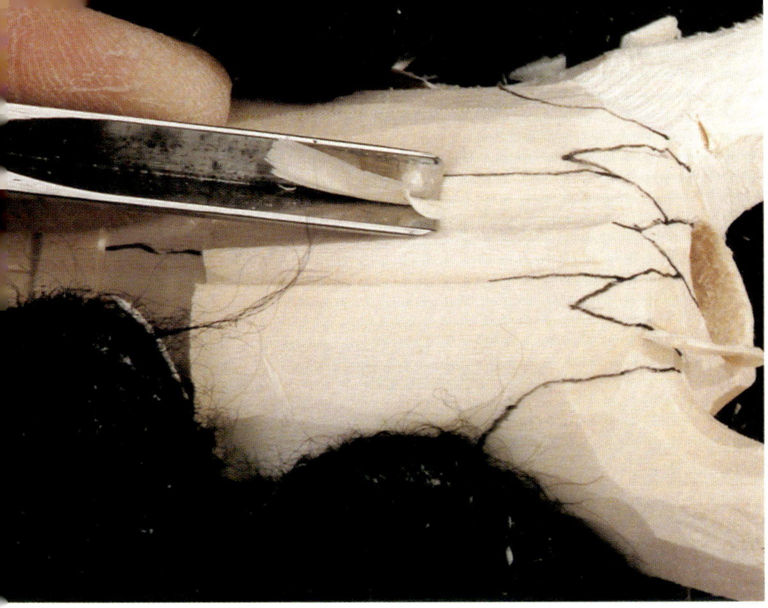

Use your large V tool to cut in the front of the vest.

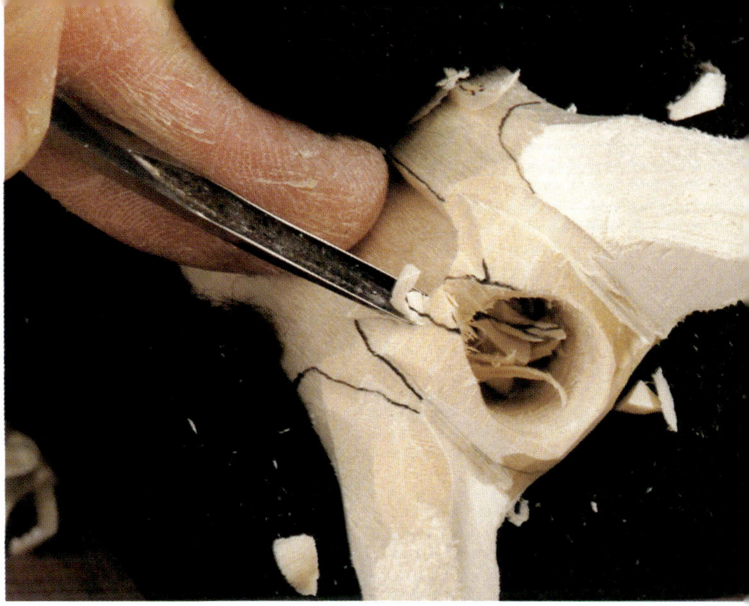

Using your 1/8" V tool, carve in the collar line, front and back.

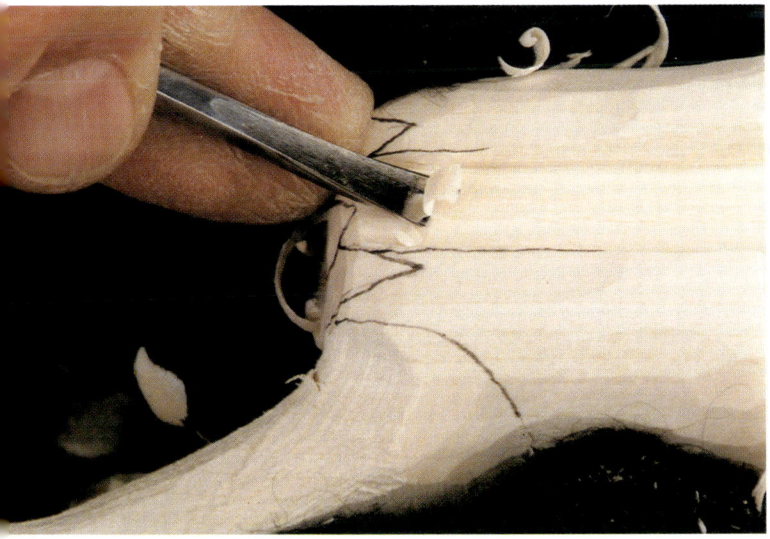

Using a small, shallow gouge, extend the plane of the shirt front to the top of the collar.

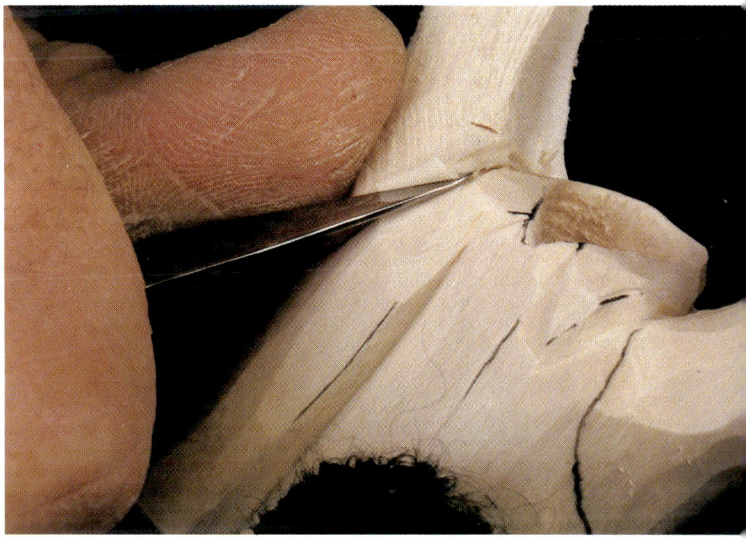

With your detail knife, relieve wood from the vest to the shirt collar.

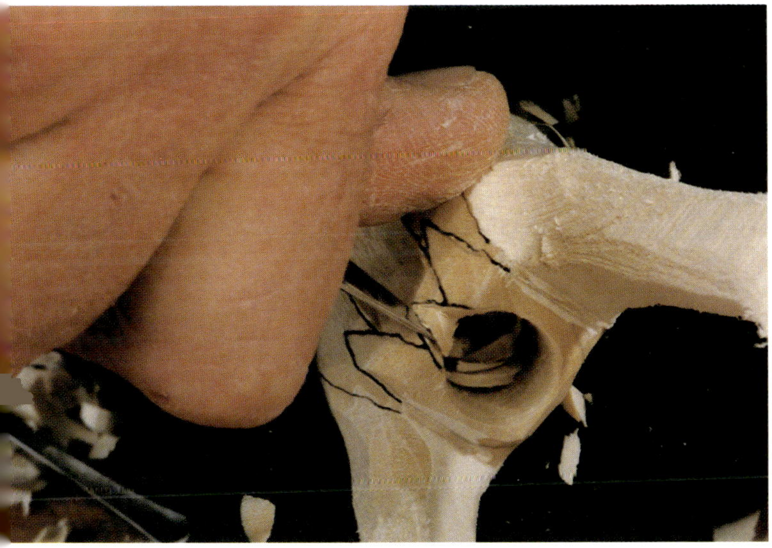

Chip out the neck-hole to the front of the shirt.

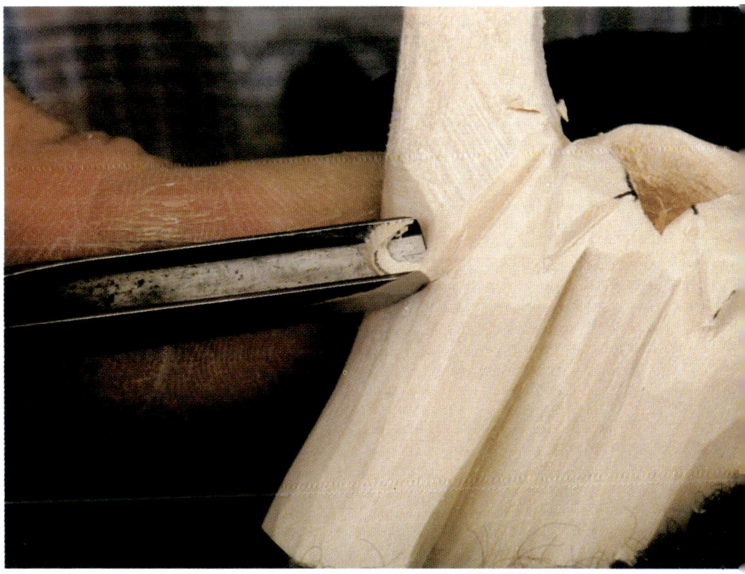

Use your large V tool to cut in the arm holes in the vest.

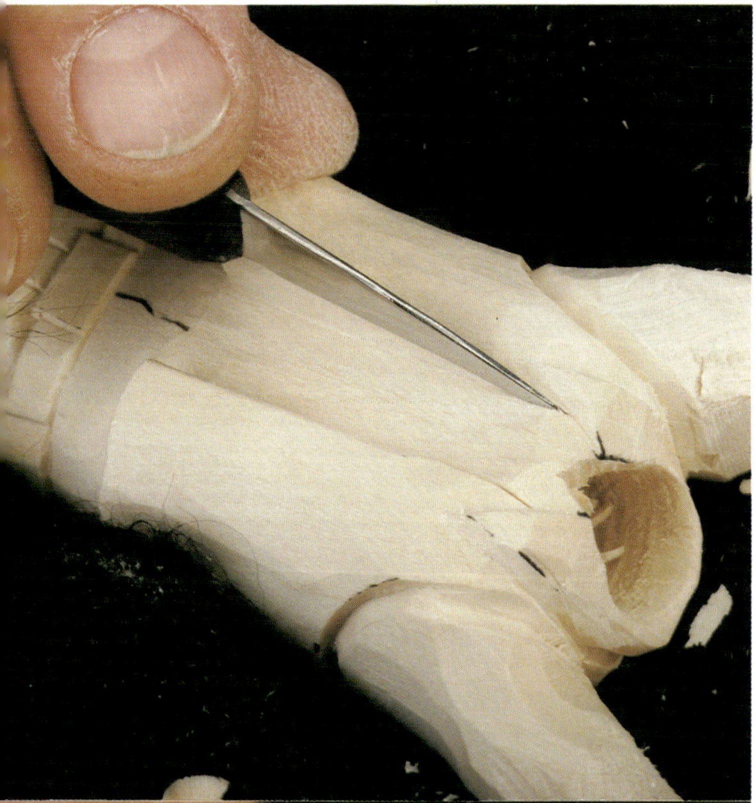

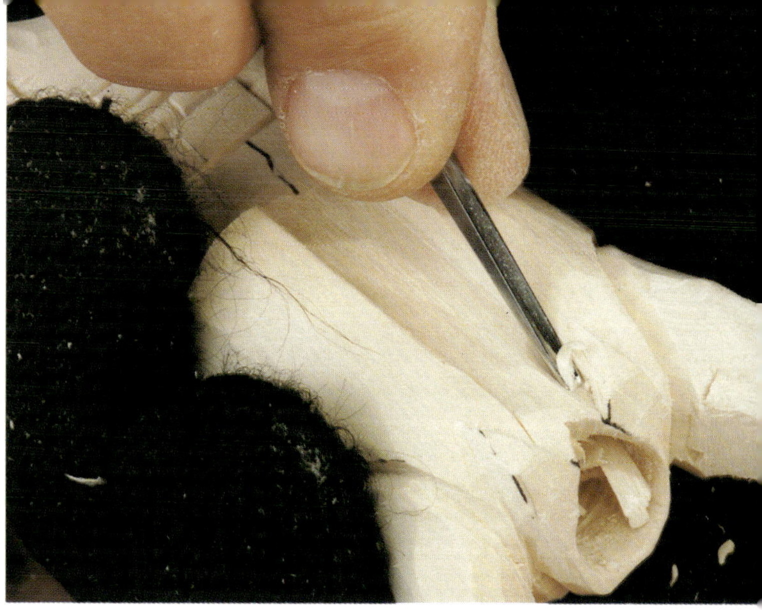

Use your small, shallow gouge to remove wood from the shirt front up to the two previous cuts to raise it up above the vest. Repeat for the other collar.

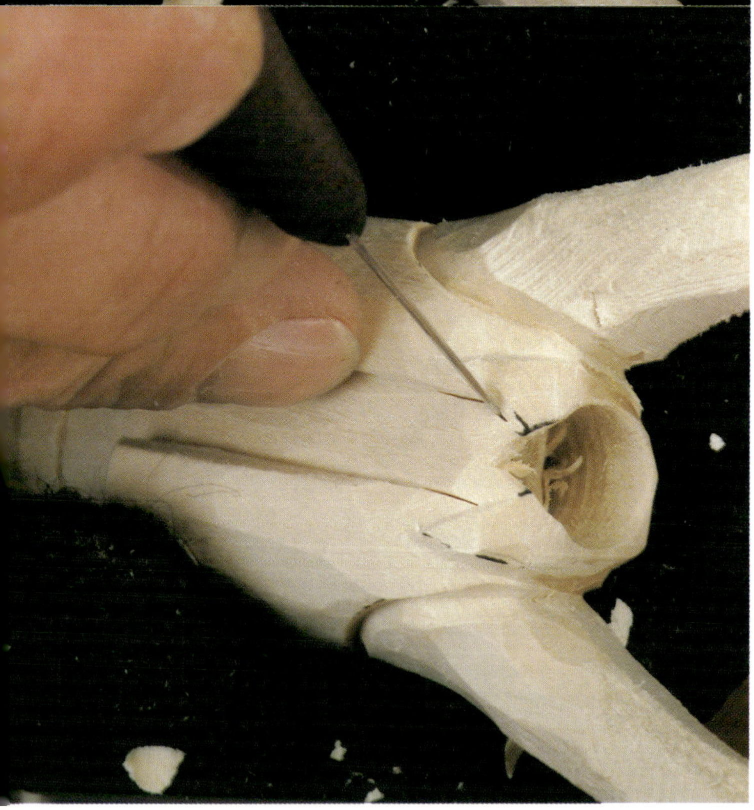

With the point of your detail knife, make a V cut along the leading edge of the vest and the tip of the shirt collar.

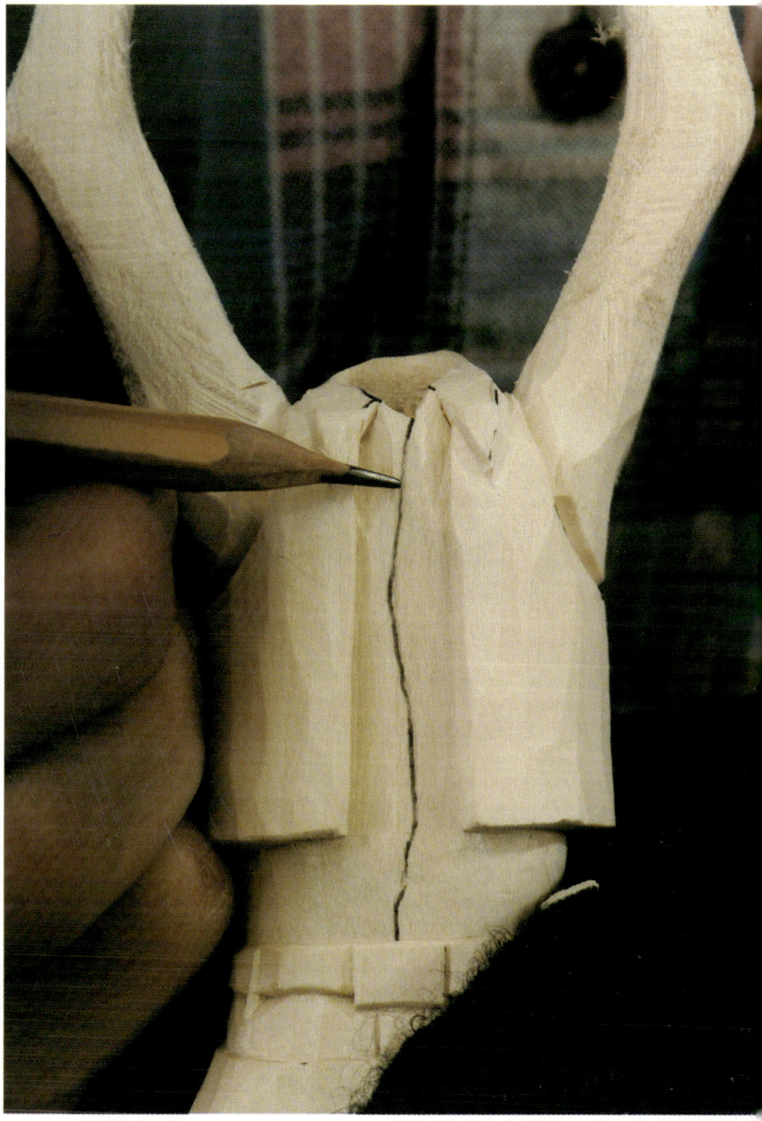

Sketch in the shirt placket.

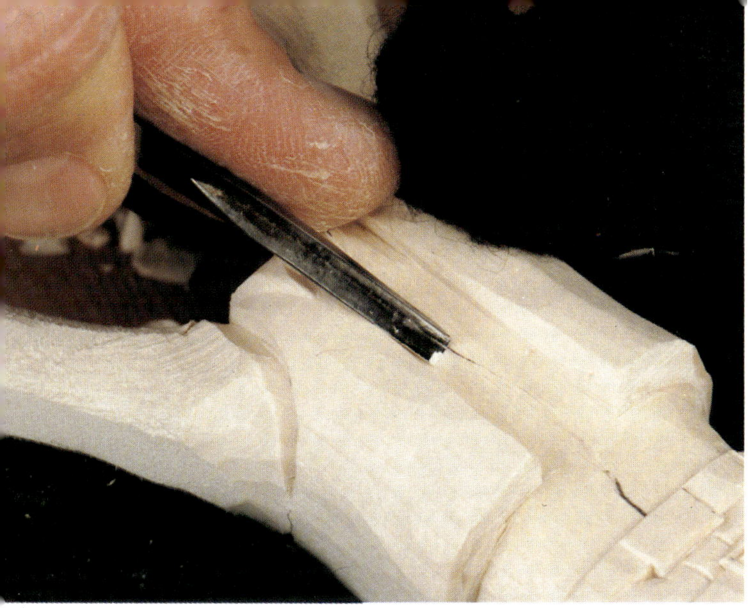

Lay the side of your medium V tool flush with the surface of the shirt and the sharp point along the placket line. Follow the line from the collar to the belt buckle.

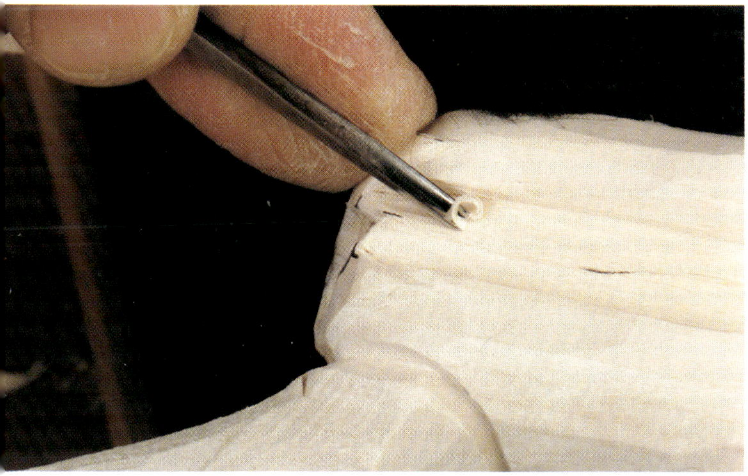

Use your small 1/8" shallow gouge to shape the shirt front.

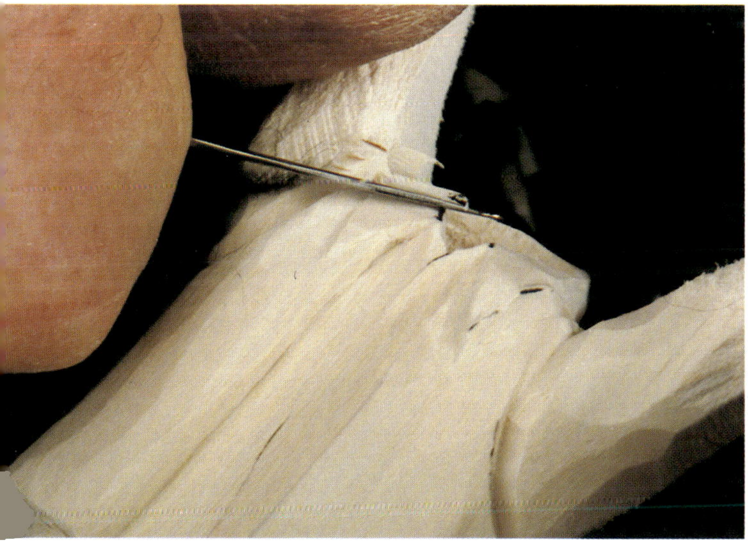

Thin the collar with your detail knife. Don't forget the back of the collar.

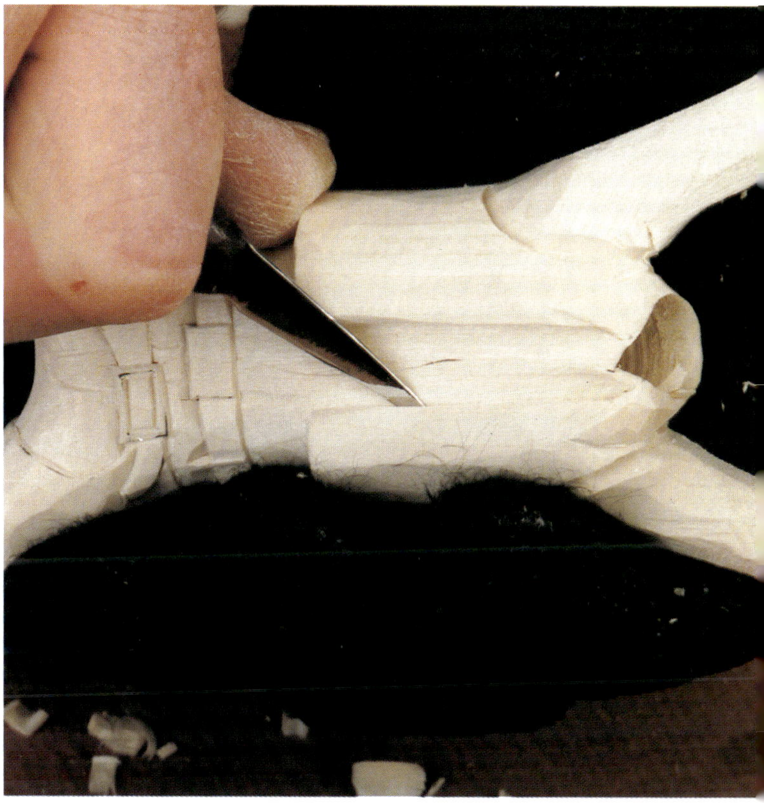

We want the vest to appear as if it is hanging unrestrained from the cowboy's body. Since the cowboy is hanging precariously from a limb on the side of a cliff, there will probably be wind blowing under the vest so we will want to undercut very deeply along the front and bottom of the vest. Lay one side of your detail knife flush with the front of the shirt and insert it deeply into the vest from the shirt collar all the way down to the bottom of the vest.

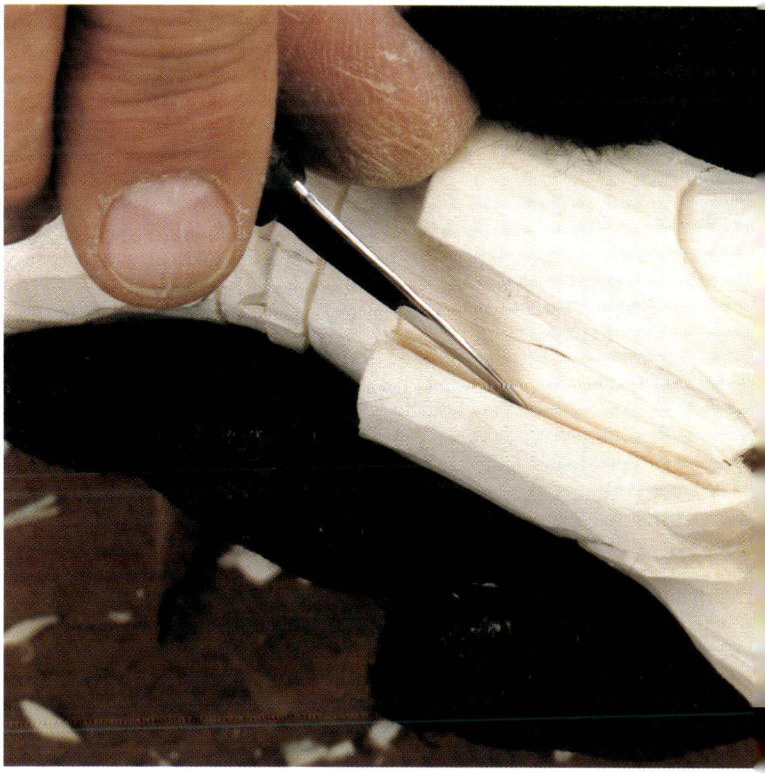

At an angle of about 45 degrees, intersect the first cut and remove the sliver of wood.

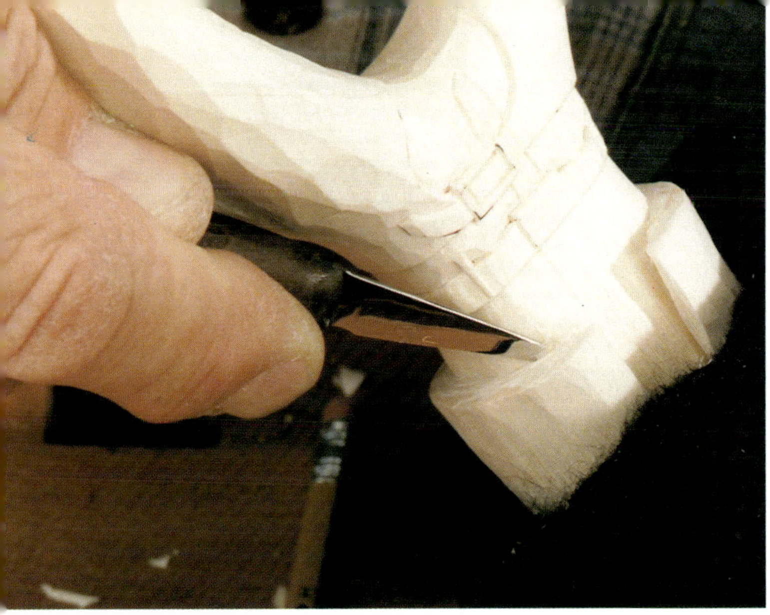

Continue undercutting around the bottom of the vest.

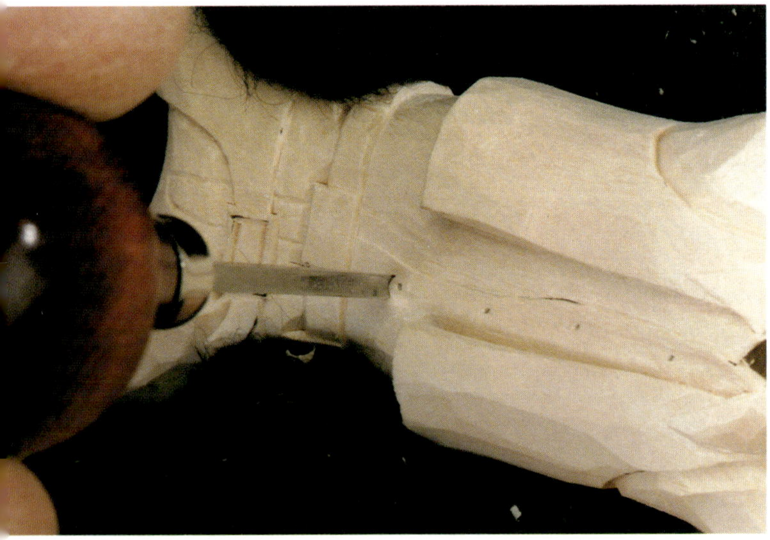

Locate 4 or 5 buttons along the shirt front. Stick your small 1/8" gouge perpendicularly into the shirt front to a depth of about 1/16" at both the bottom and the top of the button.

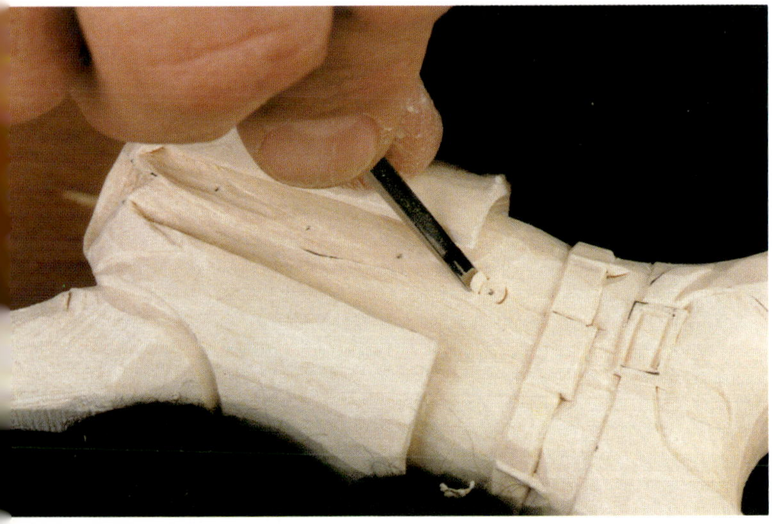

Use that same gouge to relieve a sliver of wood above the button ...

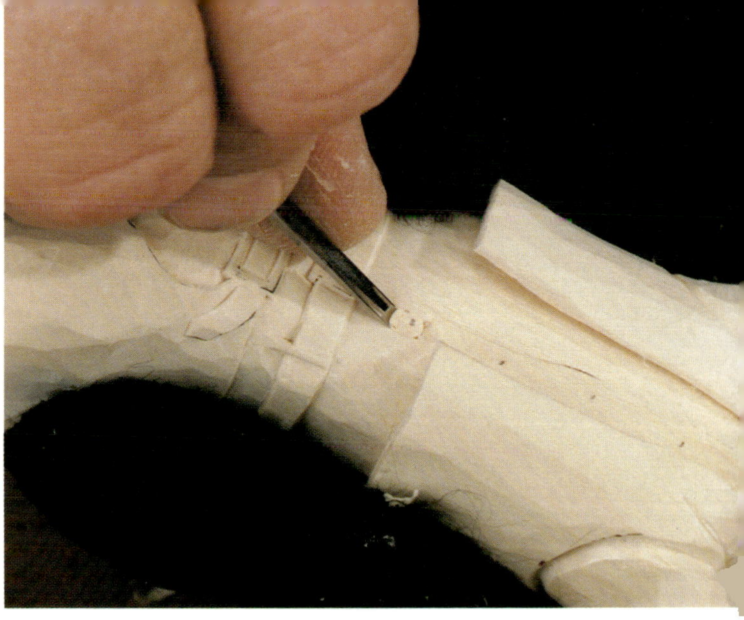

... and below the button as well. Repeat these steps for the other buttons on the front of the shirt. Add a couple to the vest.

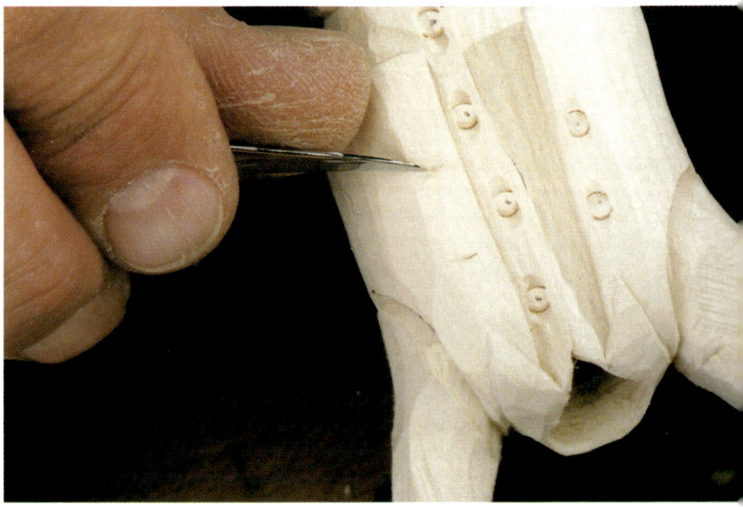

Don't forget to mark the button holes on the left side of the vest.

Use your detail knife to clean away saw marks and to shape the arms from the armholes in the vest to the hands.

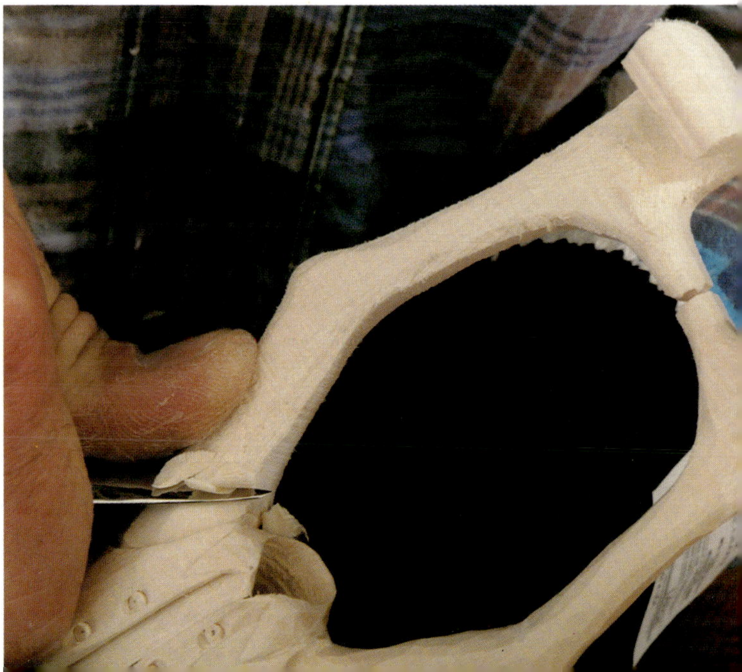

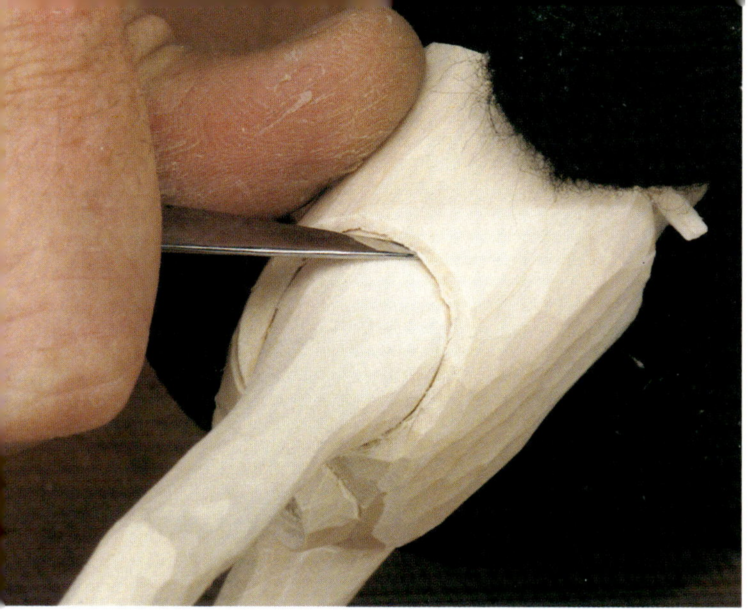

Once the arms are cleaned off, undercut the arms into the armholes of the vest. First slip your knife tip into the armhole with one side of the blade flush to the shirt.

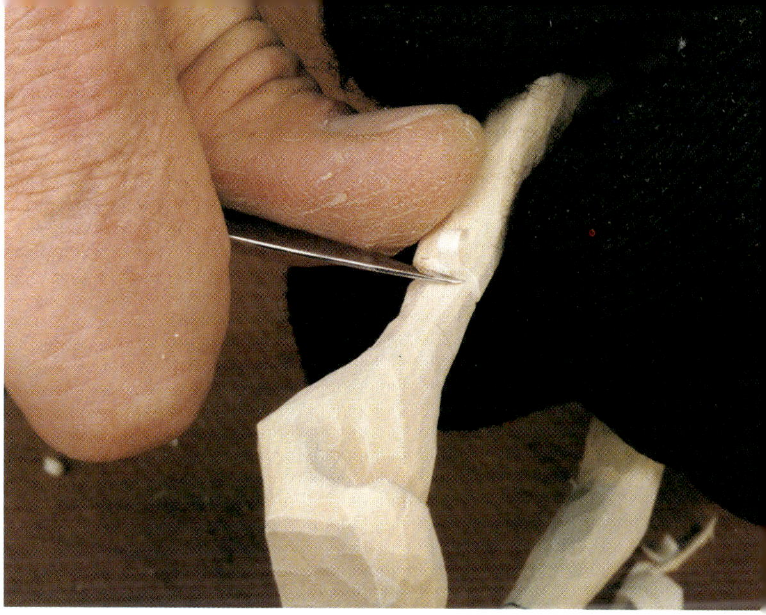

Relieve the wrist to the cuff line cut. Wrists and arms can be thin because we have the grain working in our favor.

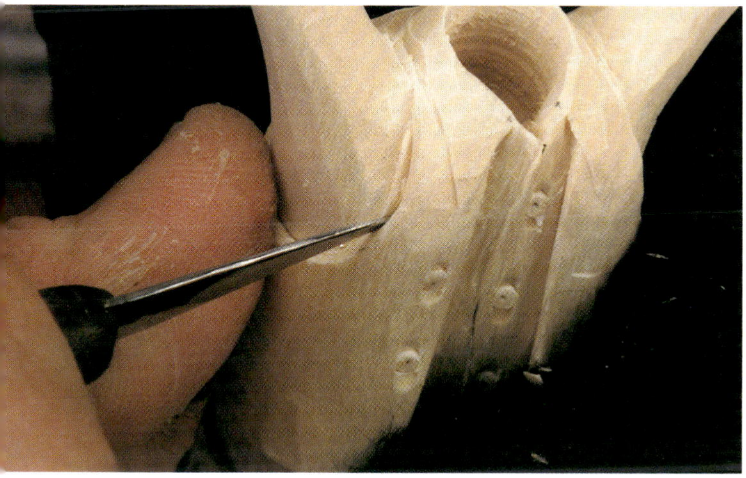

With your knife at roughly 45 degrees to the first cut, remove an undercut sliver.

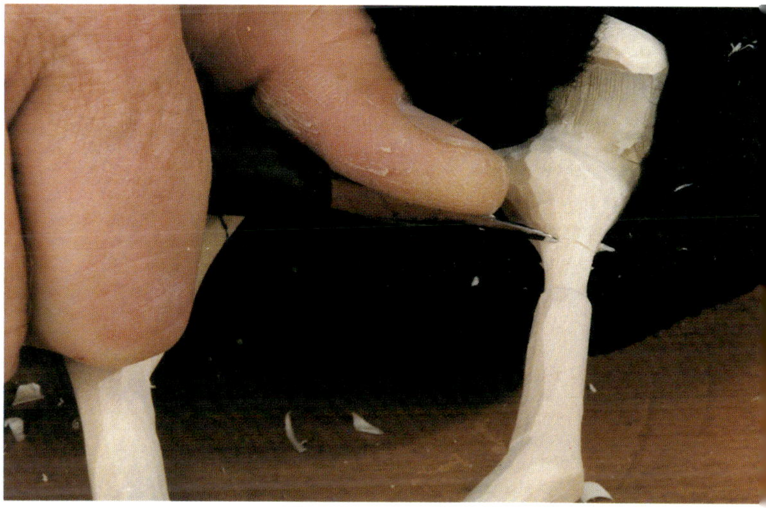

With your knife tip, score along the top of the cuff.

Sketch in the cuffs of the shirt. Note the bulk of wood that I have left for the hands. This is necessary because of the direction of the grain through the fingers which must hold both the cowboy's and the horse's weight once we attach them to the limb. Use your 1/8" V tool to score around the cuff line.

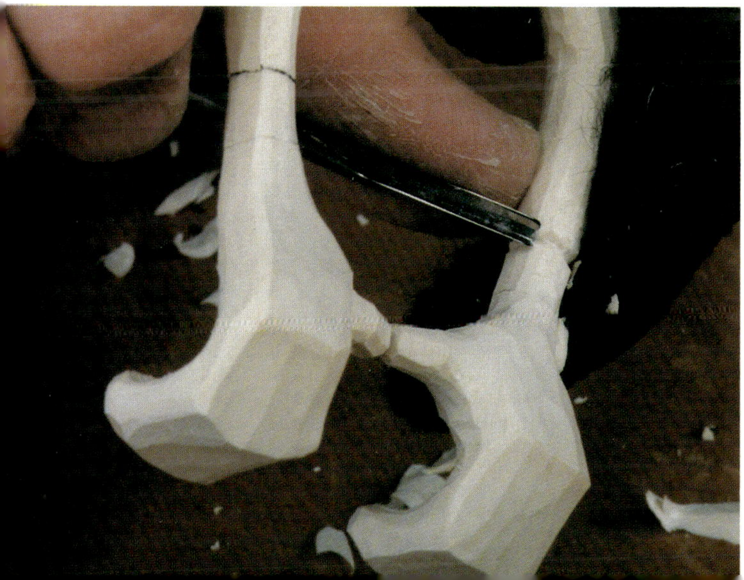

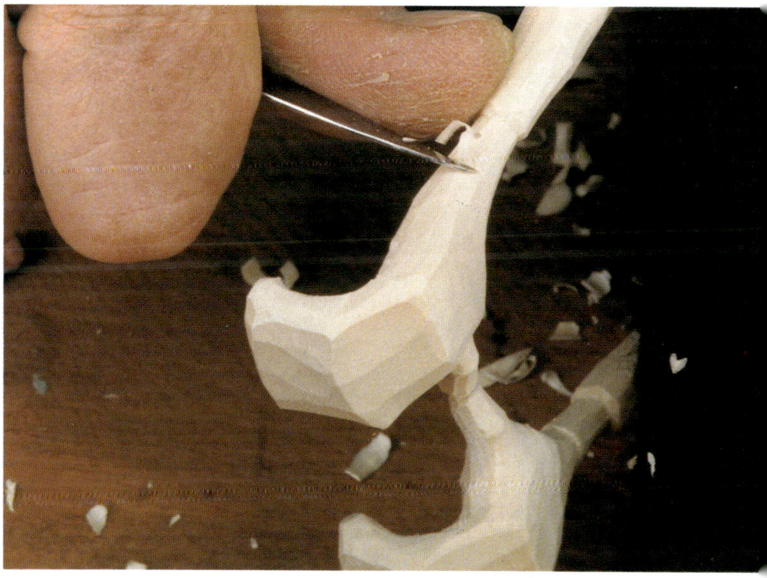

Relieve the hand and wrist to the bottom of the scored cuff line.

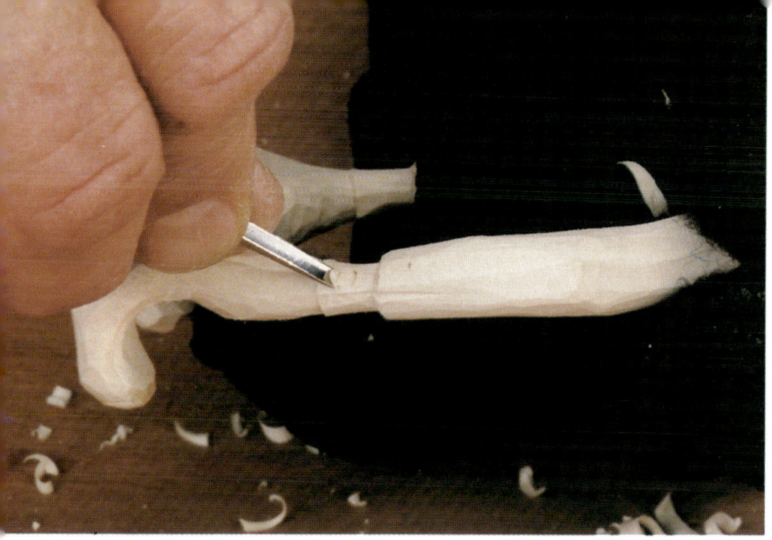

With your 1/8" V tool, one edge of V tool laying on the cuff, cut the cuff placket. Carve a button on each cuff using the same technique we used on the front of the shirt.

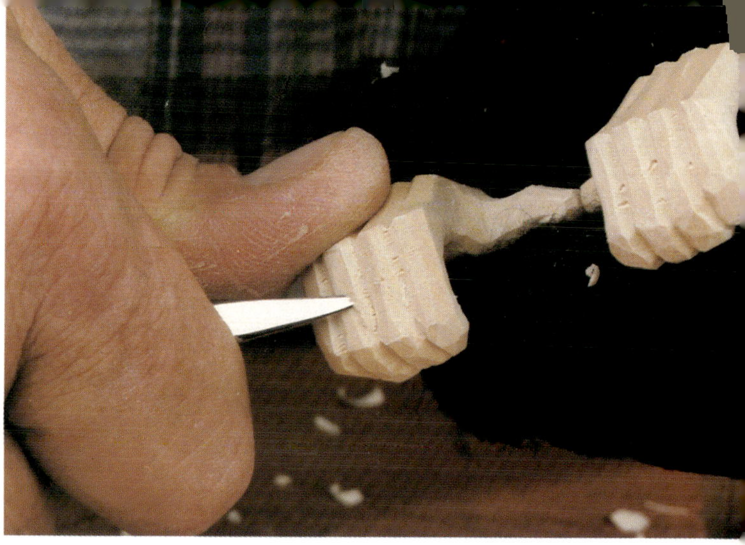

Using your detail knife, begin to round each finger.

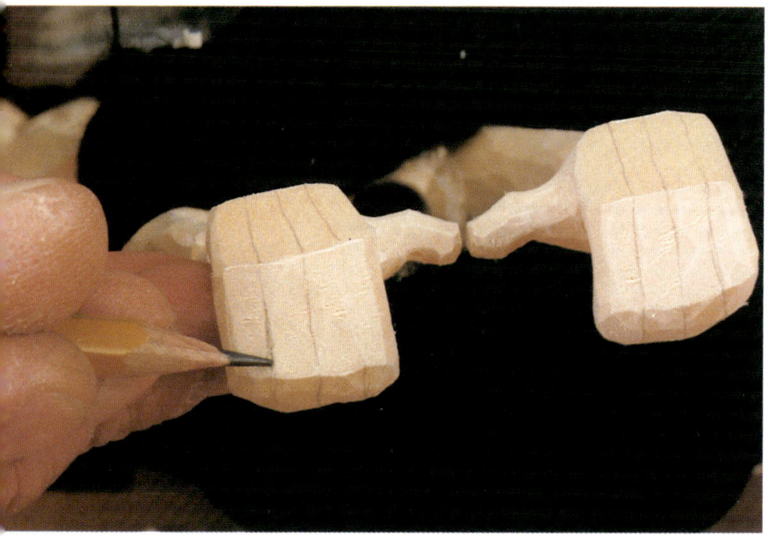

Draw the four fingers on each hand.

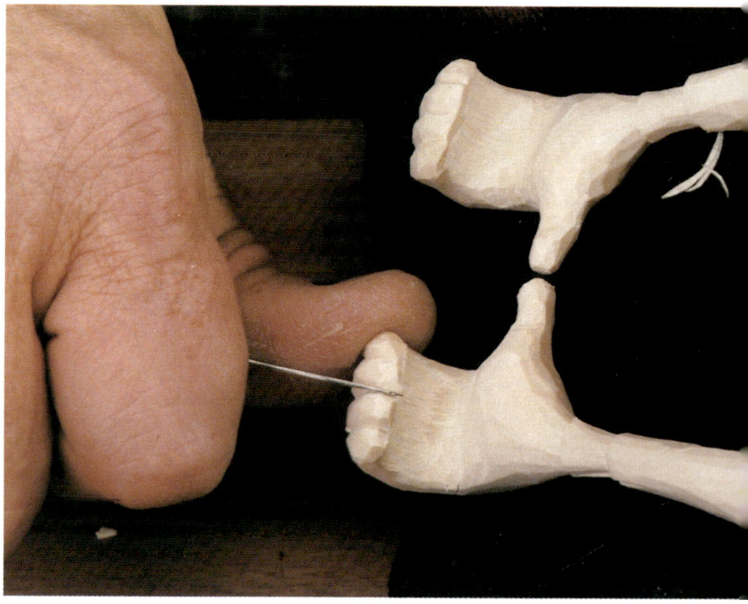

Use your knife tip to shape and separate the finger tips.

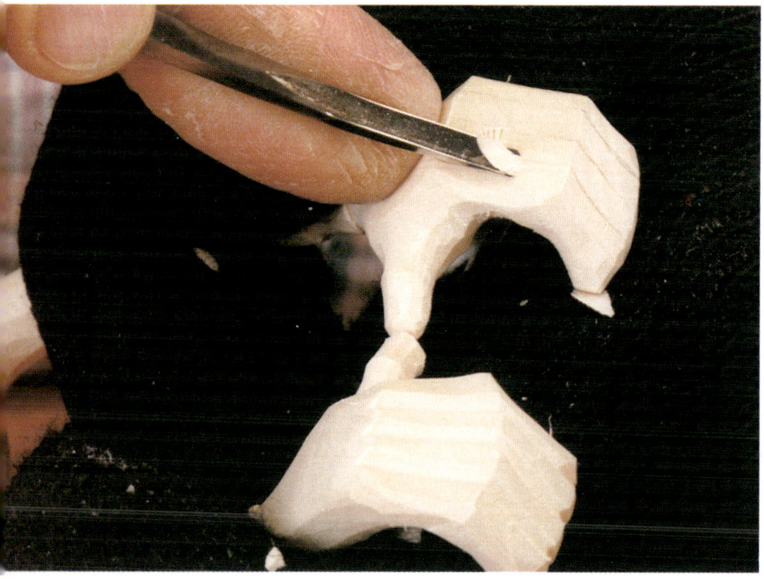

Use your 1/8" V tool to separate these fingers.

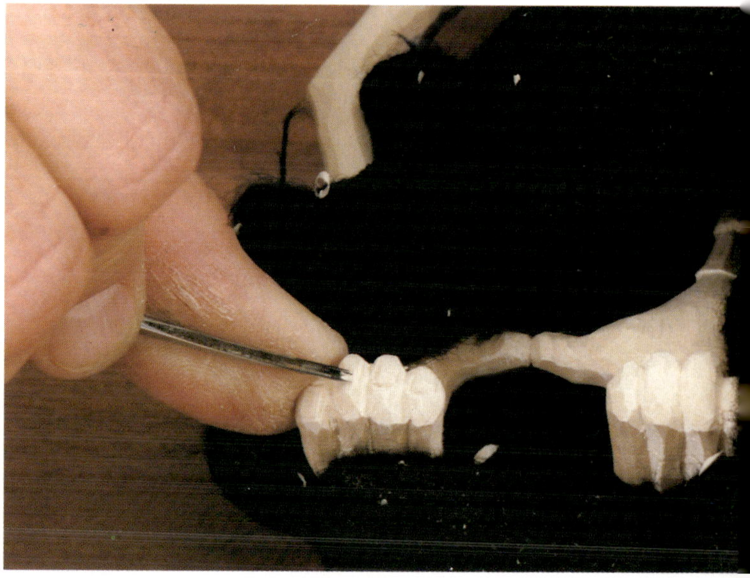

Add fingernails with your small V tool.

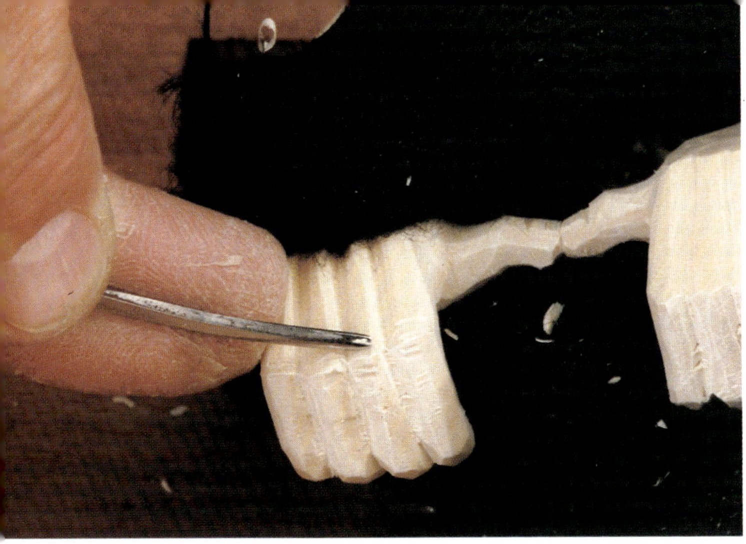

Use your small V tool to indicate skin folds around finger joints.

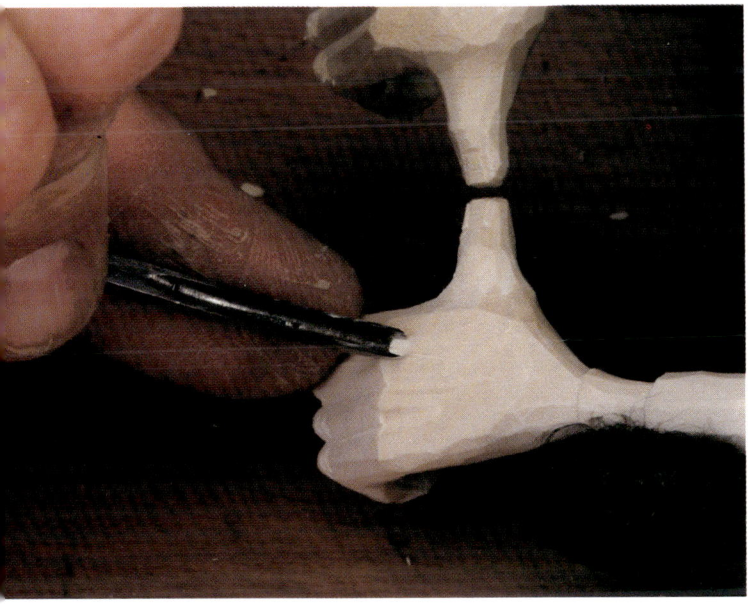

Indicate ligaments on the back of hand with a small deep gouge.

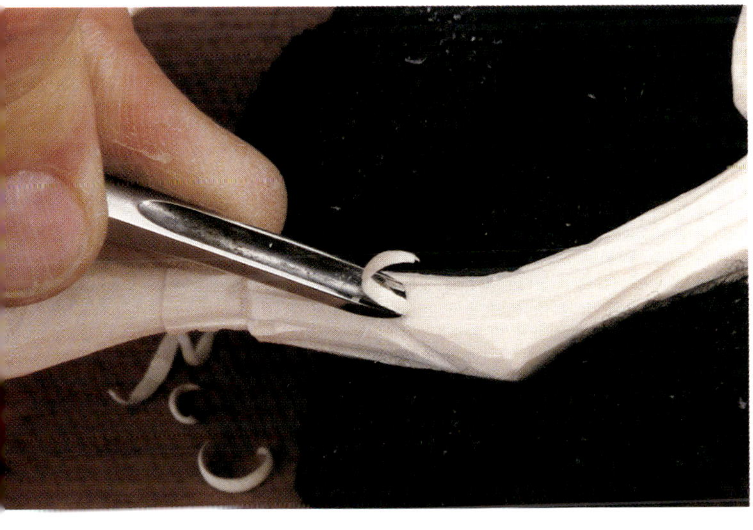

Finally, to finish the cowboy's body, use a combination of a medium V tool and a 3/16" deep gouge to carve creases and crevices down the lengths of each arm. These cuts simulate folds in the shirt.

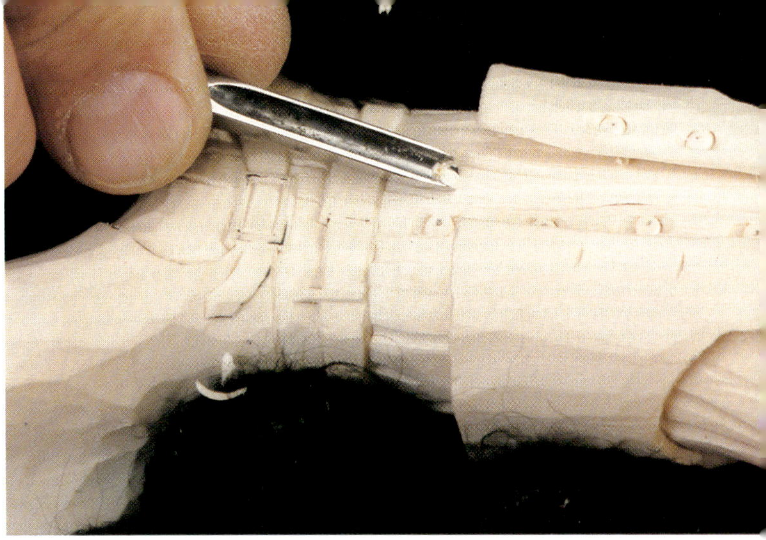

Don't forget some very shallow folds in the shirt as it enters the pants.

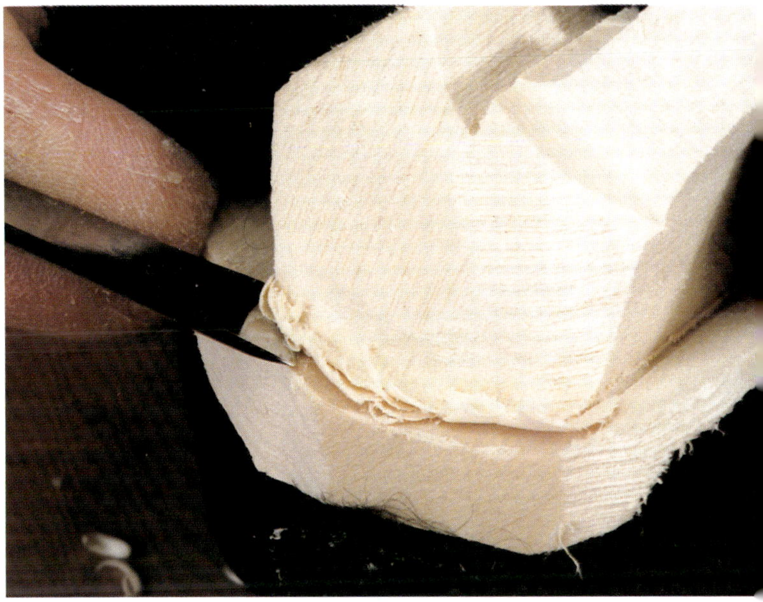

We will begin cleaning saw marks from the head using the 1/2" fishtail gouge. Start by inserting the gouge into the head along the bottom of hat brim to establish at stop cut.

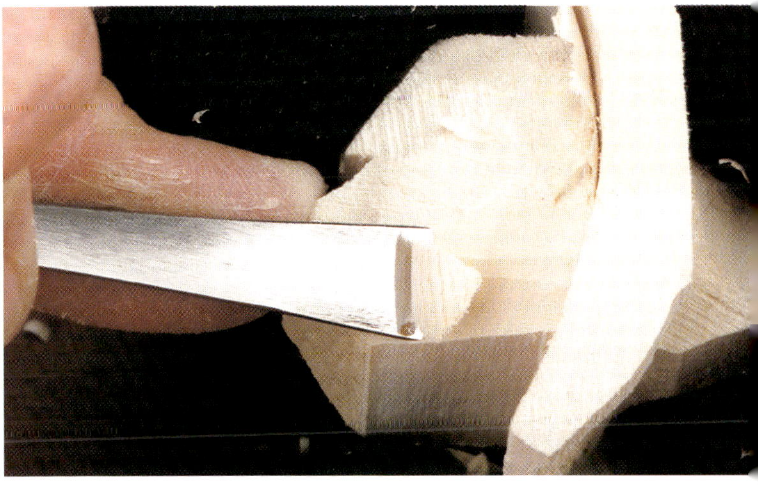

At the front of the head we must carve from the neck toward the hat brim and the stop cut.

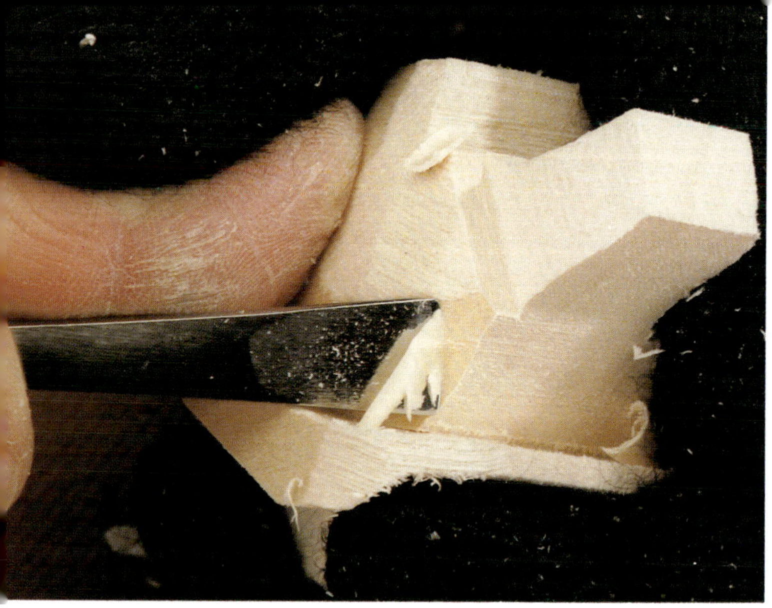

At the back of the head we must cut from the hat brim toward the neck. This way we follow the grain orientation, producing a smooth cut.

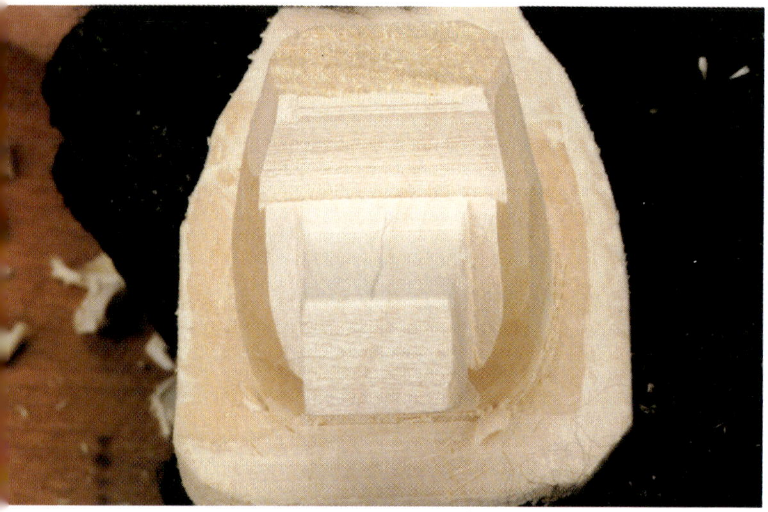

Our objective at this stage is two fold. We wish to remove saw marks and to begin shaping the head into an oval when viewed from the base of the neck up toward the hat brim.

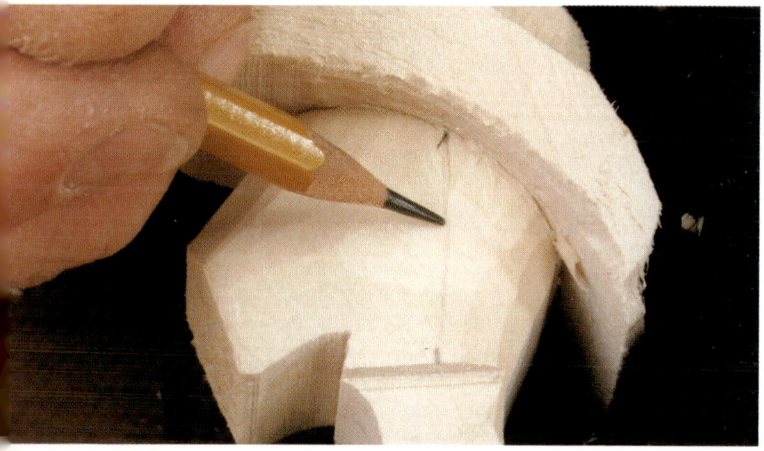

Locate a point along the head—just under the hat brim—that divides the head into two equal parts, front to back. Locate the same point along the neck, dividing it into equal halves as well. Draw a line between these two points, locating the leading edge of the ear.

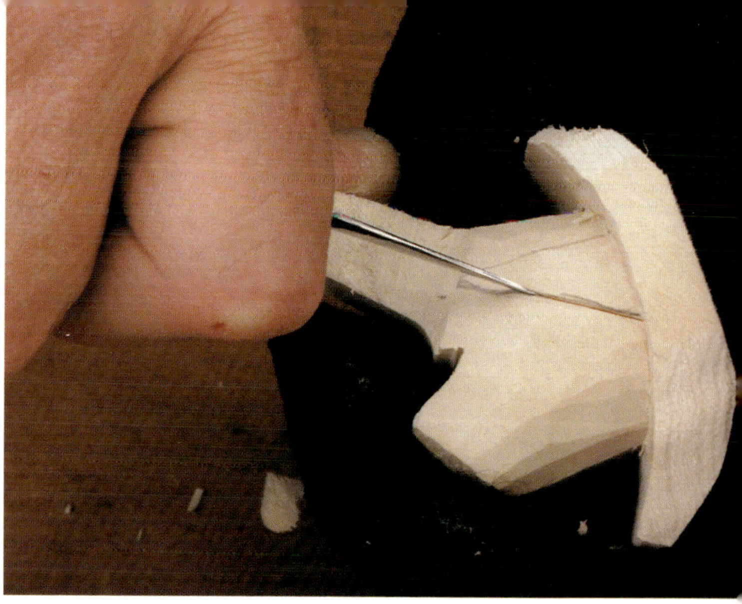

Locate a point approximately 1/2" from the top of the previously drawn line. From this new point, draw a second line to forming this triangle. You have now located the ear. With your detail knife score along each of these lines, perpendicular to the surface of the head.

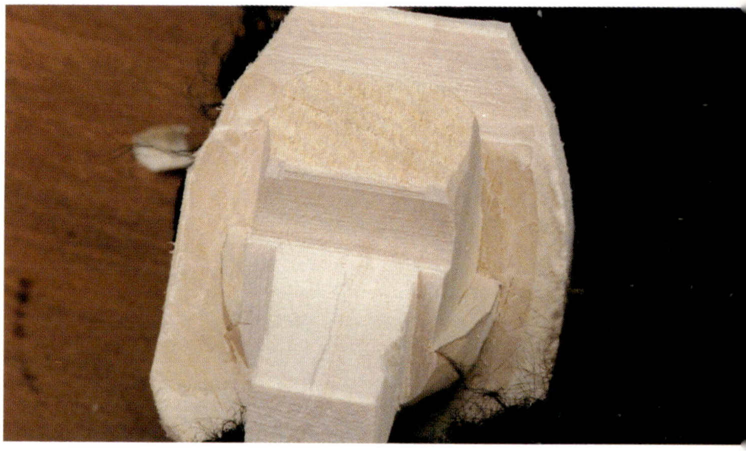

Cutting from the front of the head in toward the ear, remove the excess wood on the face to the depth of the front of the ear. These cuts should be made so that they are parallel to the outer surface of the ear triangle and subsequently parallel to each other.

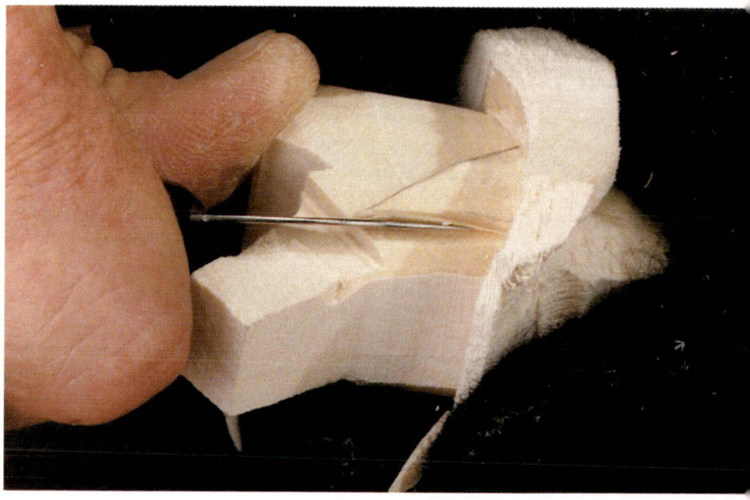

Chip the wood from behind the ear.

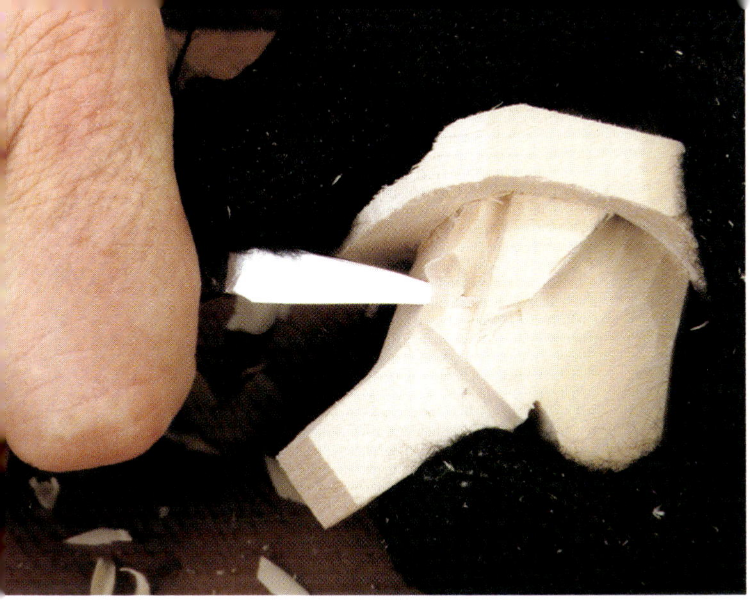

Round the back of the head by cutting down from the top of the head toward the neck.

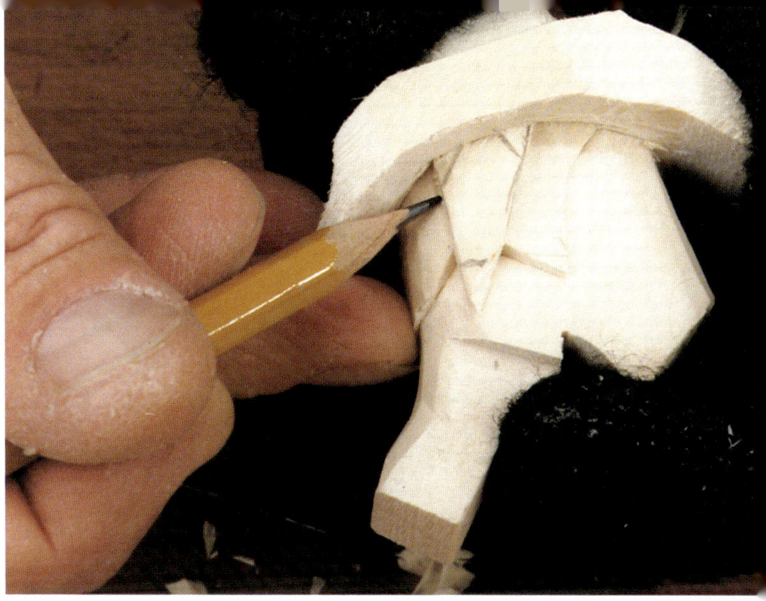

Draw triangles at each of the corners of the ear triangle as shown.

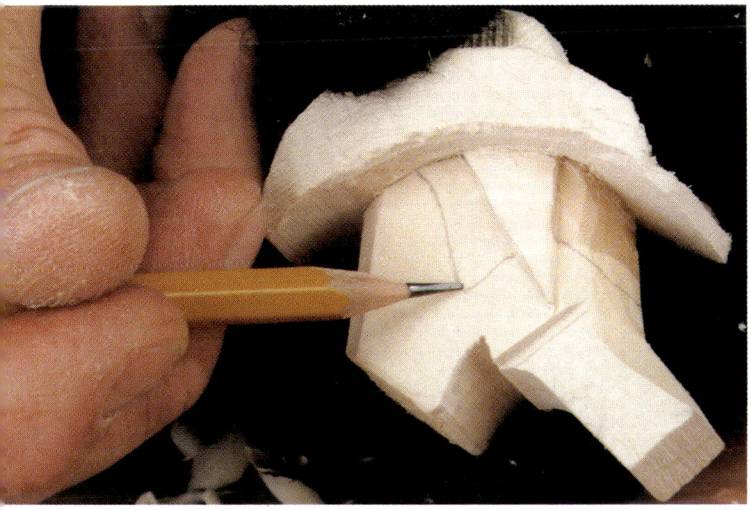

Sketch in the sideburns and the hairline around the back of the head.

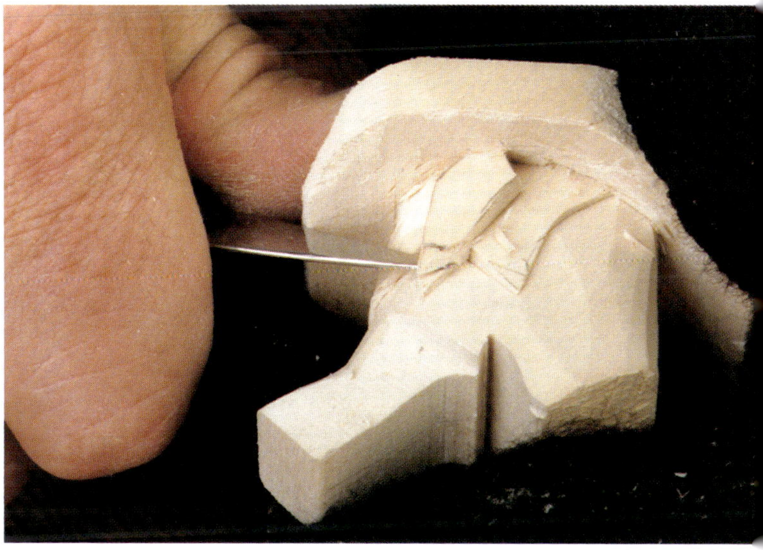

Remove these small triangles with tip of your detail knife.

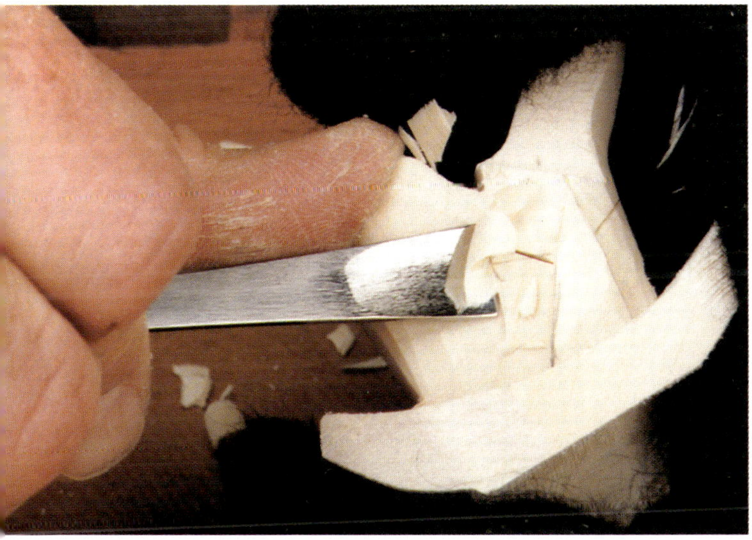

Score along the hair line and relieve the wood on the face to the depth of these scored hair lines.

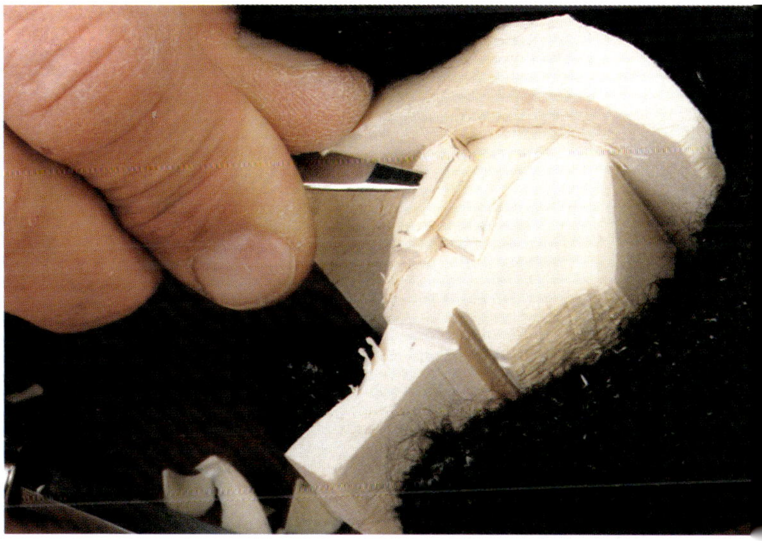

With the tip of your knife blade cutting at an angle of about 45 degrees, remove the excess wood from the leading edge of the ear.

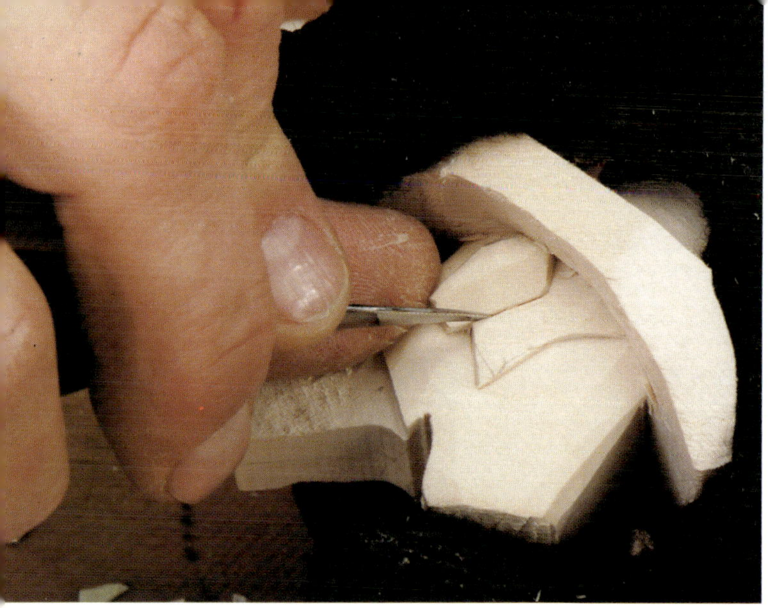

Score along the front of the ear to the depth of the sideburn.

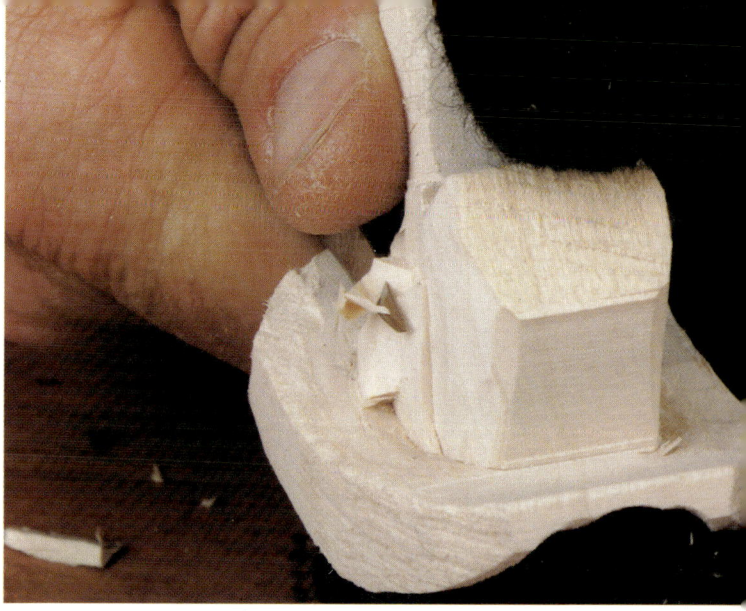

To keep the ear from looking like a stiff appendage attached to the side of the head, let's add a little looseness to it by sloping it from the top to the earlobe.

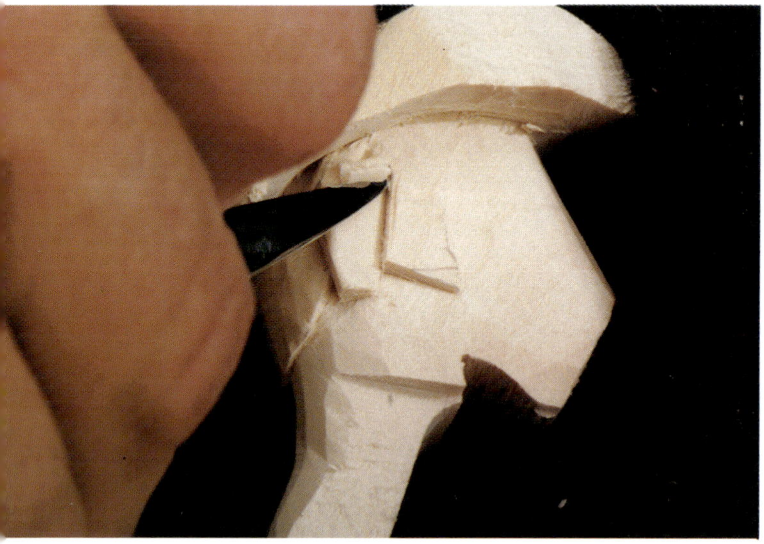

Again with your knife tilted at about a 45 degree angle, slice along the front edge of the ear to the depth of the sideburn. This separates the sideburn from the ear.

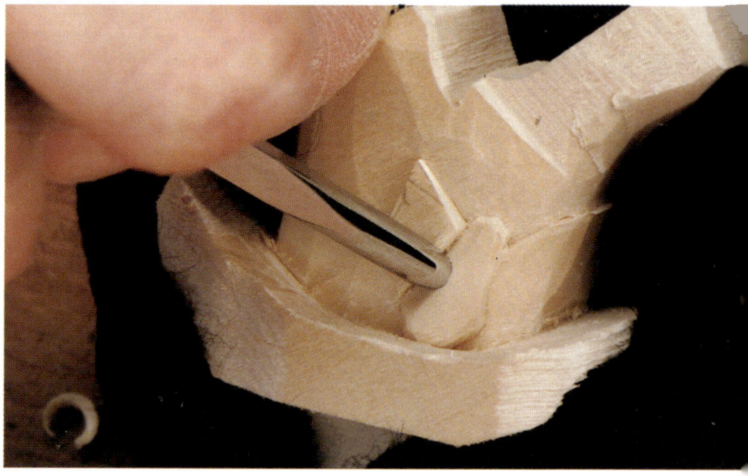

Form the tragus in the ear with your 3/16" deep gouge by inserting the gouge into the ear to a depth of about 1/8".

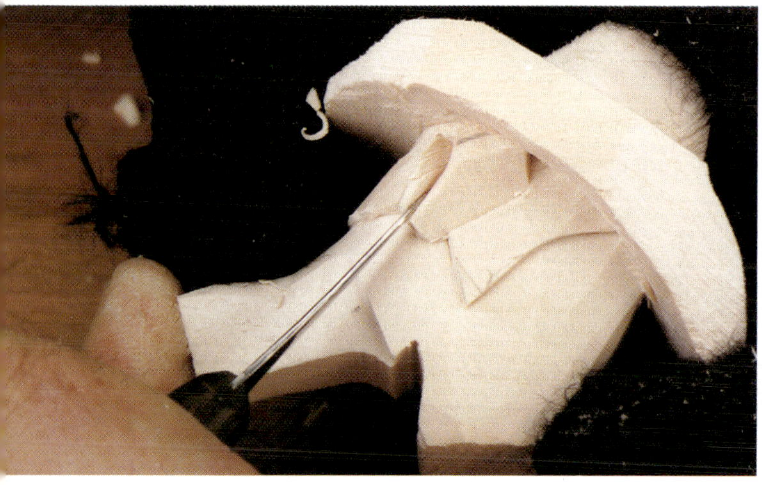

Shape the rear of the ear so that the ear looks almost like a backward question mark.

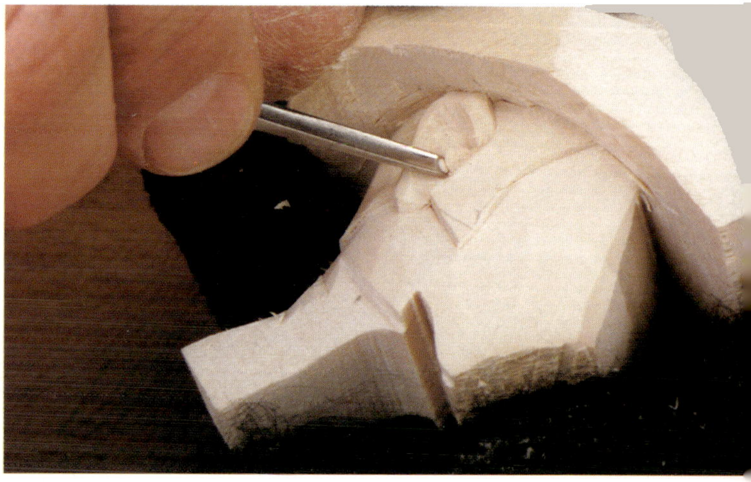

With your small, shallow gouge, remove wood from inside the ear to the depth of the tragus cut.

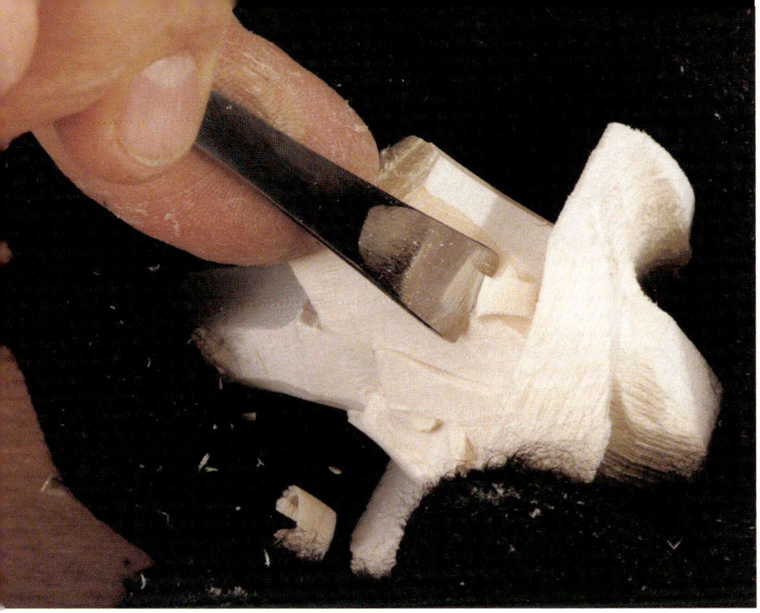

Use your fishtail gouge to reshape the front of the head into an oval.

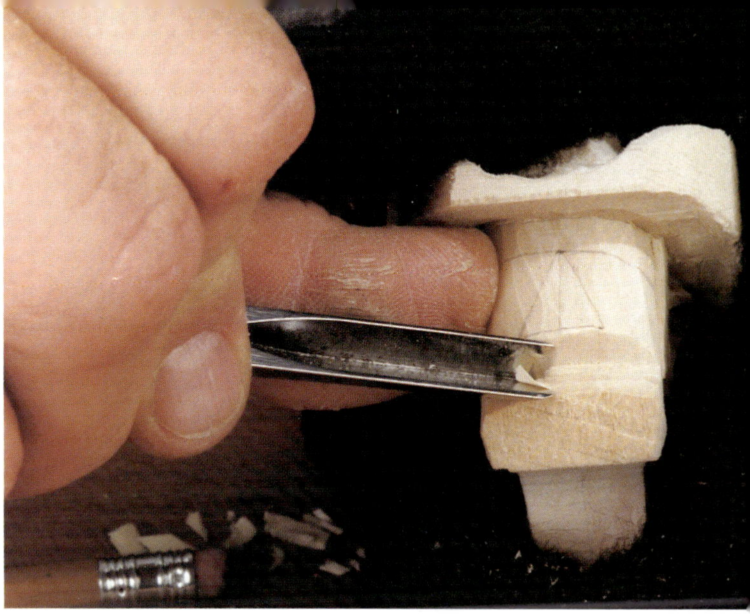

Using your large V tool, cut in the bottom of the nose.

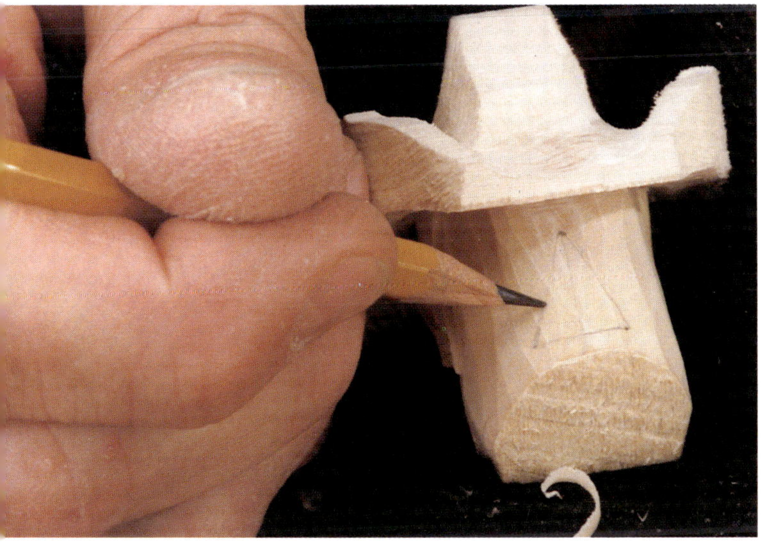

Place a point about 3/16" below the edge of the hat brim along the centerline of the face. Mark the width of the nose below. Lay out a triangle for the nose.

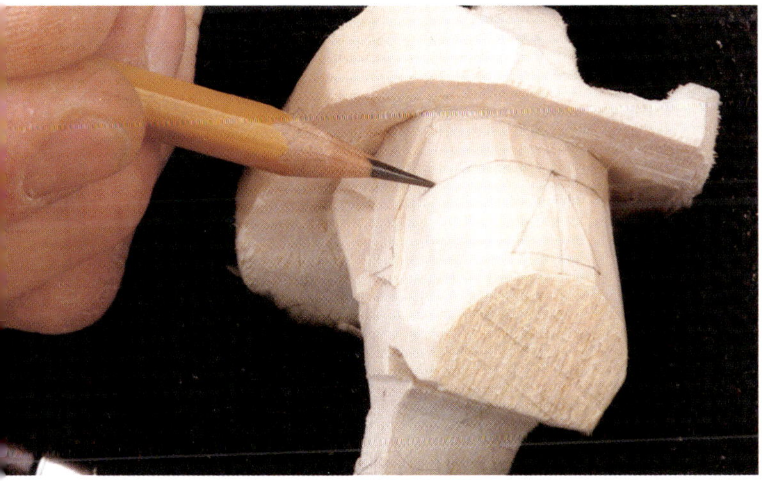

Extend a line from either side of the apex of this nose triangle to locate the bottom of each eyebrow.

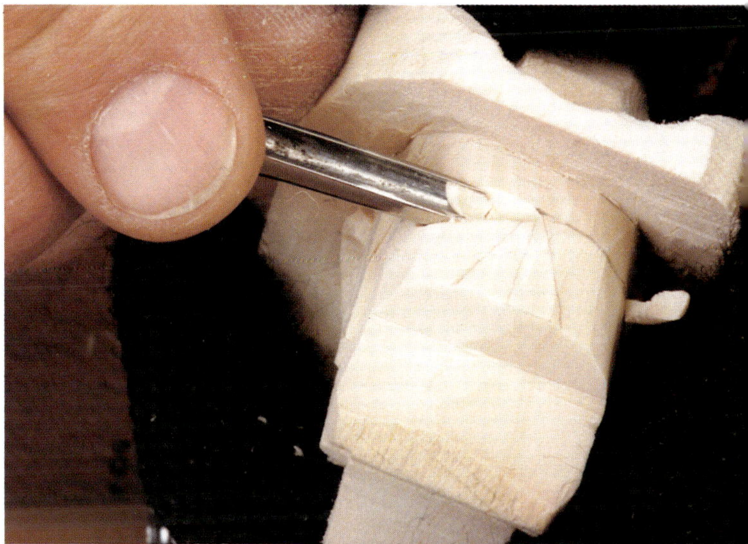

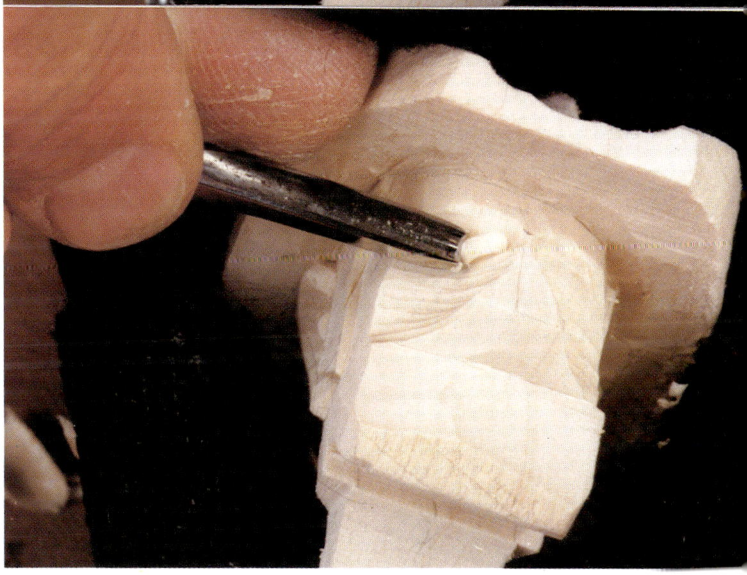

Remove wood from between the eyebrow line and each side of the nose with your 3/16" gouge. Carve parallel to the plane of the nose triangle. As you approach the side of the nose turn the cut outward from the face to exit the cut. The two concave surfaces you are carving will become the eye sockets.

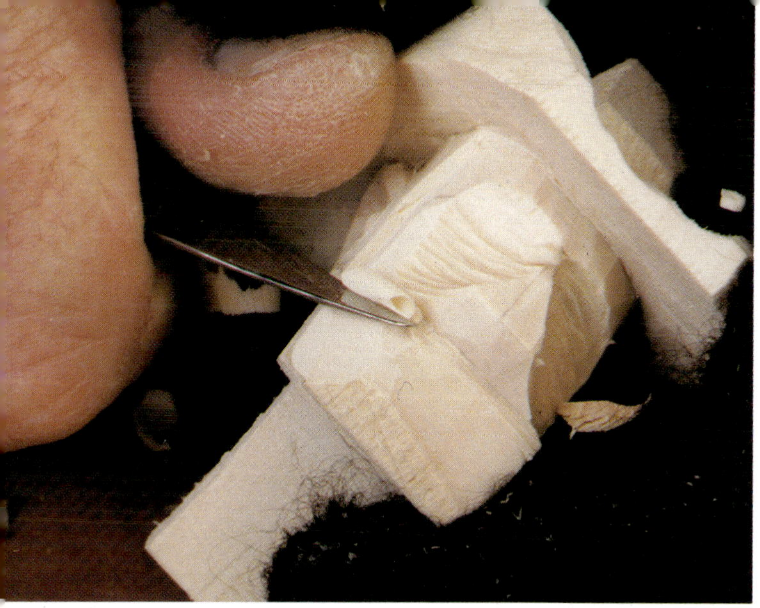

Round each side of the head from the chin to the forehead with your detail knife.

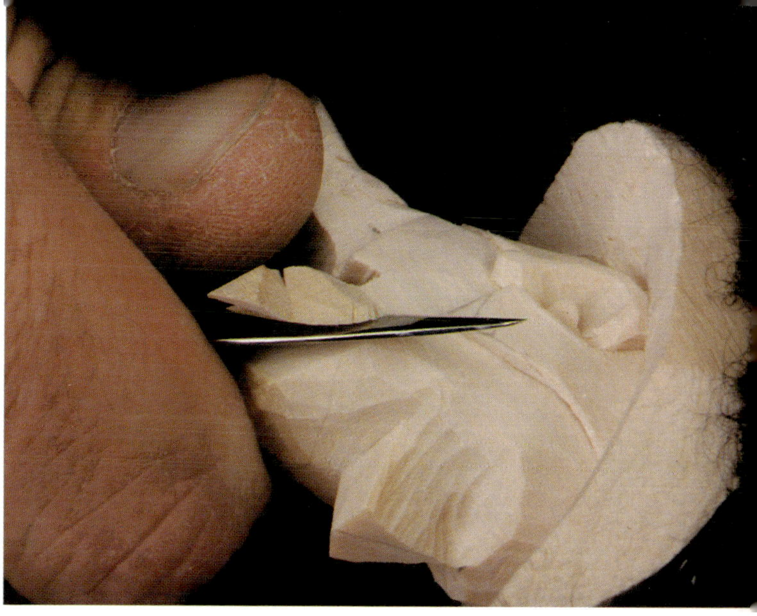

Begin to shape and round the chin and neck with your knife.

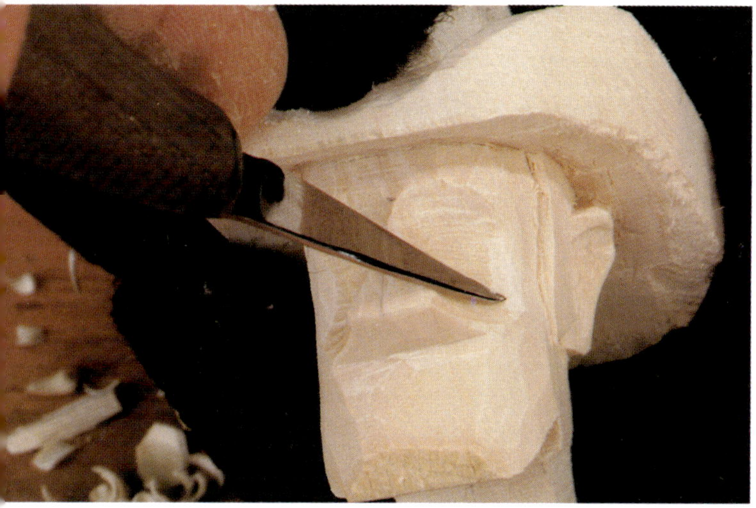

Note the indentation made at the outer edge of the eye socket for the temple area.

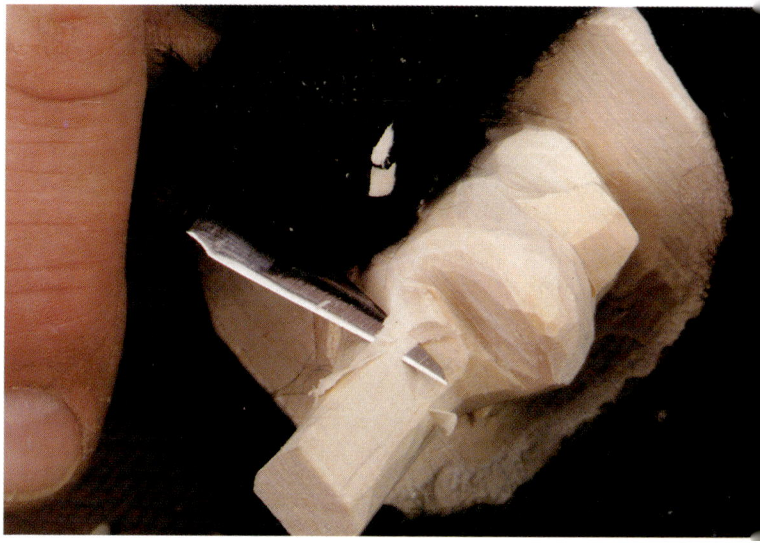

While we're down in this area, let's shape the adams apple and finish rounding the neck.

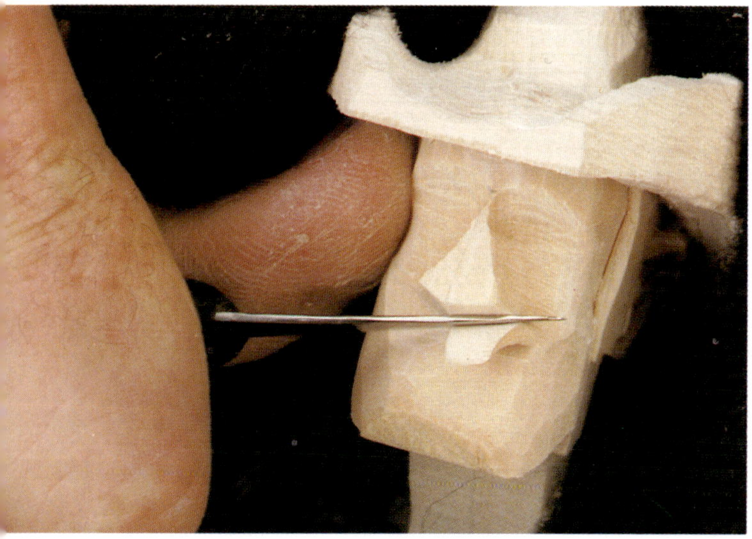

Clip each side of the base of the nose as shown.

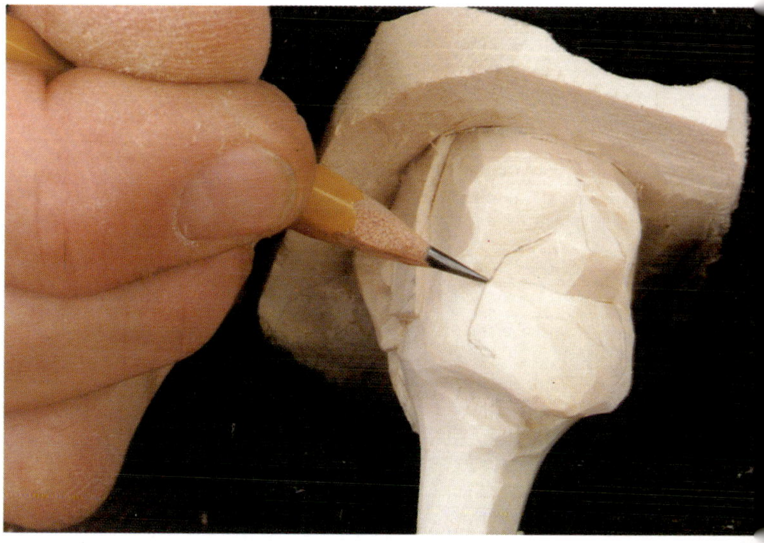

Draw in the smile lines.

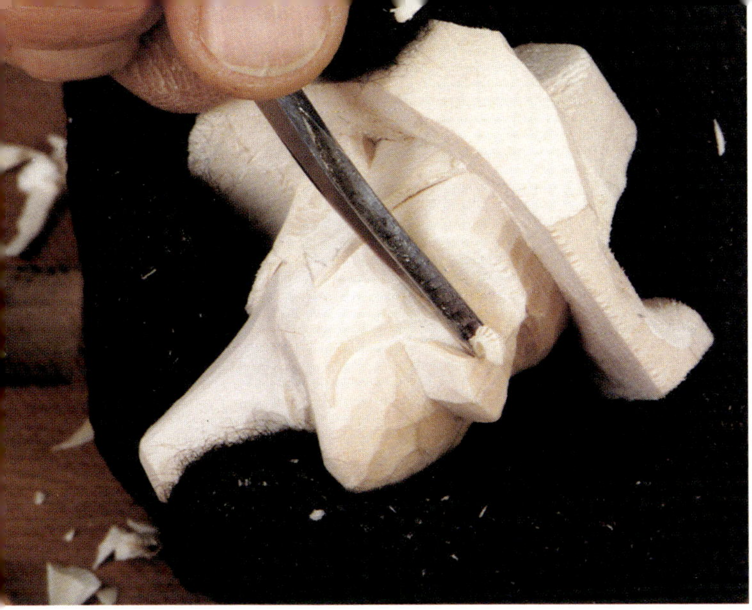

With your 1/8" V tool, follow these smile lines into the nose.

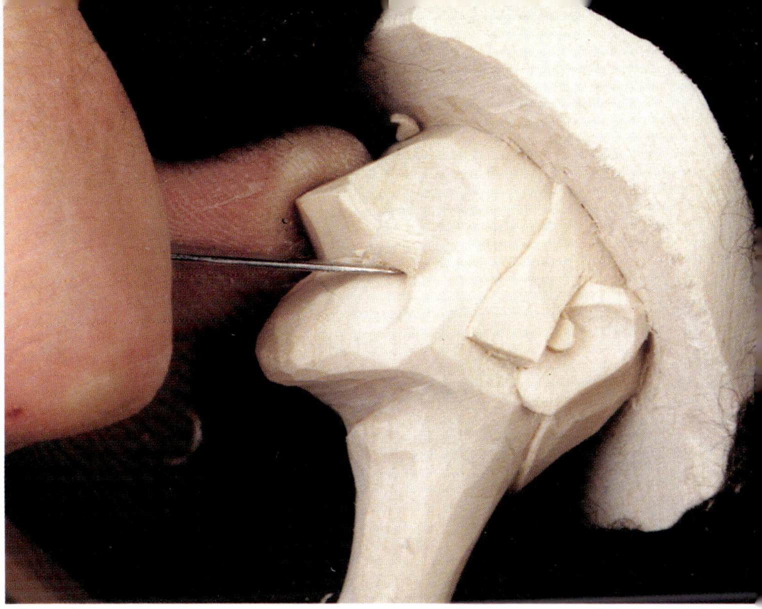

With the tip of your detail knife, one edge flush with the mouth area, remove wood to the depth of the smile line cut from the chin up to the base of the nostrils.

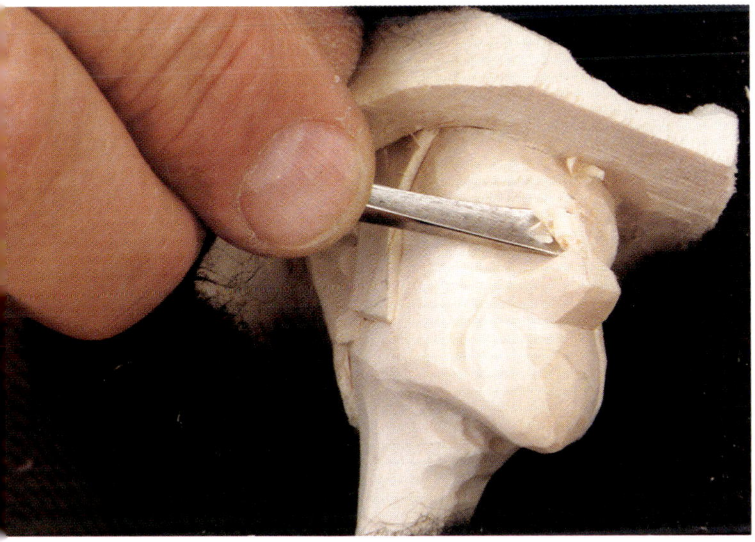

Remove the wood from above each nostril with your small, shallow gouge.

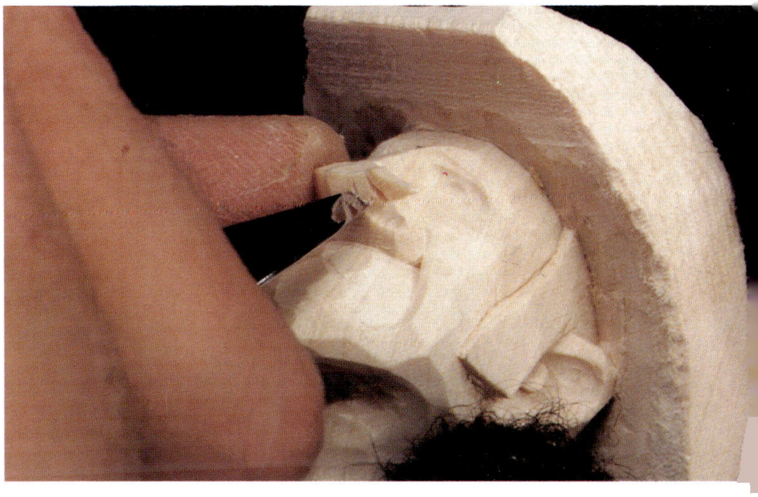

Shape the nostril with your knife tip by cutting a concave plane toward the center of the nose.

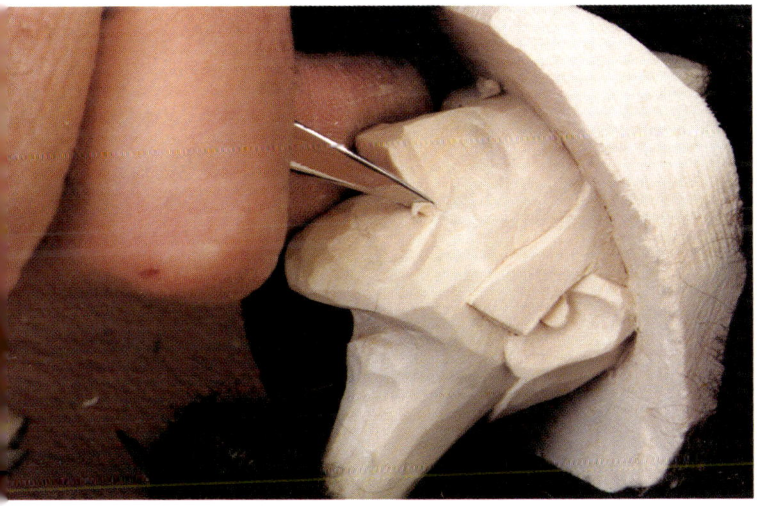

Clip the tip of the nostril off to the smile line cut with the tip of your detail knife.

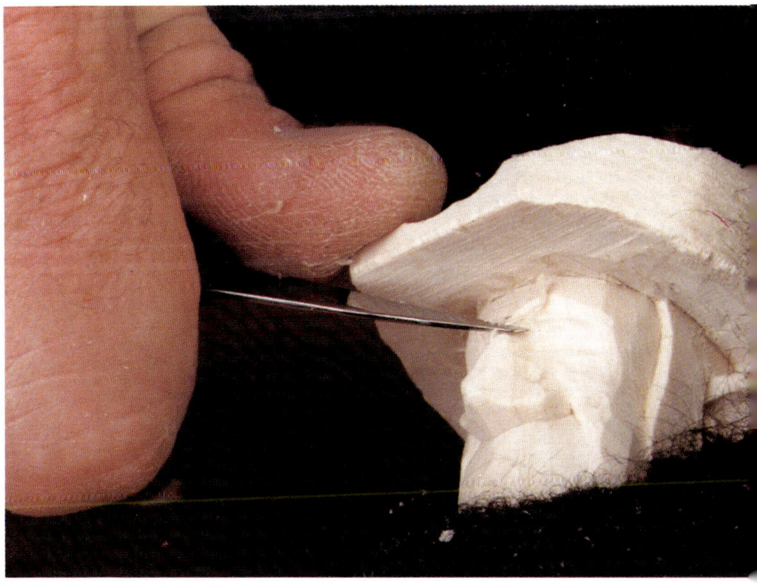

Round the nose.

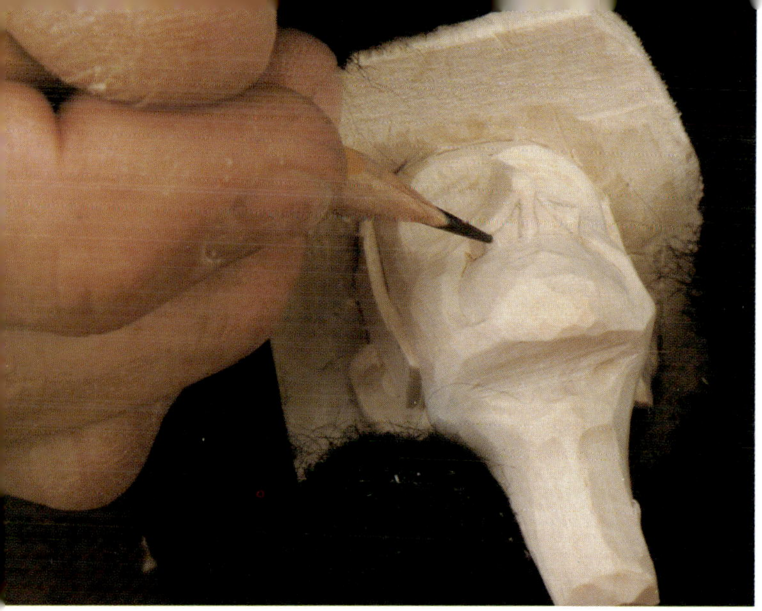

Sketch in the septum and the entrance to the nostrils on both sides of the nose.

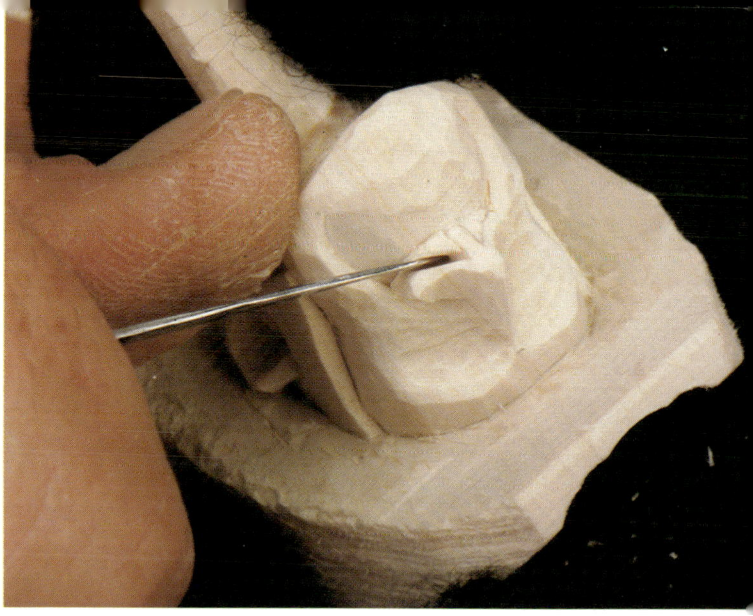

Remove a chip by inserting your knife tip along the top of the nostril opening.

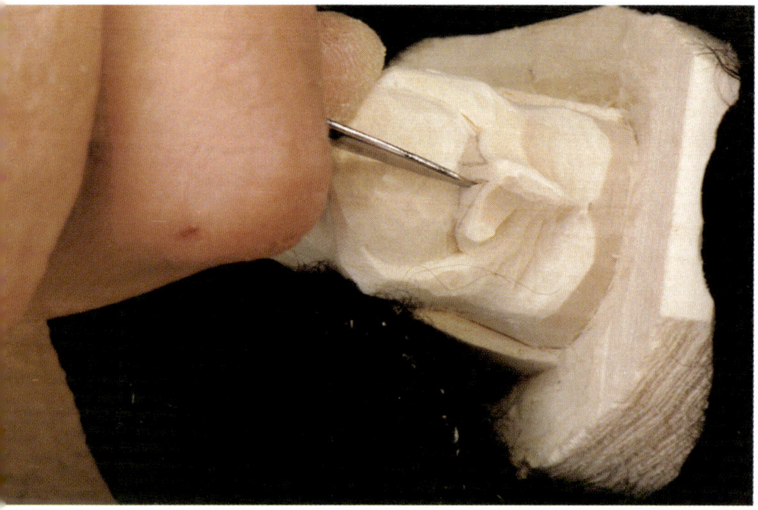

Slip the knife tip along one side of the septum to a depth of about 1/8".

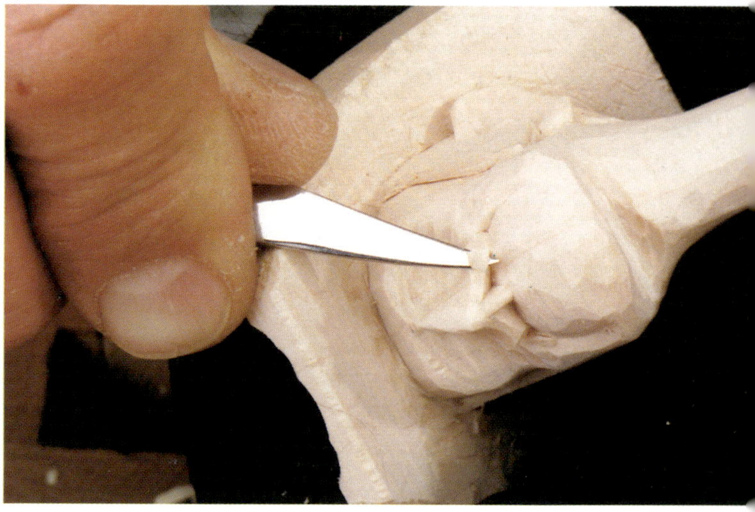

Removing wood from this area accents the septum. When the nose is viewed from the profile, the septum can now be seen—as is the case for most noses.

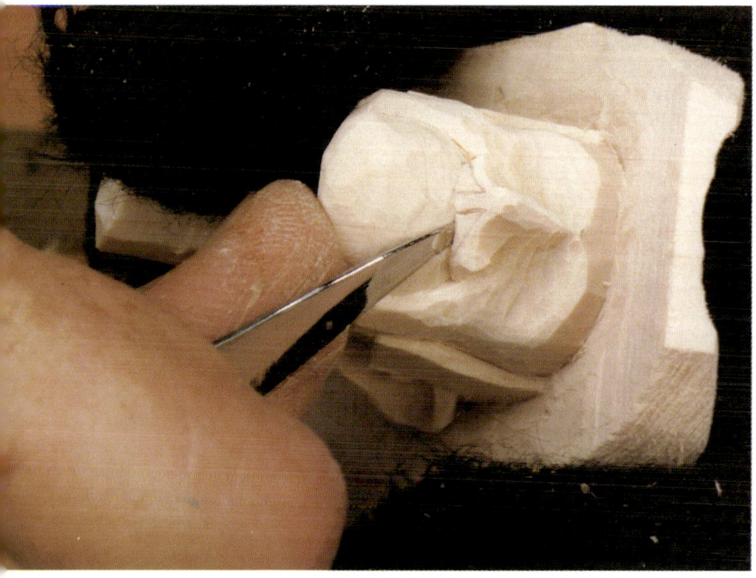

Intersect that cut with one along the bottom of the nostril opening.

Cut in the bridge of the nose with your knife.

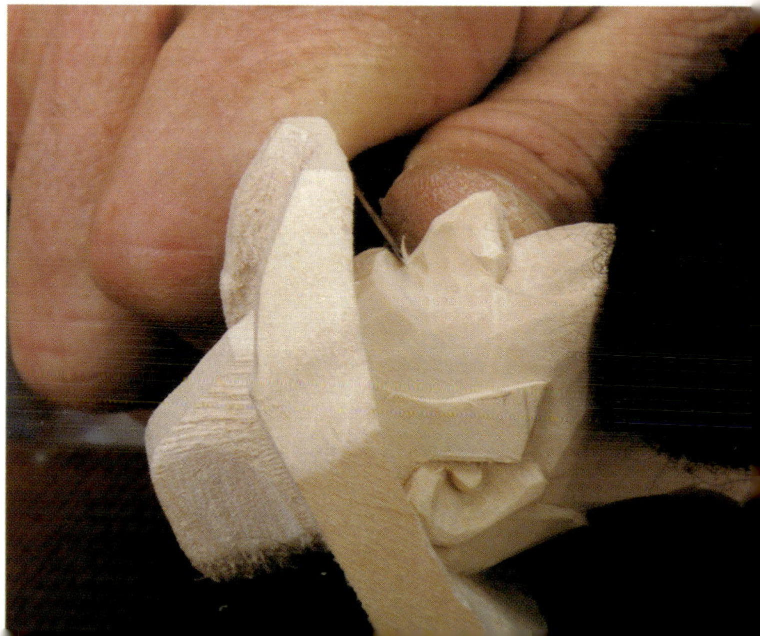

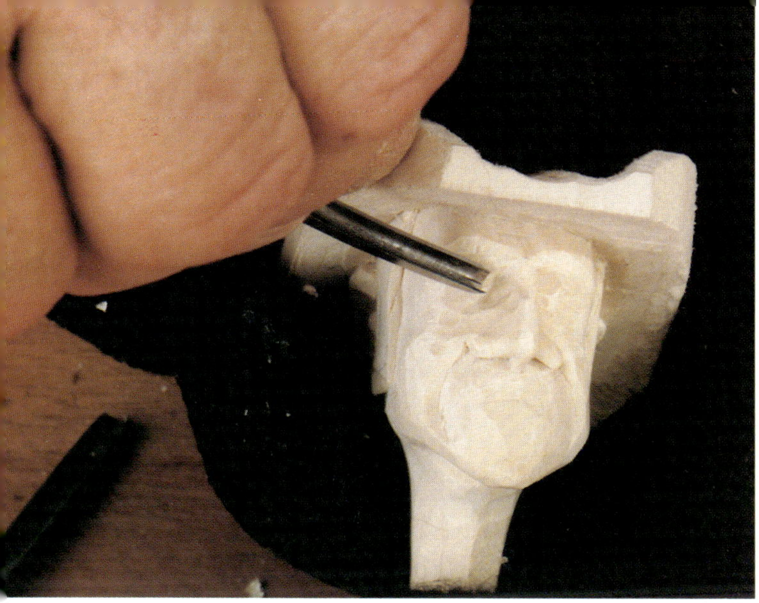

Let's carve the eyes next. Remove wood from the area of the inside corner of the eyeball with a small deep gouge. We want to dig out a considerable amount of this wood so that we can carve the finished eye in such a way that it protrudes from the face more than is usual. In other words, we want to carve him "bug-eyed" to indicate fear and amazement at his situation.

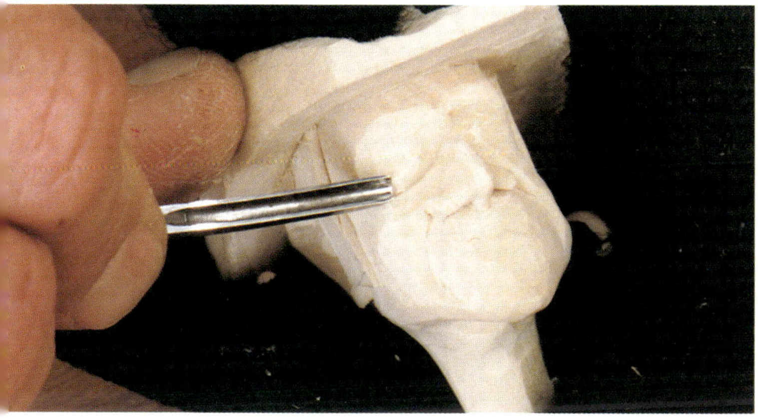

Form a mound into which the eye will eventually be carved with the small deep gouge.

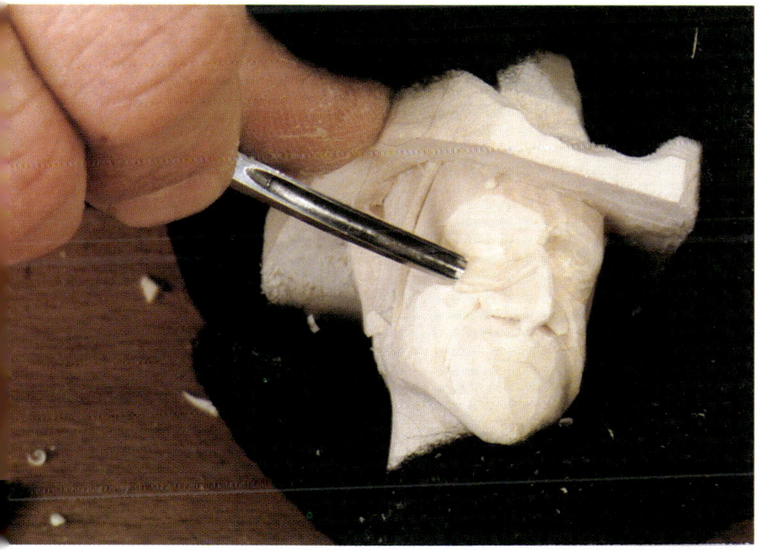

Shave off wood below this mound.

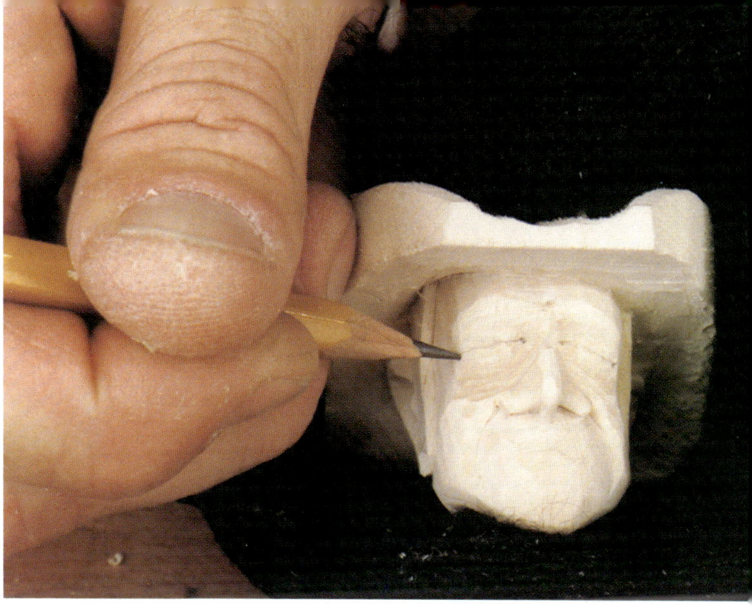

Mark the inside and outside corners of each eyeball with a dot. Connect these dots with a straight line.

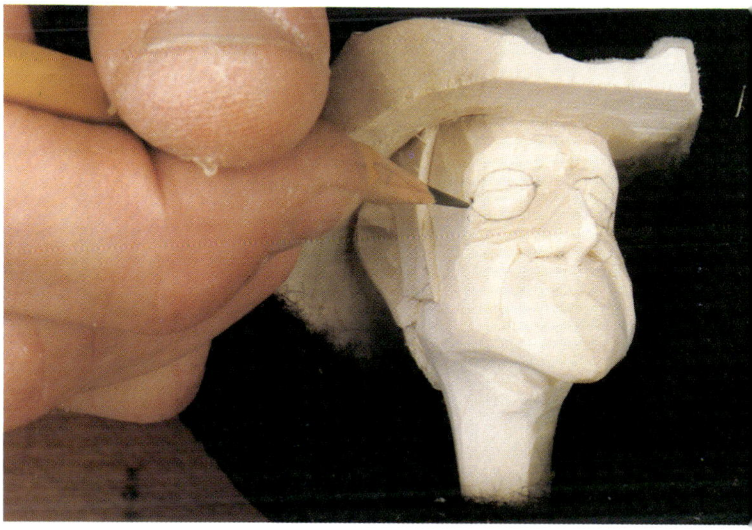

Using this straight line as the major axis, draw an ellipse that approaches a true circle.

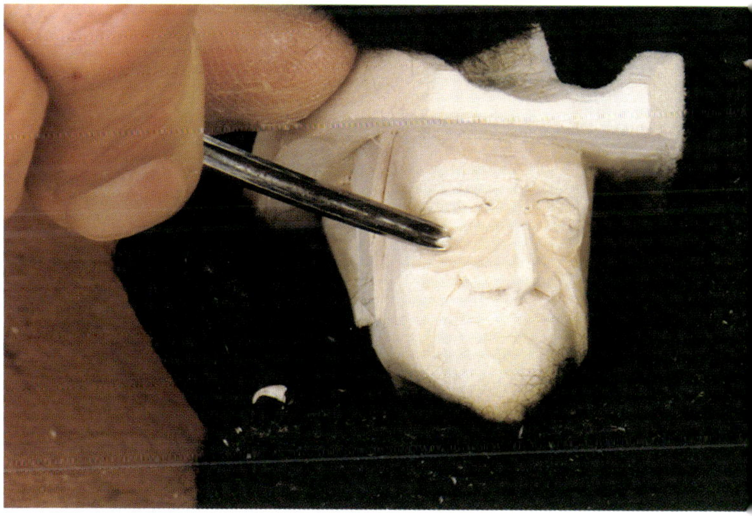

With the smallest deep gouge you have, follow the bottom line of your ellipse from the inside corner to the outside corner of the eye.

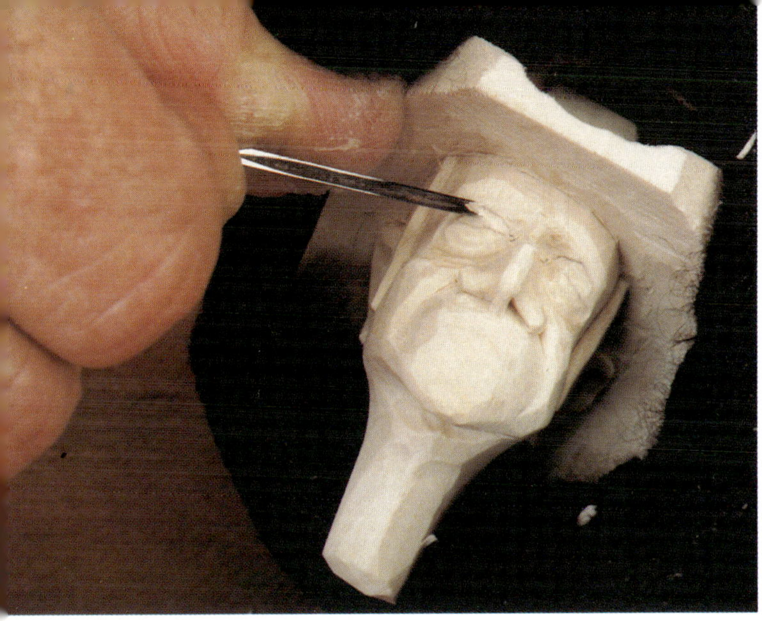

Follow the upper arc from outside corner to inside corner of eyeball with your small V tool.

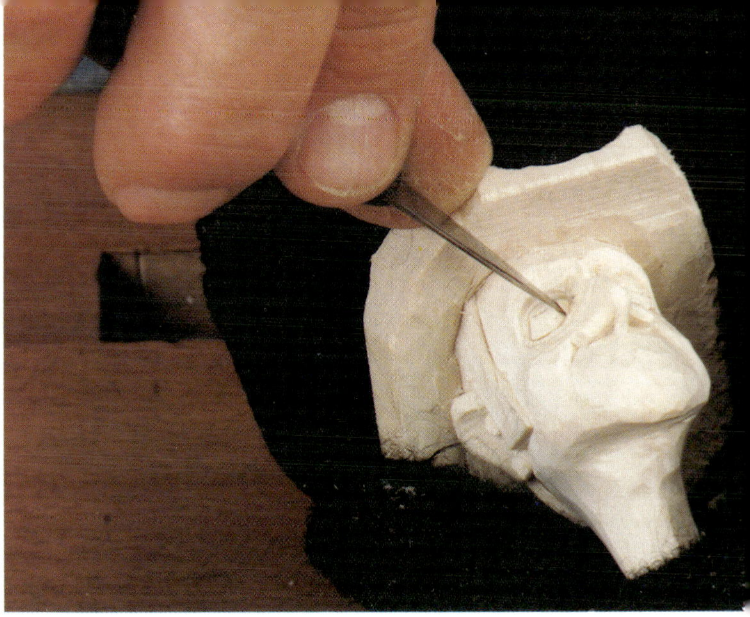

Clip out small triangles from the inside and outside corners of each eye with your knife tip.

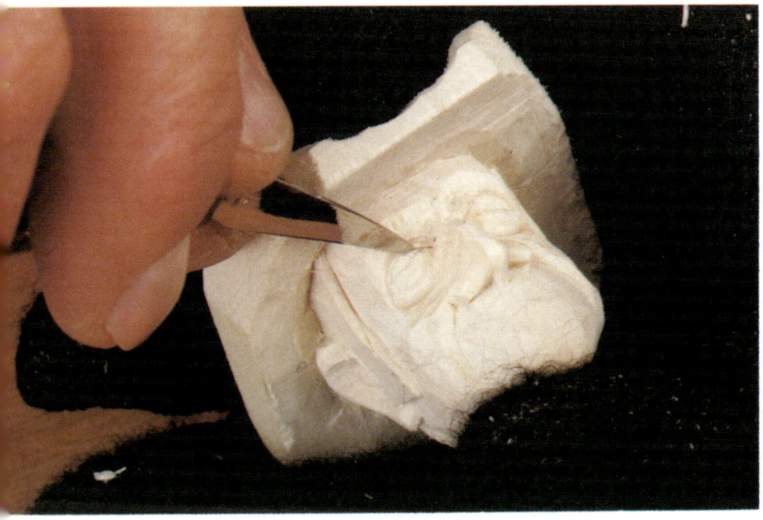

Following the lower ridge of that last V cut, cut in the bottom of the upper eyelid.

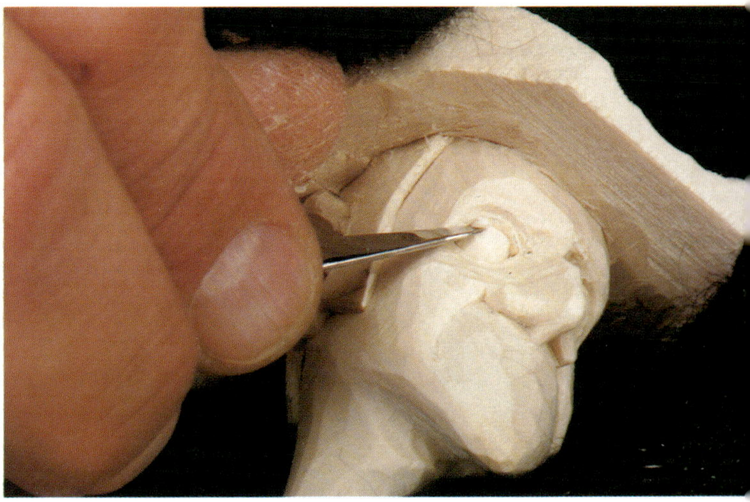

Relieve the eyeball between the lower and the upper lids.

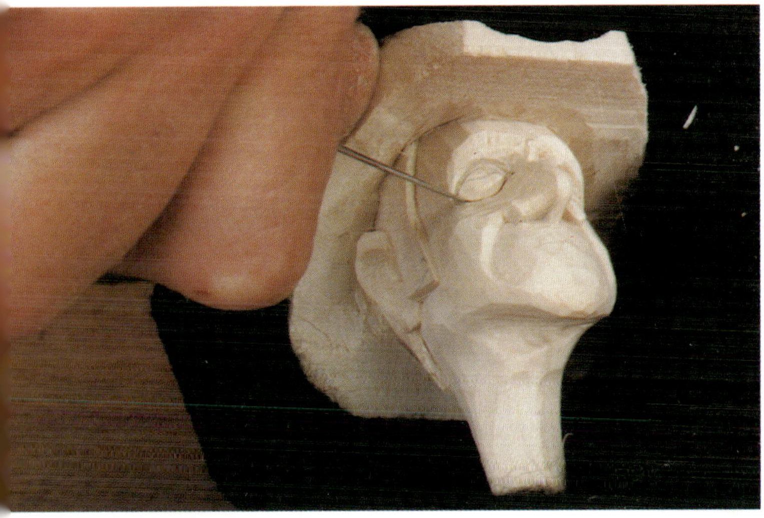

In the middle of the trough formed as you cut in the bottom arc of the eye, cut the lower eyelid with your detail knife.

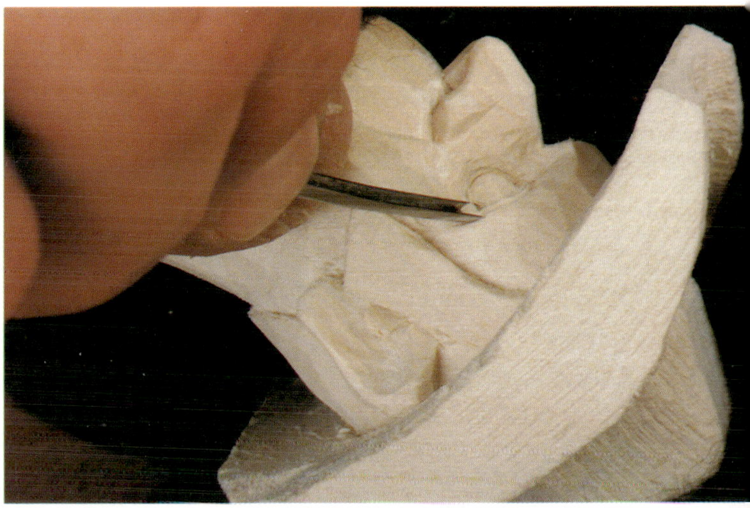

Our objective is to carve eyes with as much eyeball showing as was possible. This is nature's way of indicating fright. With your small V tool, extend the upper lid at the outside corner so that it appears to overlap the lower lid.

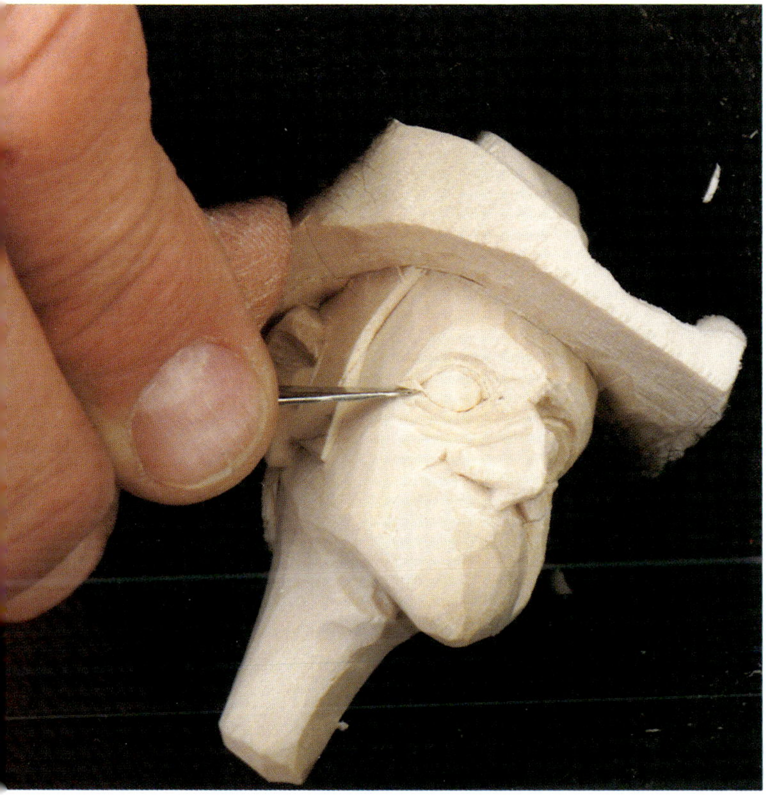

Remove the outside portion of the lower lid below the upper lid with your knife tip.

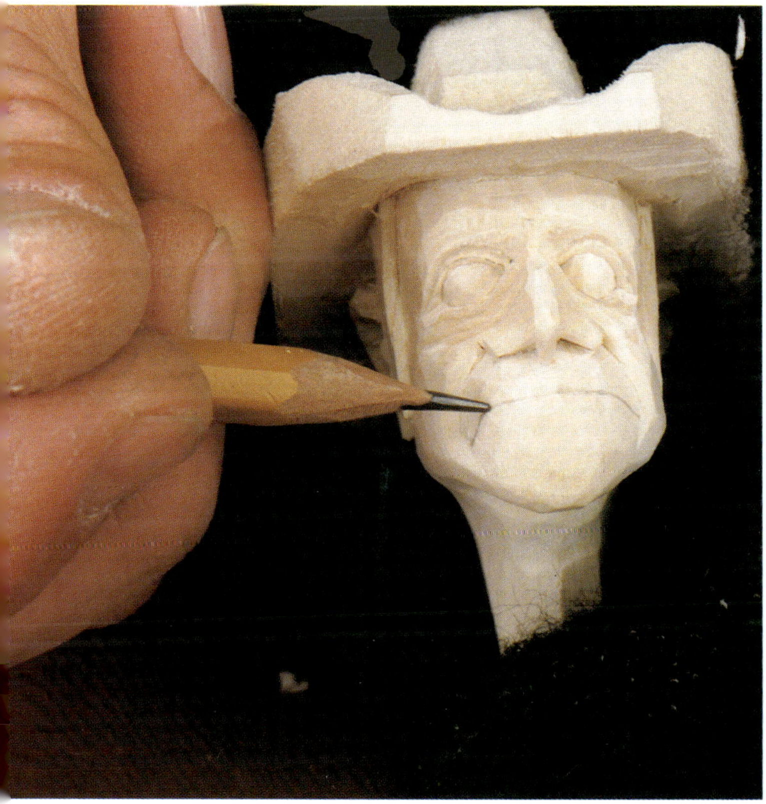

Sketch in a mouth indicating a disgusted frown.

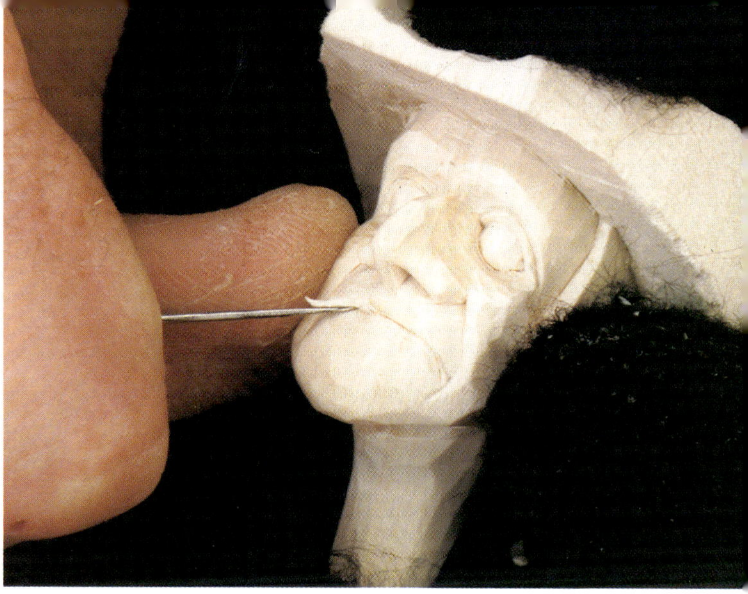

With your knife tip, cut this mouth line to a depth of about 1/16". Cut again at an angle of about 60 degrees along the tip of the bottom lip.

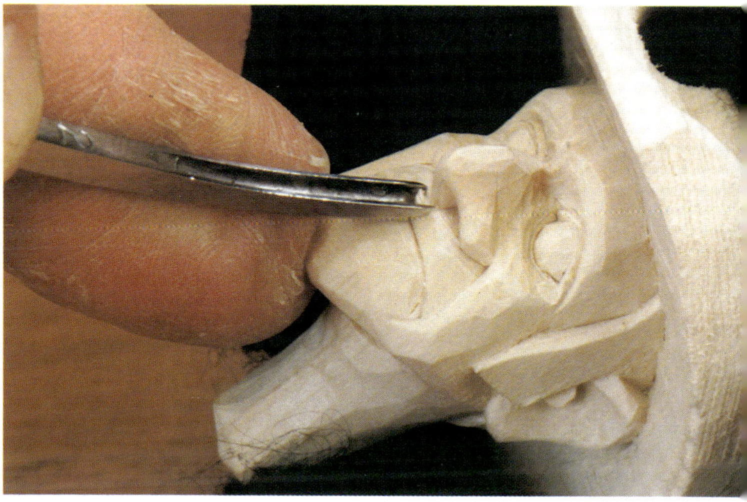

Using a small deep gouge, cut the philtrum from the upper lip to the septum.

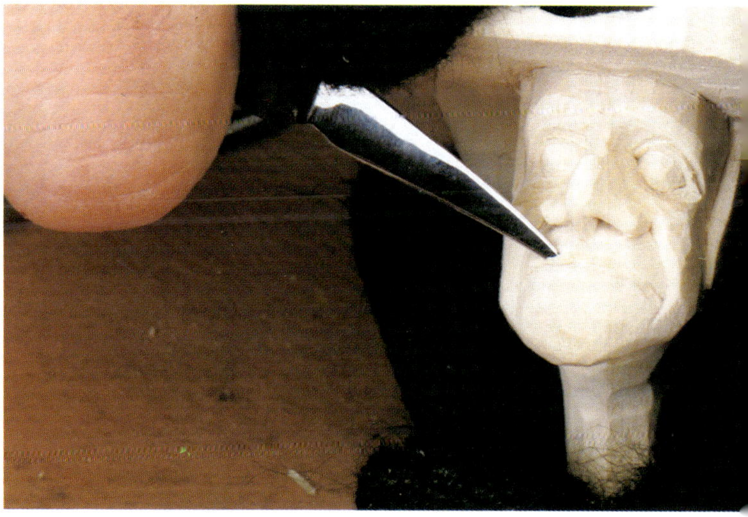

Shave a short length from the top lip on either side of the philtrum with your knife tip.

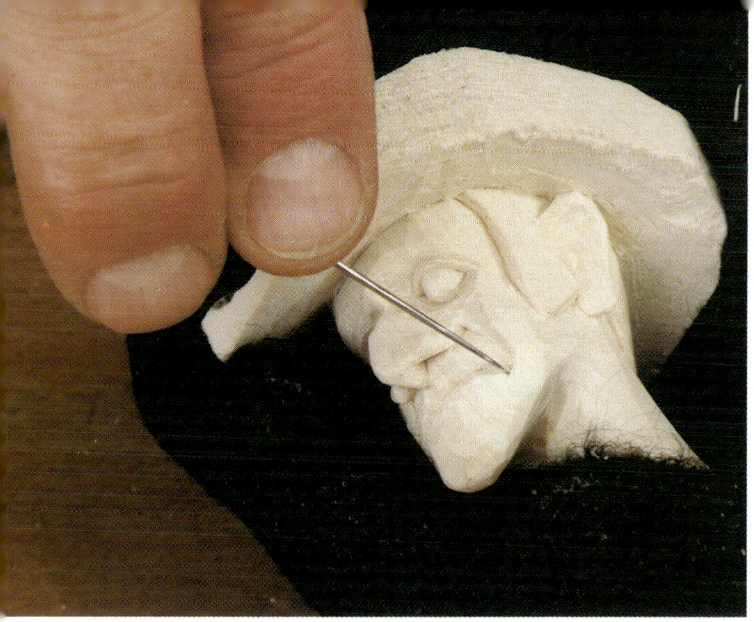

We can add to the perplexed expression of this cowboy's mouth by clipping small triangles from each corner of the mouth.

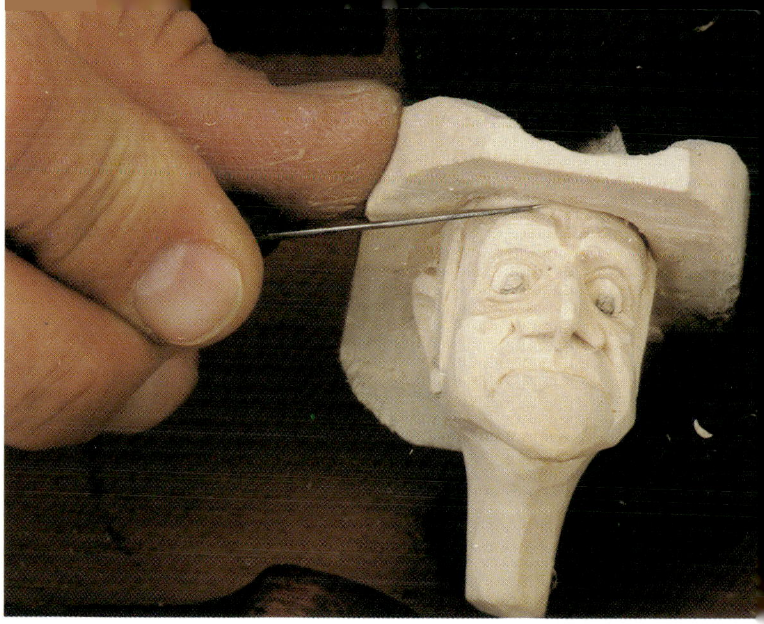

Complete the formation of the eyebrow by removing wood from beneath the hat brim to the top of the eyebrow mound.

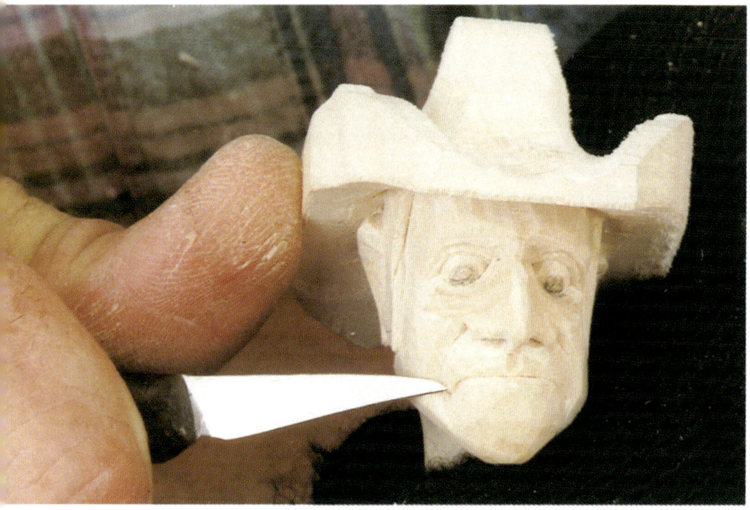

Since the lips are pulled tight across his teeth, we would not be able to see an indention along the lower lip.

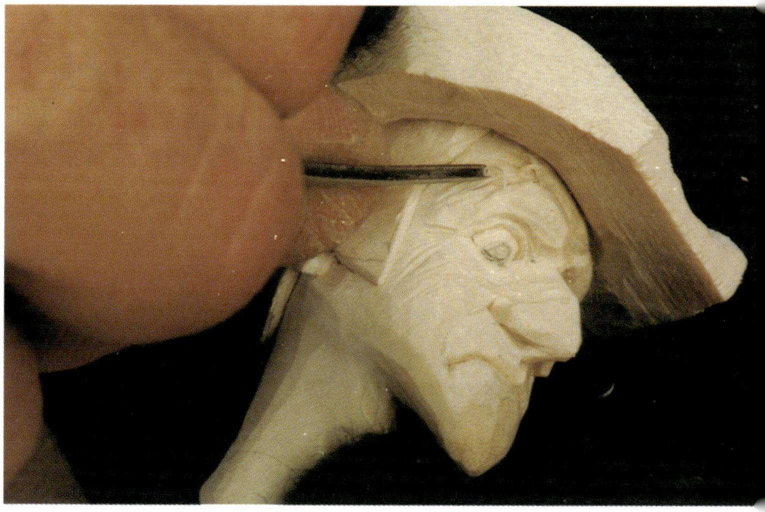

Using your small V tool, add lines radiating from the outside corner of each eye, along the brow, and under each eye. Due to the precarious circumstance this old boy finds himself in, we should probably have more worry lines than usual.

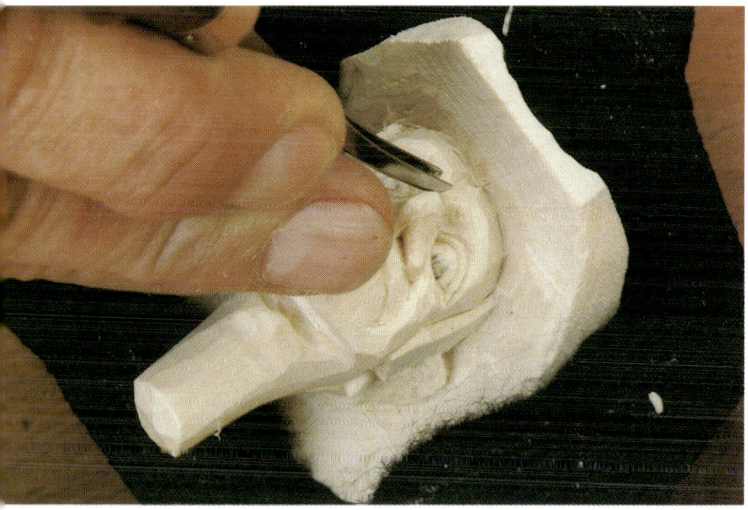

Form the eyebrows by first separating them with a cut directly above the nose to the bottom of the hat brim.

Shape the bottom of the hat brim with your knife, cutting from the front of the head back toward the rear.

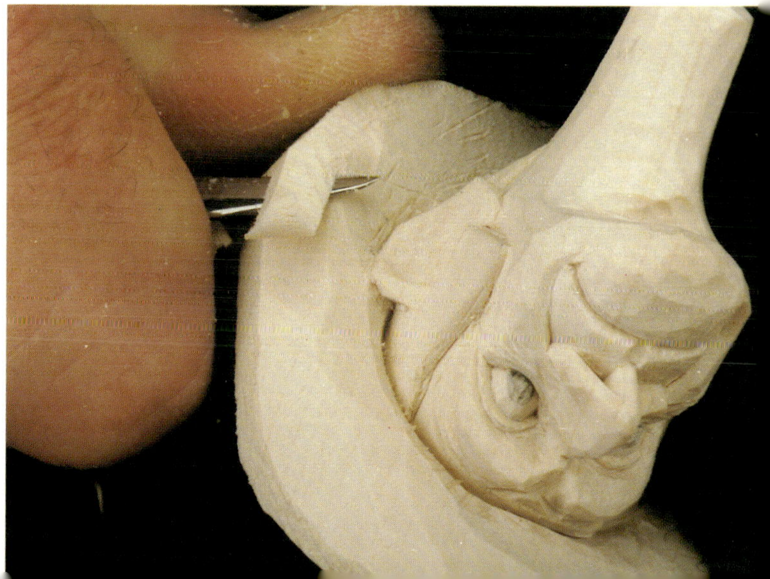

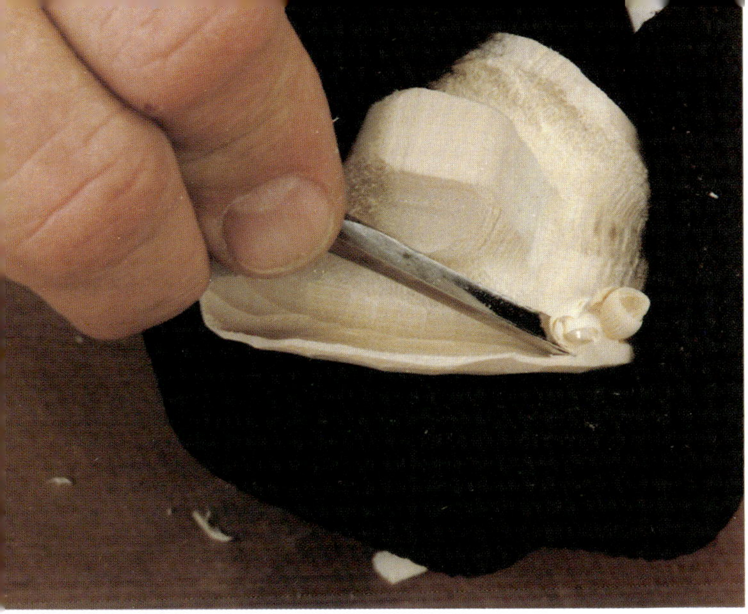

Using the 1/4" shallow gouge, remove saw marks and burr marks from the curl in the upper hat brim. Cut from the rear of the head toward the front.

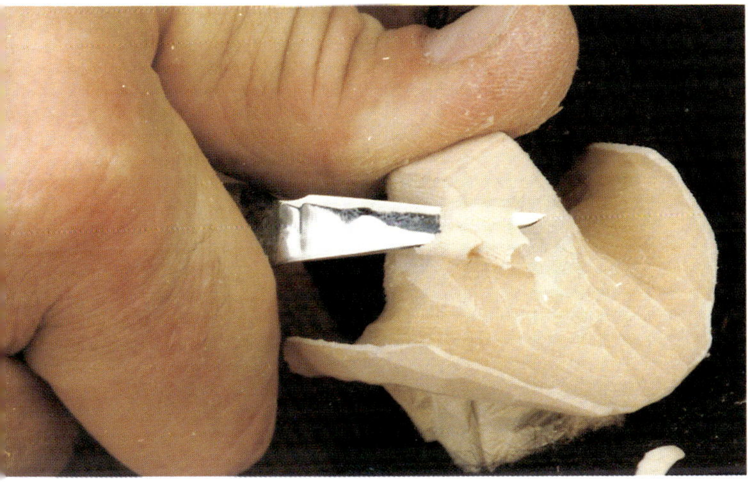

Use your knife to shape the crown of the hat. Because of the grain orientation, we must carve from the brim toward the crown in the front of the head and from the crown to the brim in the back.

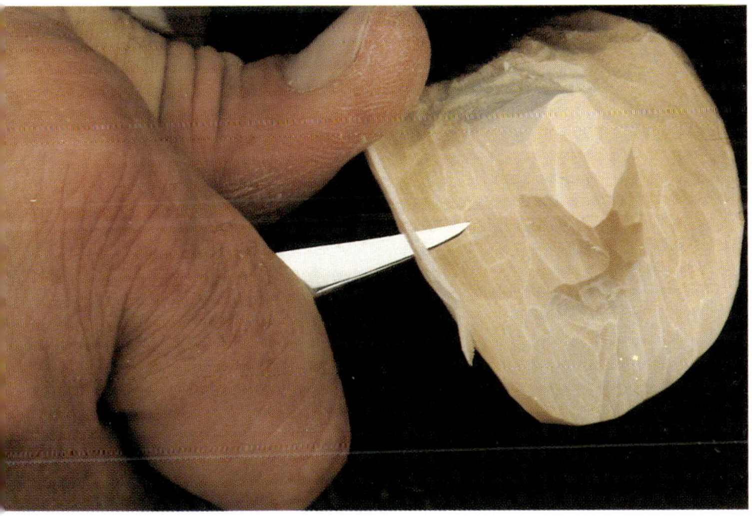

To finish the hat, use your knife and shape the outside of the brim.

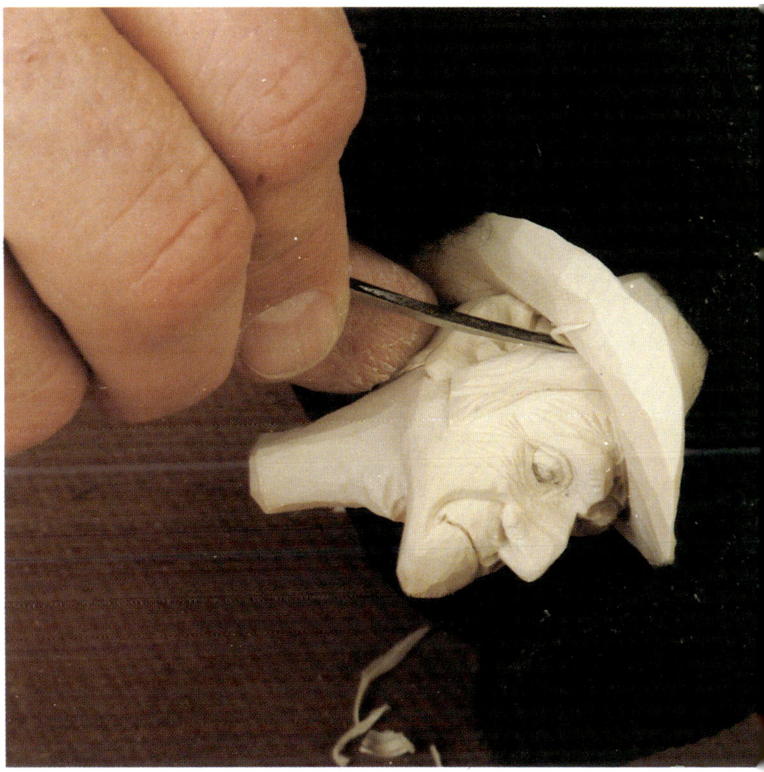

To finish this character, let's use the small V tool to texture his hair. This texturing is accomplished by varying the direction and depth of cuts.

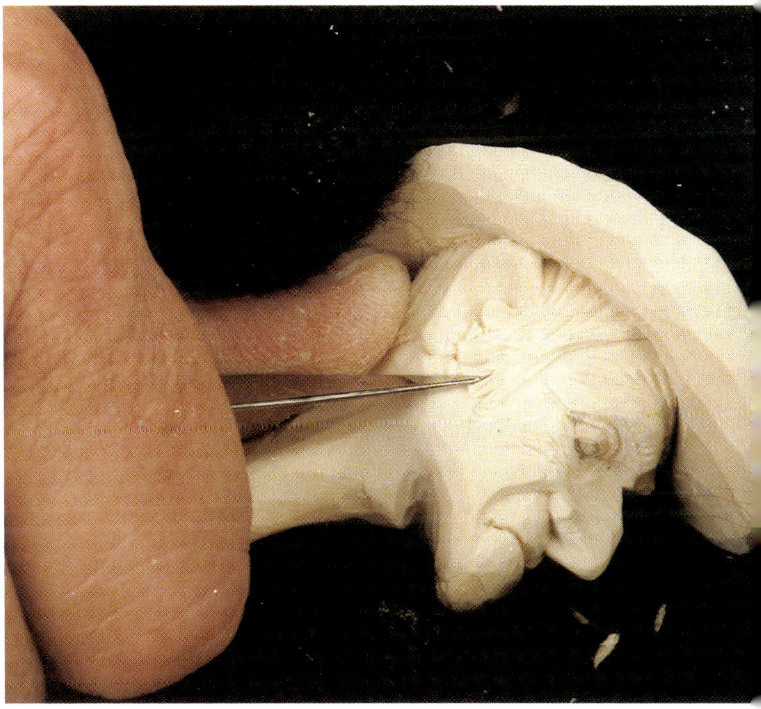

Relieve some of the hair at the bottom of the sideburns to make it appear as if he needs to visit the barber.

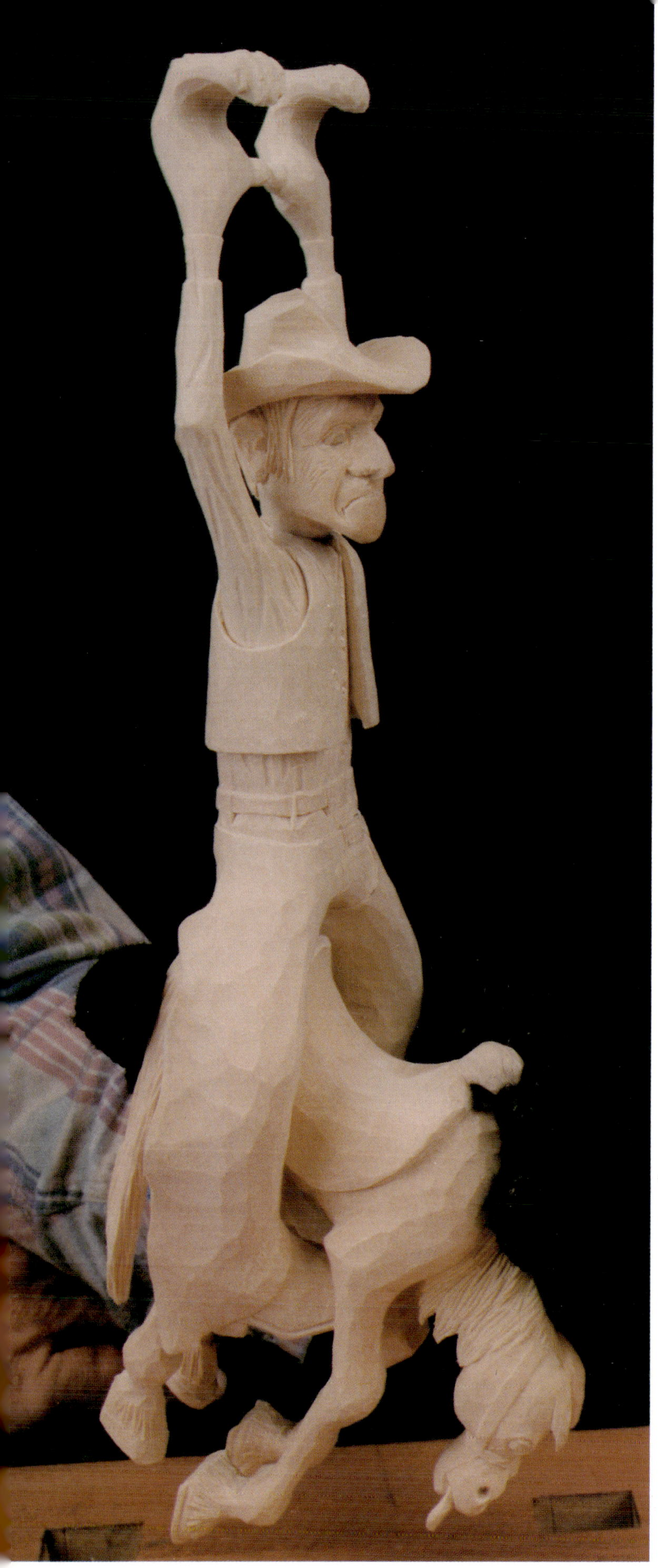

The carved cowboy and horse, together at last ... but don't glue the horse together yet.

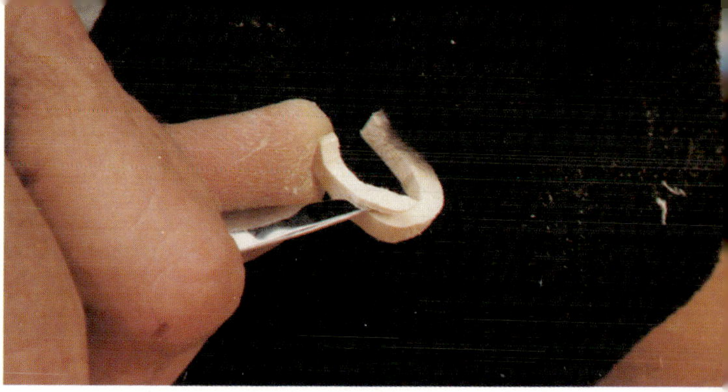

With your detail knife, clean the saw marks from the horse shoe.

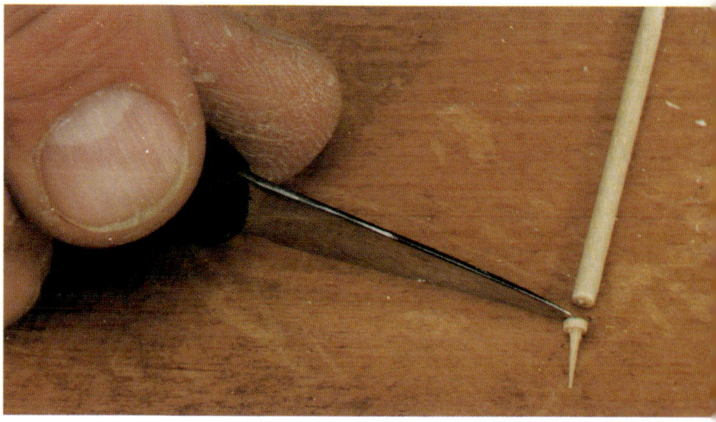

Carve a very thin nail from a round toothpick.

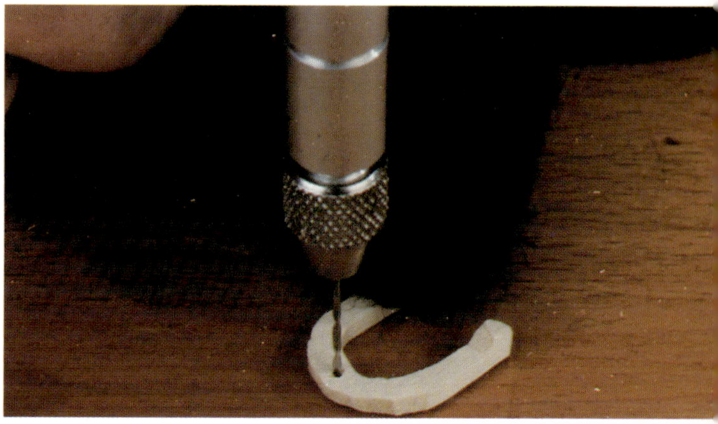

Very carefully drill a small hole into the horse shoe with a very small drill.

Insert the nail into the horse shoe and—with a small amount of Super Glue Gel—glue this horse shoe to the right rear hoof of the horse.

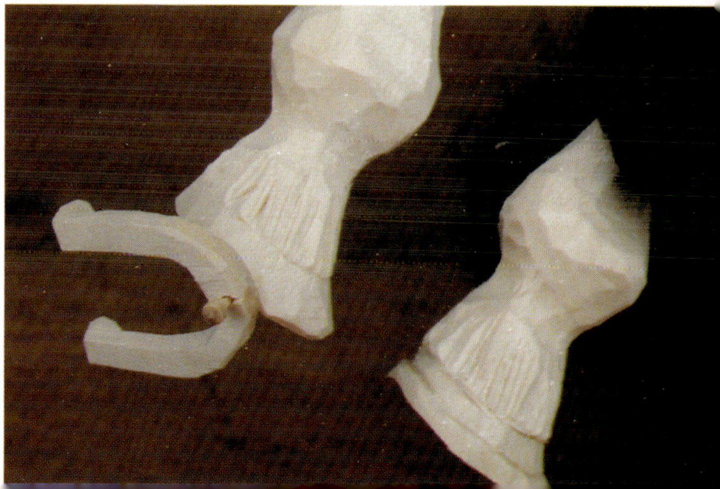

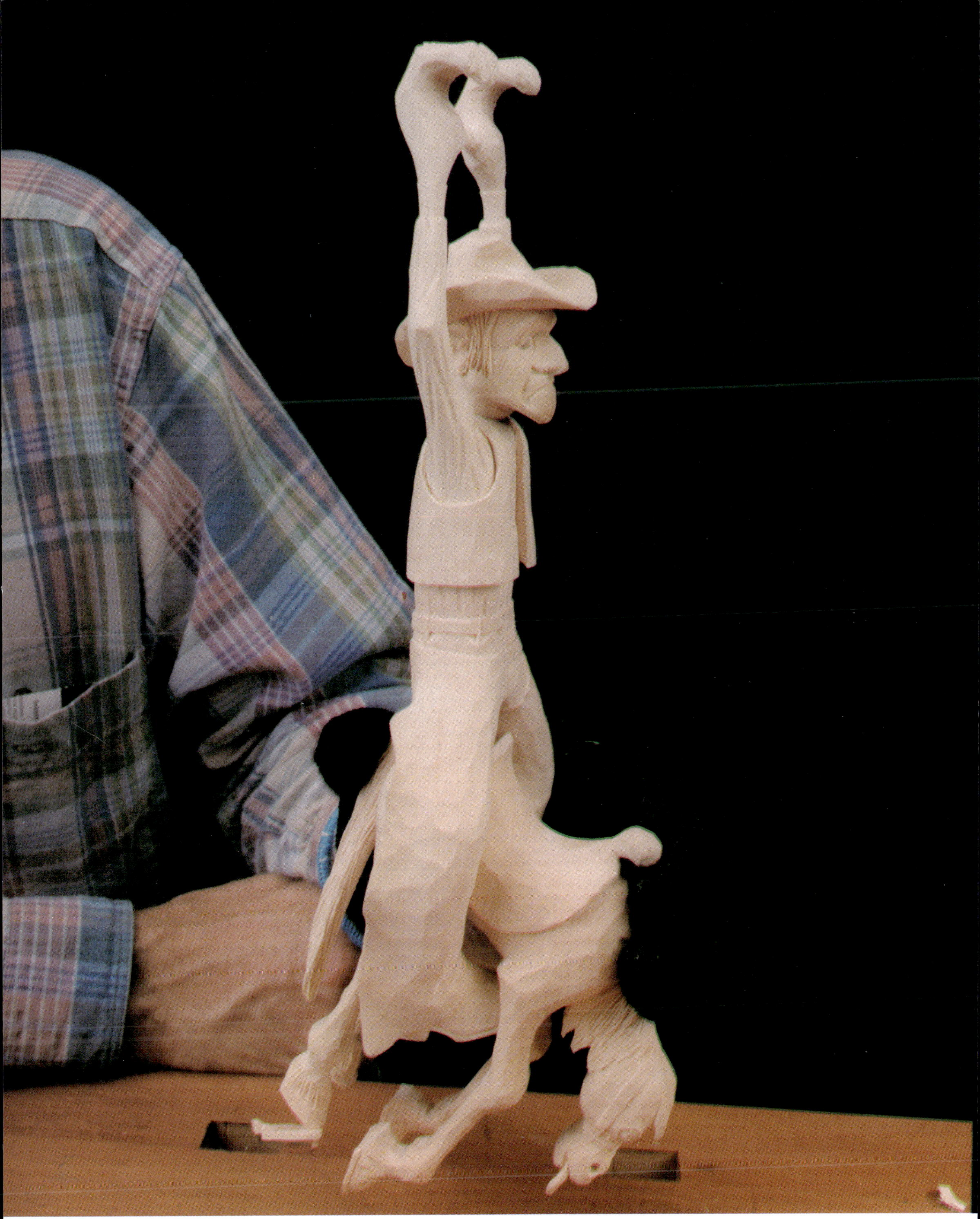

This is the complete and assembled horse and cowboy. Caution, do not attach the two pieces of the horse yet. We will do this after painting.

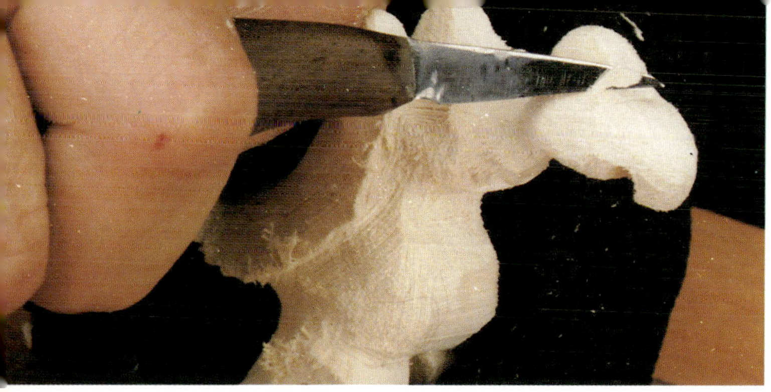

Using the detail knife and your gouges, remove the saw marks and shape the buzzard according to the drawings included in the back of the book. I'm not going to insult your carving skills by giving detailed instructions for this little guy.

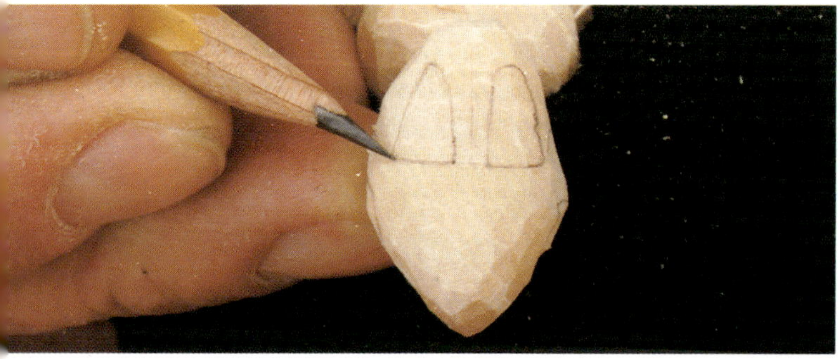

Draw the eyes in rather large.

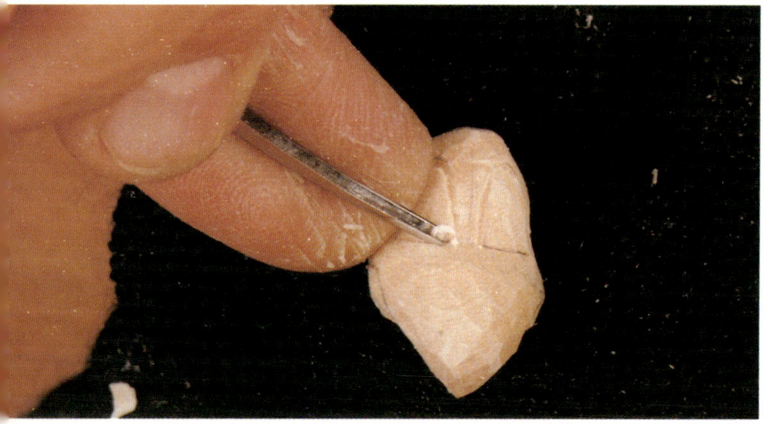

Use a V tool to cut around the eyes.

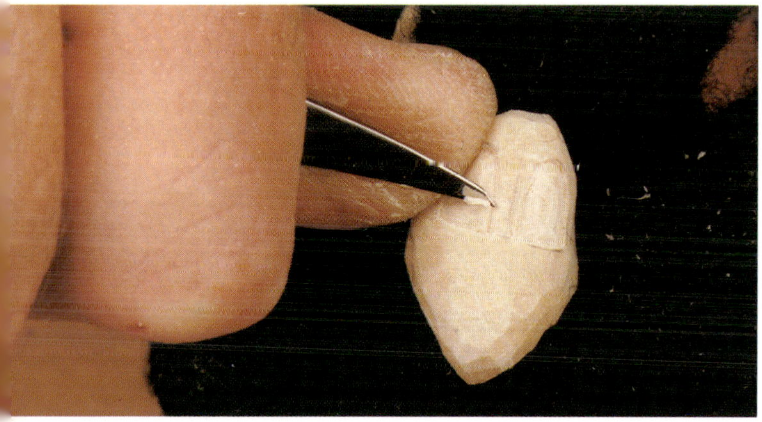

Use your knife tip to round off the sharp edges of the eyeball.

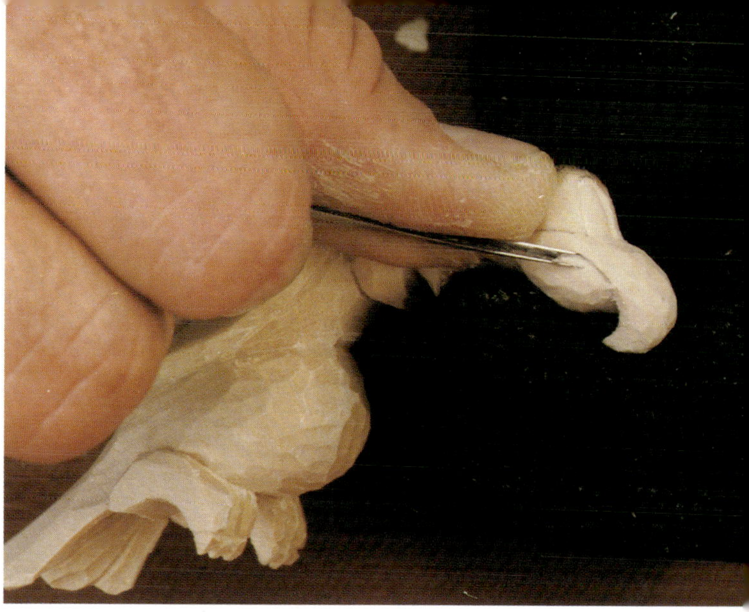

Use your V tool to separate the upper and lower beak ...

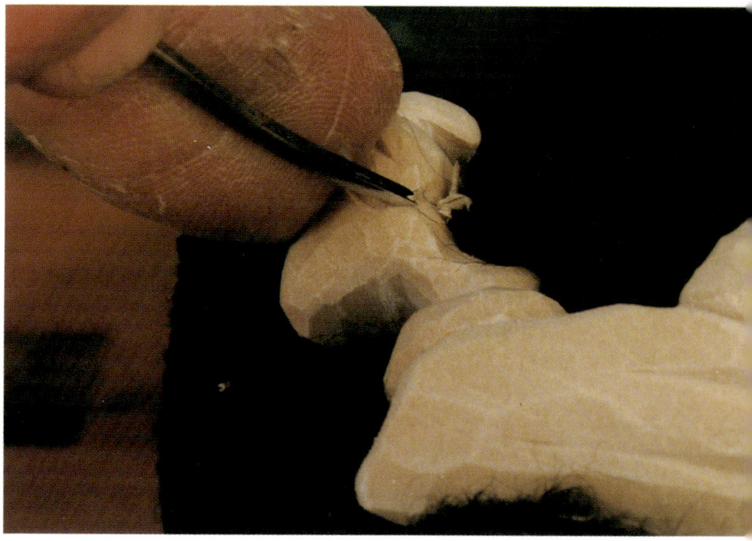

... and also to separate the beak from the head.

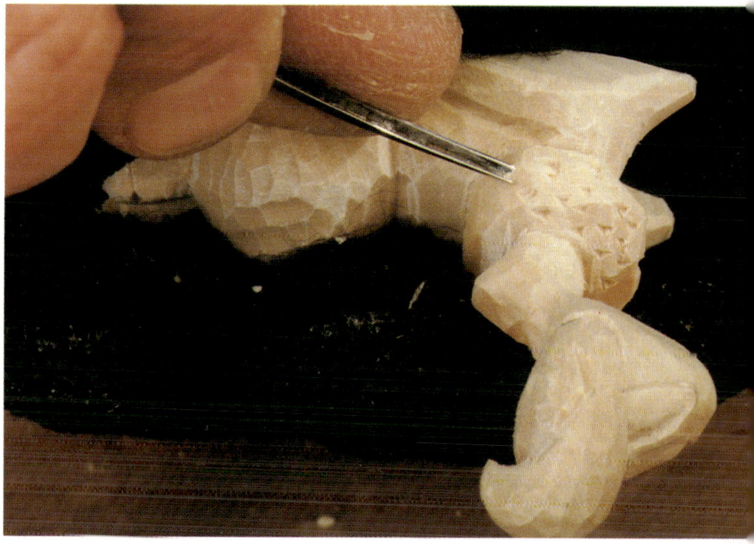

Use the same small V tool to prick the ring around the neck into buzzard feathers.

Project Painting

The brand name paint that I use is Ceramcoat. These are pre-mixed acrylics. The brush sizes you will need are #1, #2, and #000. The paint colors you will need are:

> White (no number), Black (no number), Caucasian Flesh #2029, Medium Flesh #2126, Midnight Blue #2114, Yellow #2504, Brown Iron Oxide #2023, Golden Brown #2054, Fire Red #2083, Tangerine #2043, Silver #6003, and Blue Haze #2122.

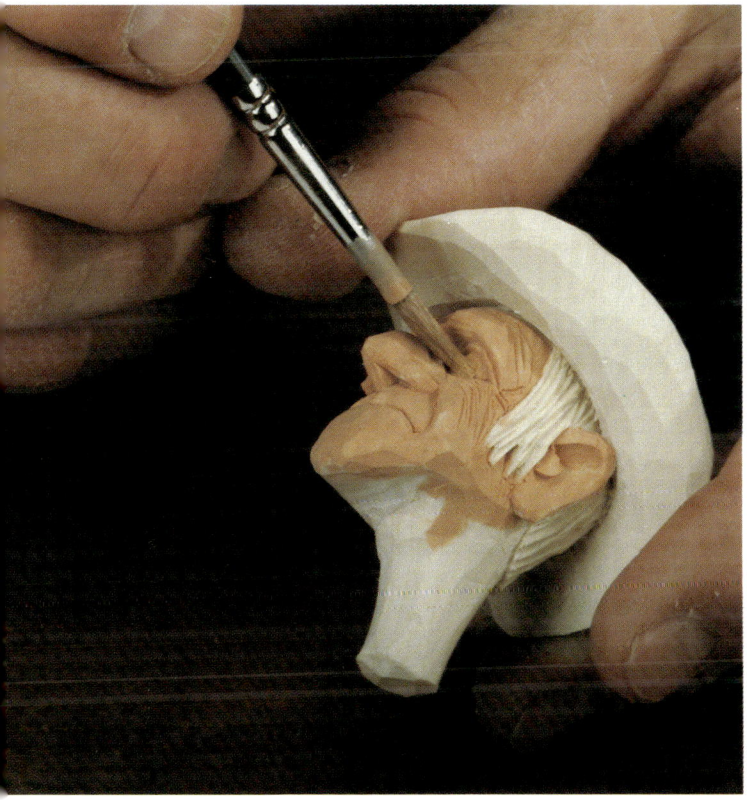

Mix four parts Caucasian Flesh #2029, one part Medium Flesh #2126, and about 6 parts water. Stir well and paint all the flesh areas of the head. Cover the eyeballs and mouth with this flesh mixture. We will use undiluted white at a later time to repaint the eyeballs.

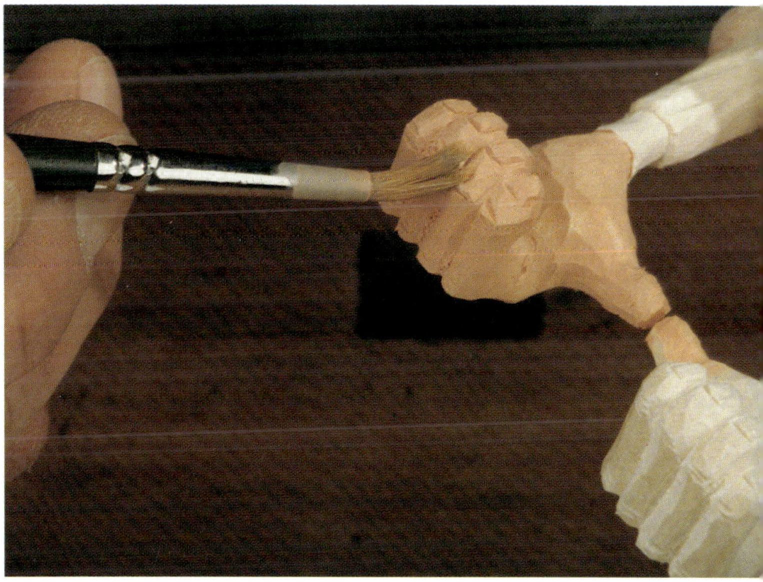

Paint the hands with the flesh mix as well.

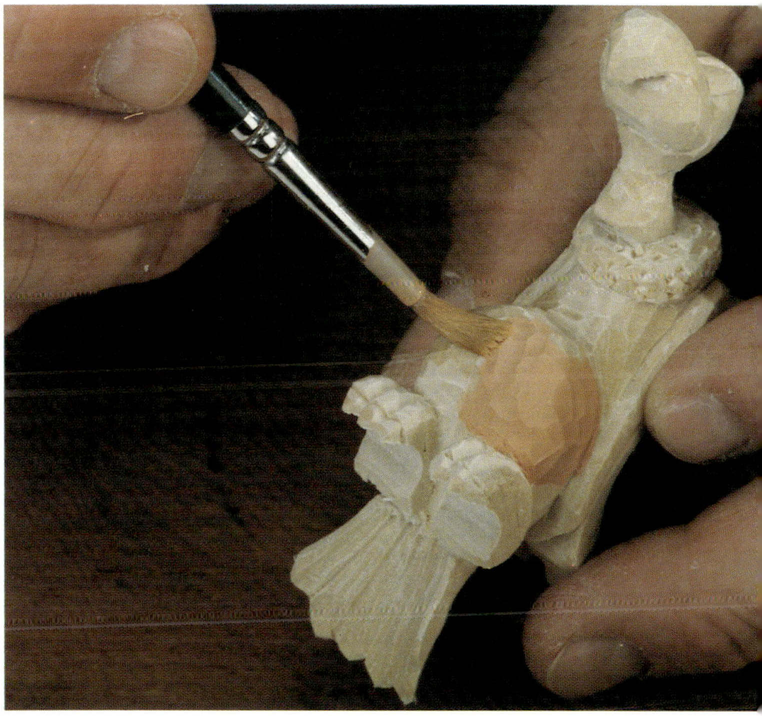

Paint the buzzard's belly with the flesh color too.

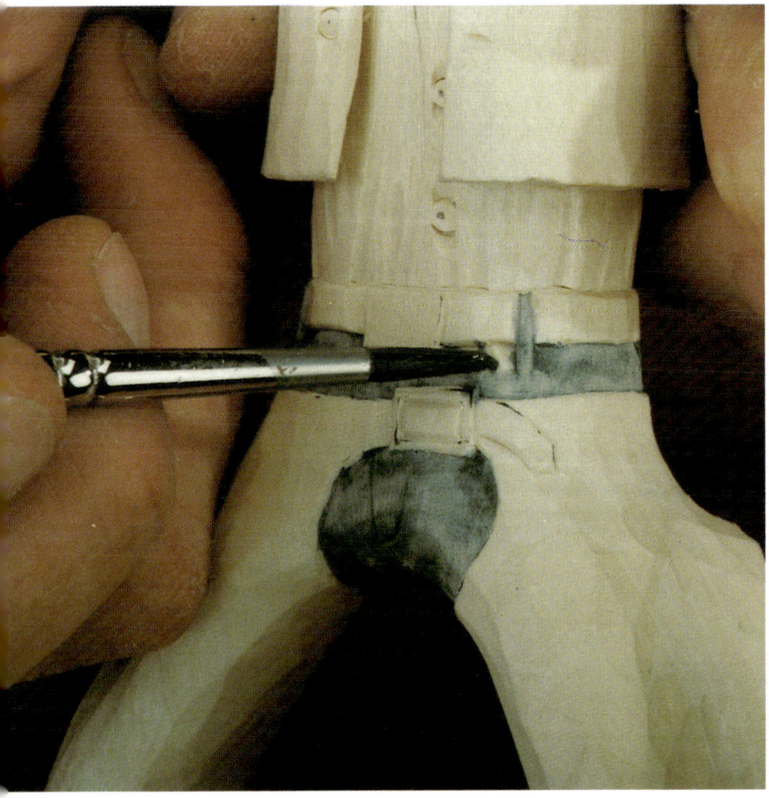

Mix one part Midnight Blue #2114 with four parts water and paint the small area of the jeans exposed beneath the chaps. Continue to paint the remainder of the jeans.

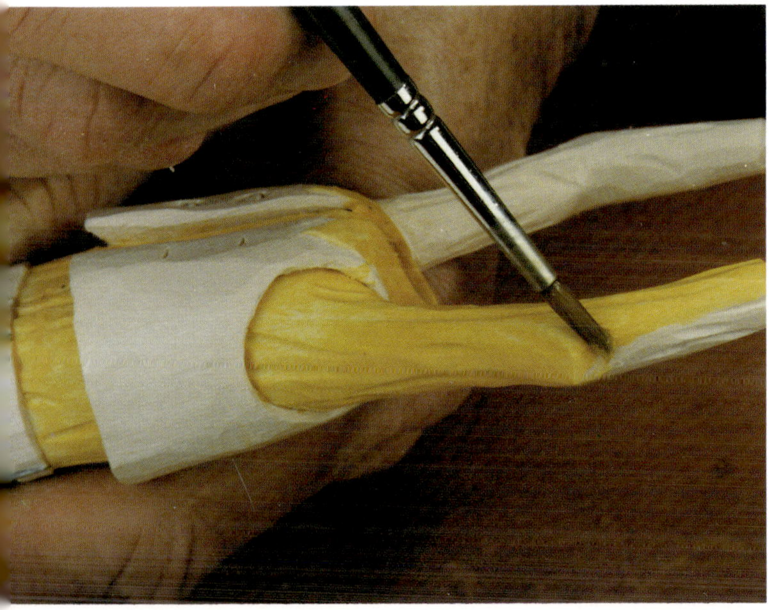

To paint the cowboy's shirt, use one part Yellow #2504 and six parts water.

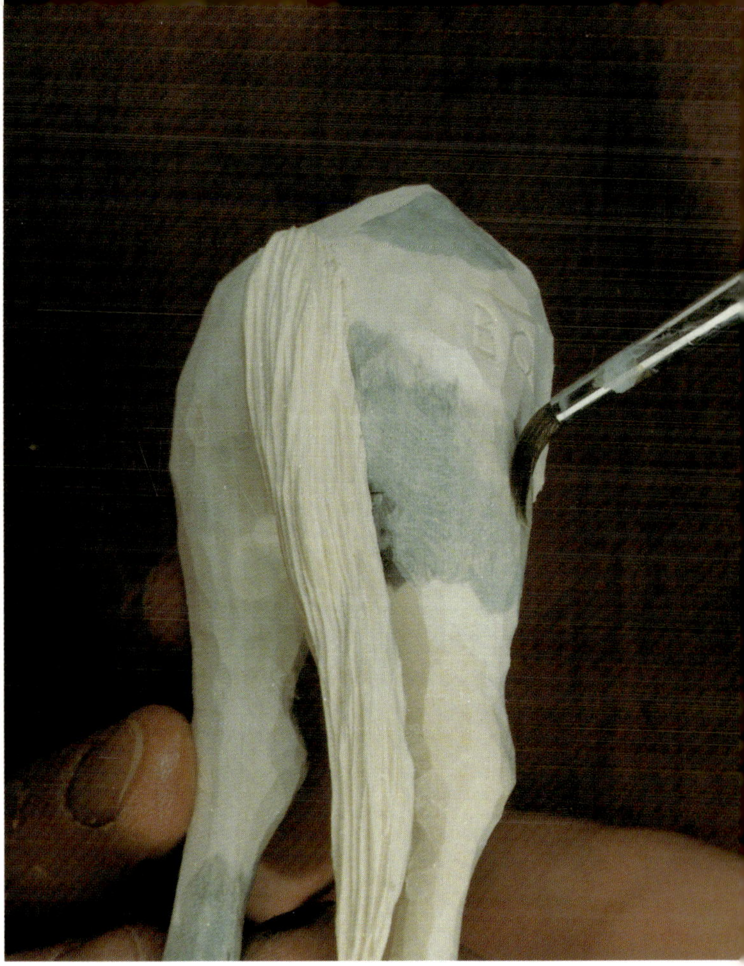

Using one part White and one part water, paint the entire body of the horse. Next, mix one part Black and six parts water. While the white paint is still wet, dip your brush into the black and touch it to the wet white wash. You will create interesting spots on the horse to break the monotony of the monotone white.

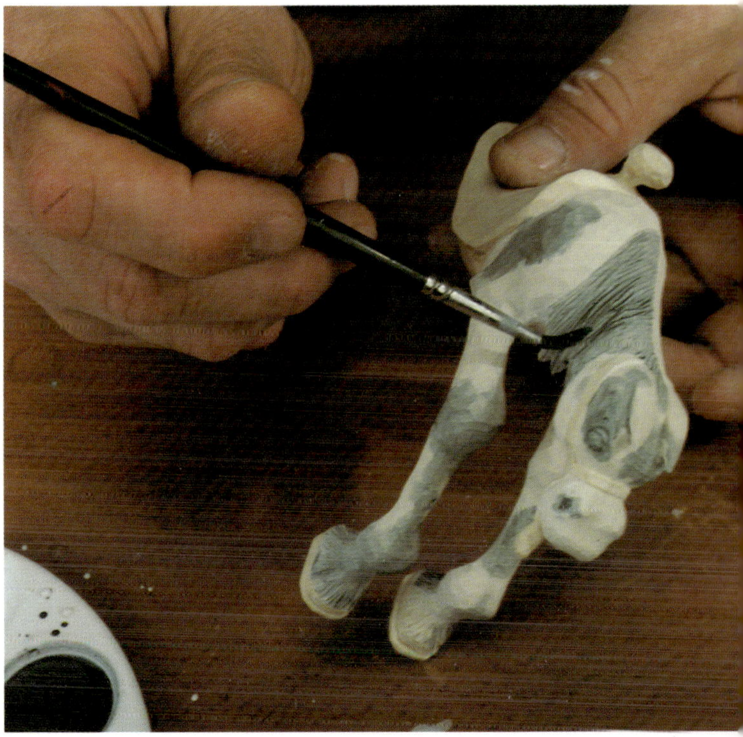

Paint the horse's tail, mane, and the area around each eye black as well.

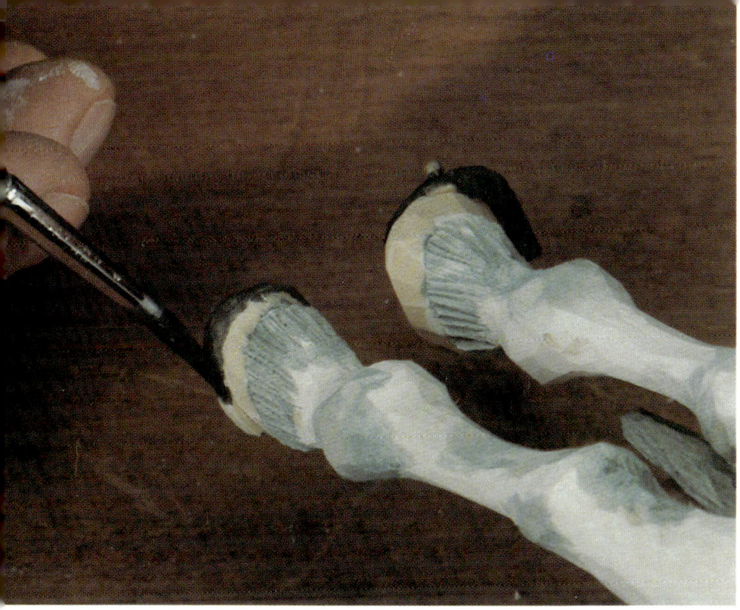

Paint the horse shoes with your black.

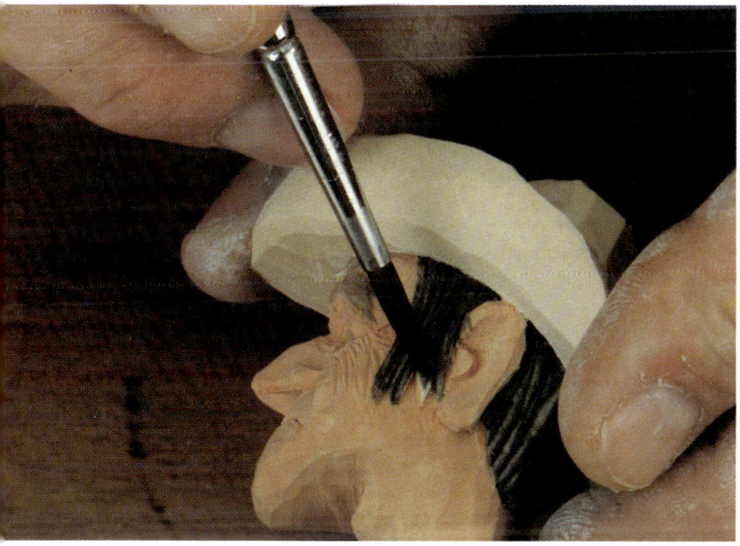

Use the black to paint the cowboy's hair and eyebrows.

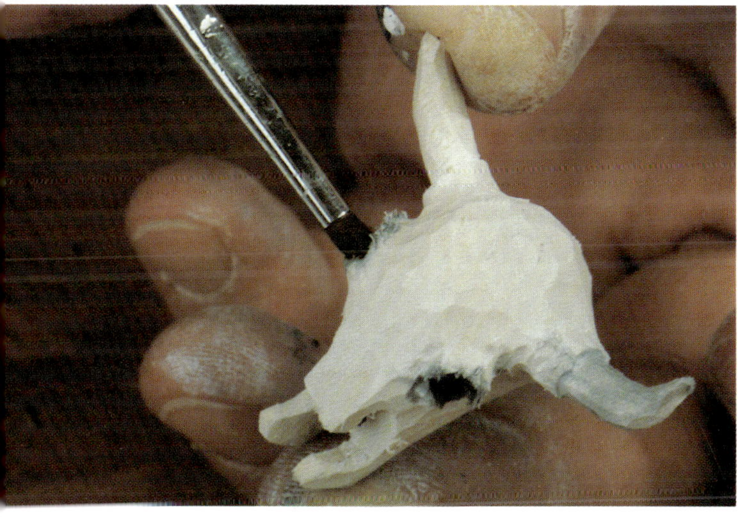

Paint the skull with one part White and one part water. While the white is wet, brush some of the diluted black mixture on the horns and into the eye sockets.

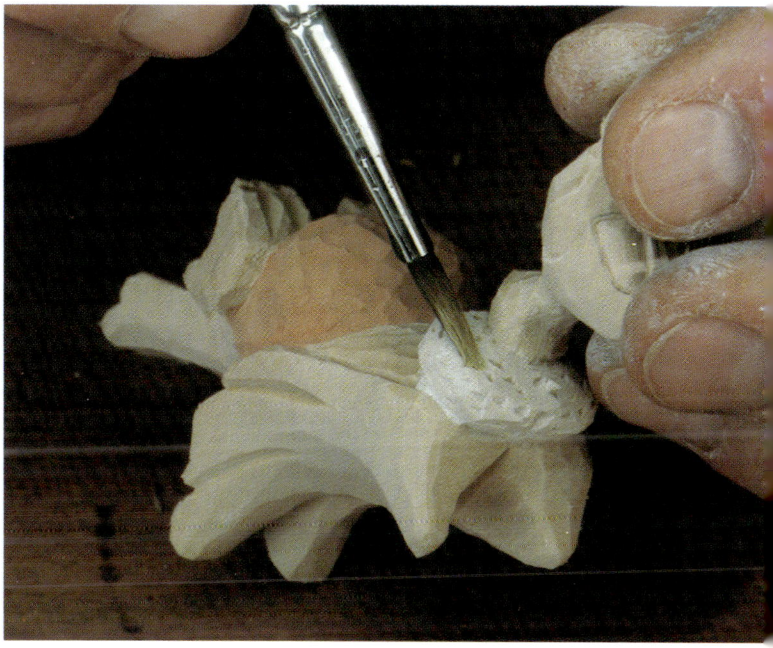

Use the white mix to paint the ringlet of feathers around the buzzard's neck.

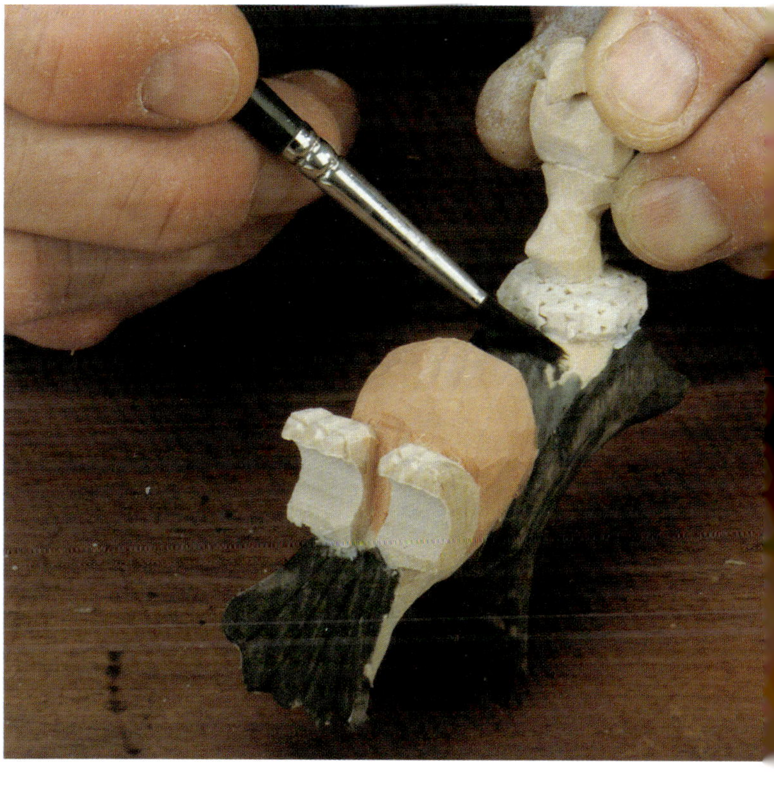

Paint the buzzard's wings, tail and chest black.

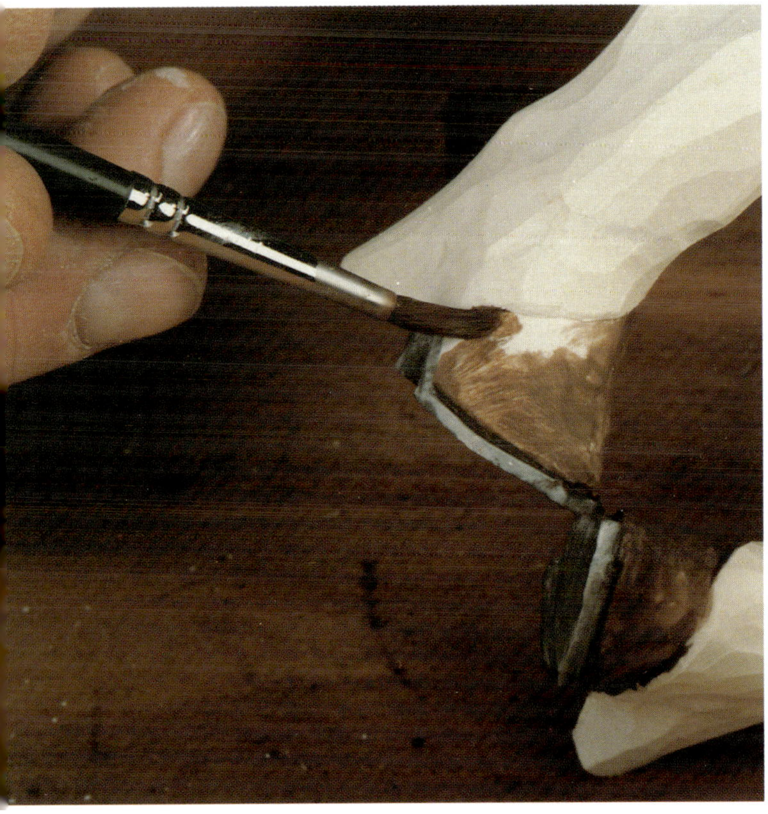

Use the black to paint the heels and soles of the cowboy's boots. Mix one part Brown Iron Oxide #2023 with six parts water and use to paint the cowboys boots, ...

... belt and vest.

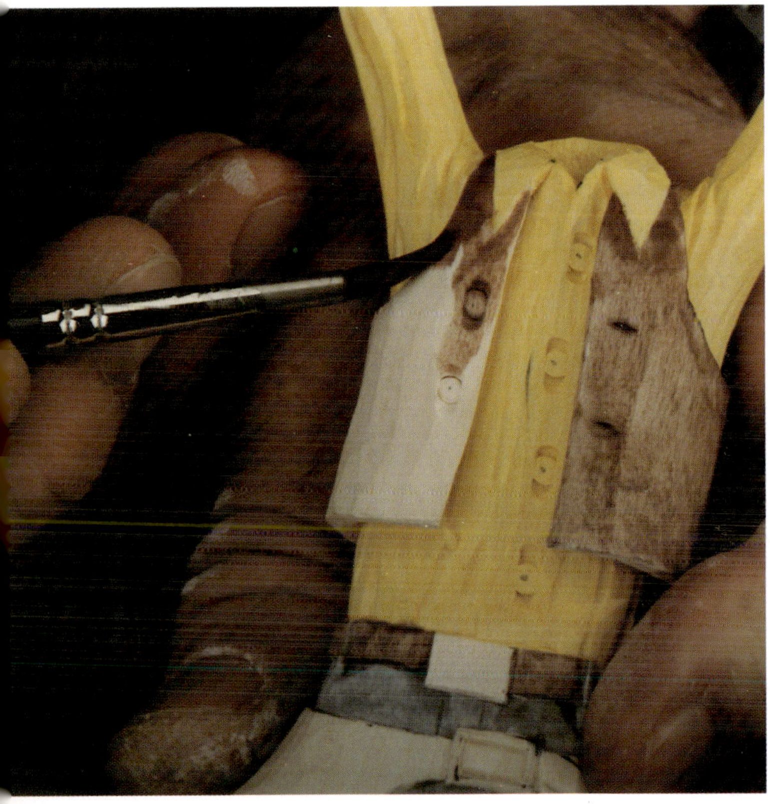

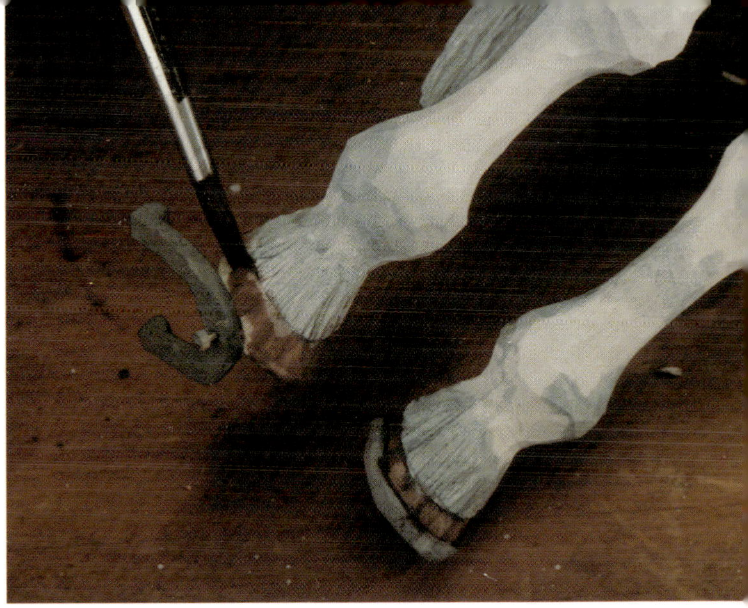

Use that same brown to paint the horse's hooves.

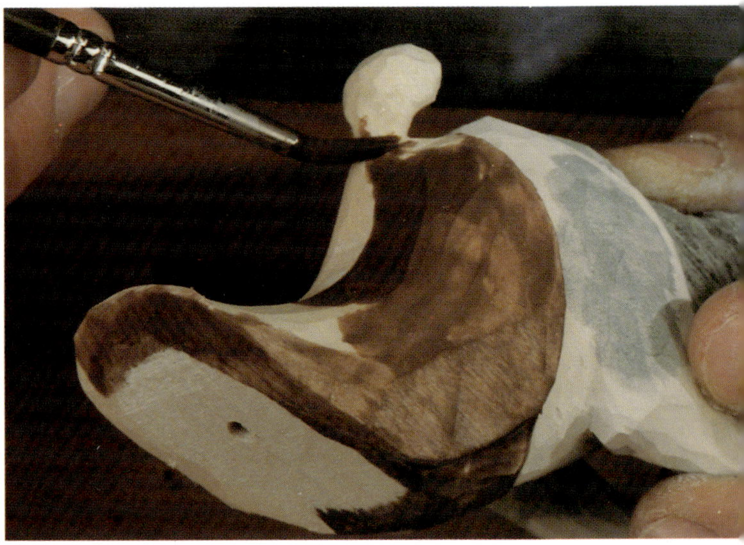

Use the brown to paint the saddle and the belly band on the horse ...

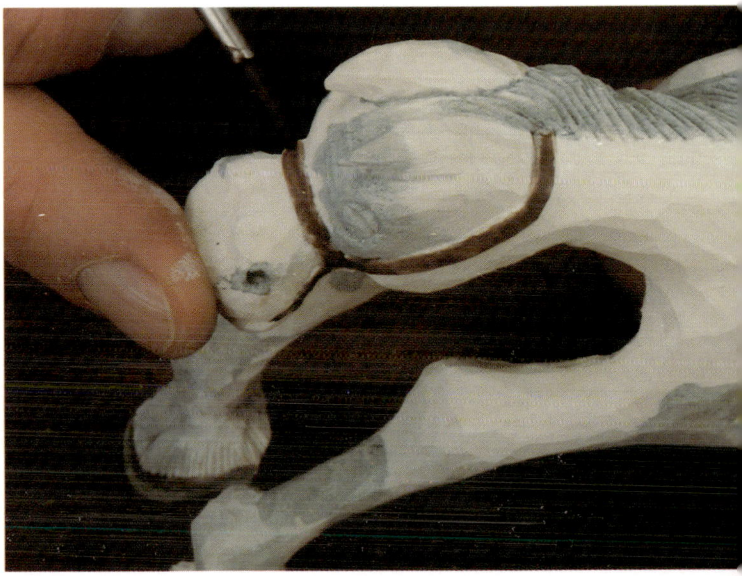

... and the bridle.

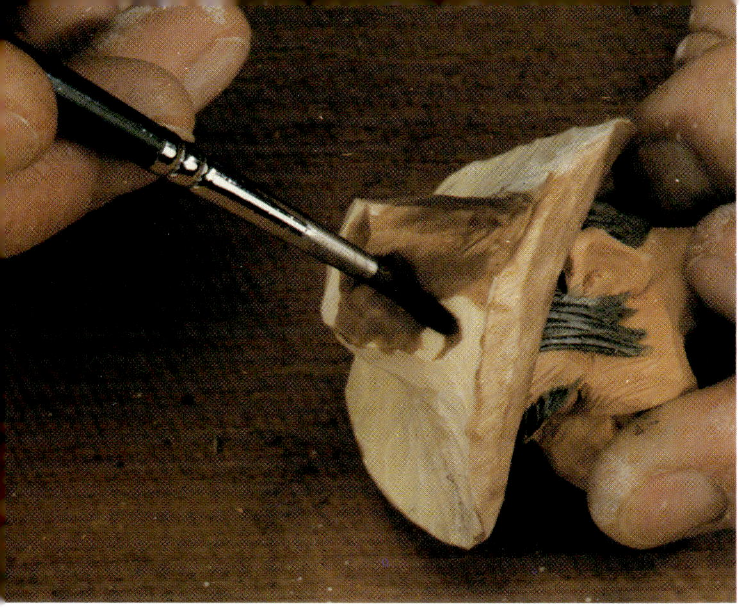

Use the brown to paint the cowboy's hat as well.

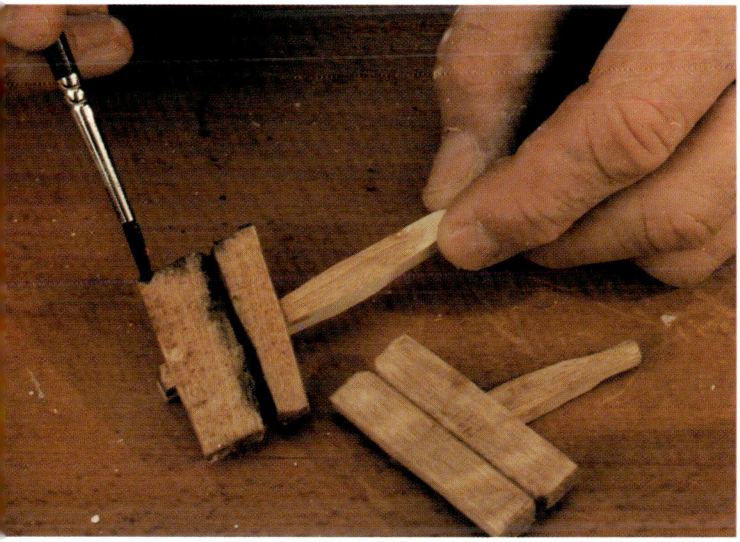

I've constructed a couple of wooden signs that will be attached to the granite cliff. They are made from scraps of basswood. Paint these with the brown mixture. While the brown is wet, bleed in some diluted black along the edges of the boards for weathering.

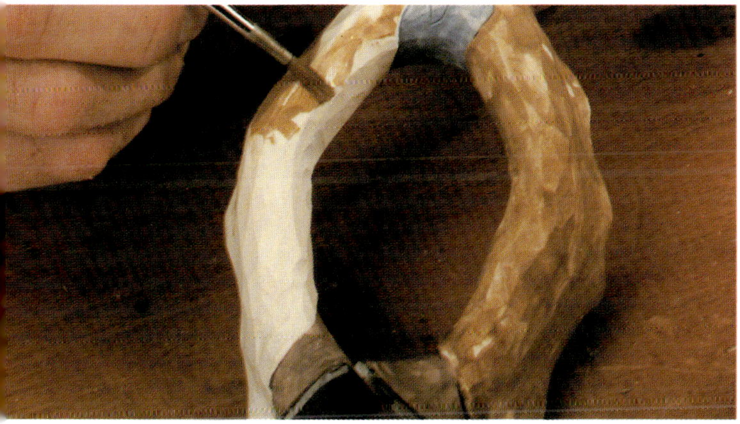

Make a mixture of one part Golden Brown #2054, six parts water, and one part Brown Iron Oxide #2023. Paint the cowboy's chaps, dabbing this color onto chaps and leaving small unpainted spots.

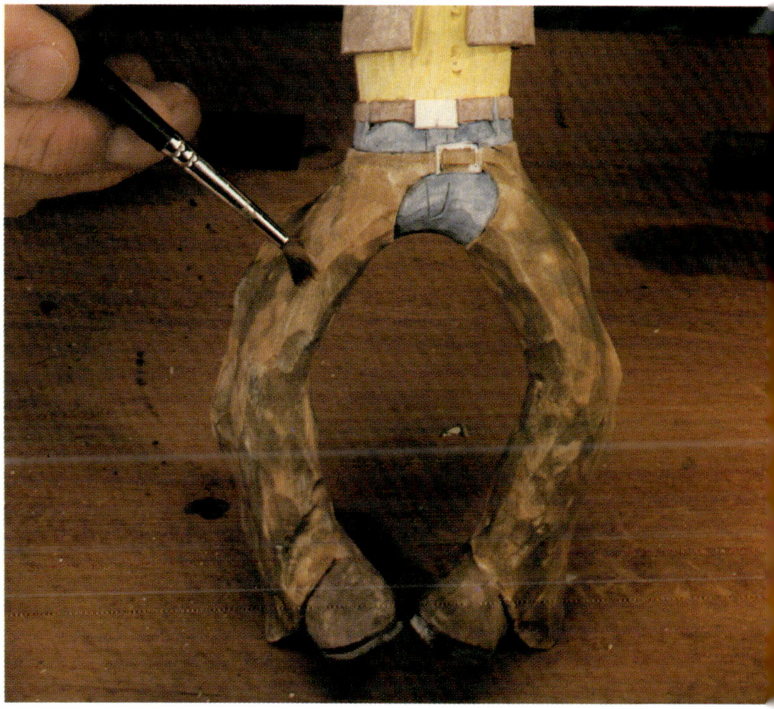

Go over the painted chaps with plain water, making sure that the chaps are wet all over. Now, with your brush fully loaded with black, go over the wet chaps rapidly. Make sure that the unpainted spots are covered with black. This effect will give the chaps a well worn appearance.

Mix one part Fire Red #2083 with six parts water. Paint the buzzards head and neck. Cover the eyes as well.

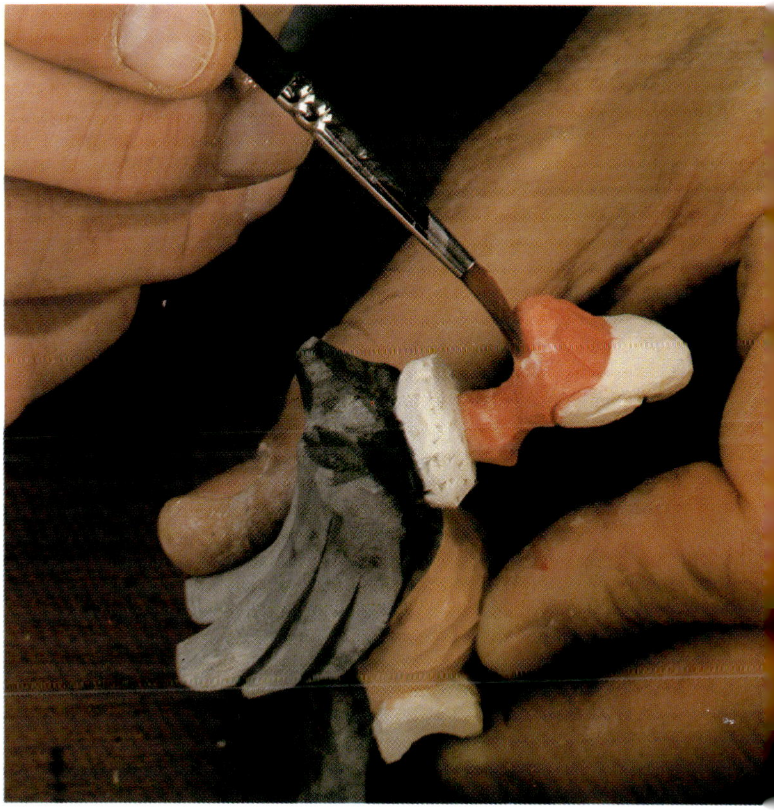

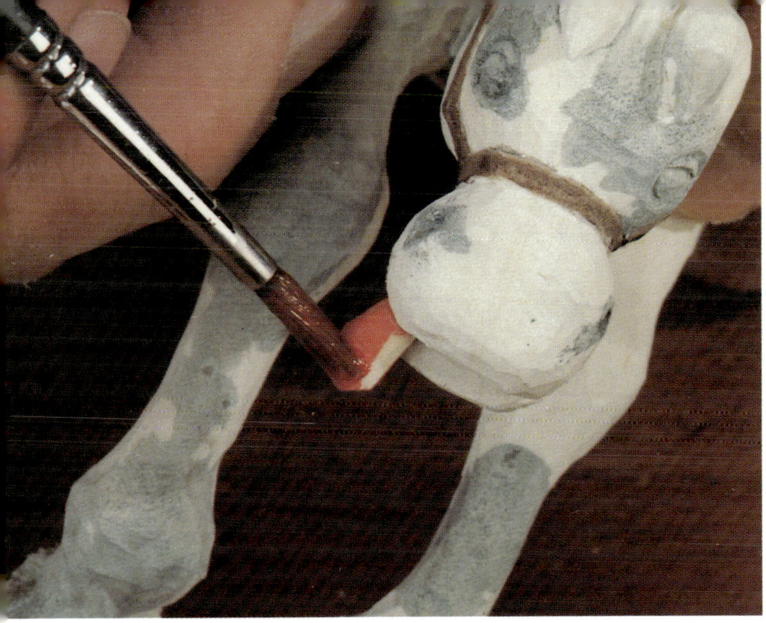

Use the same red to paint the horse's tongue.

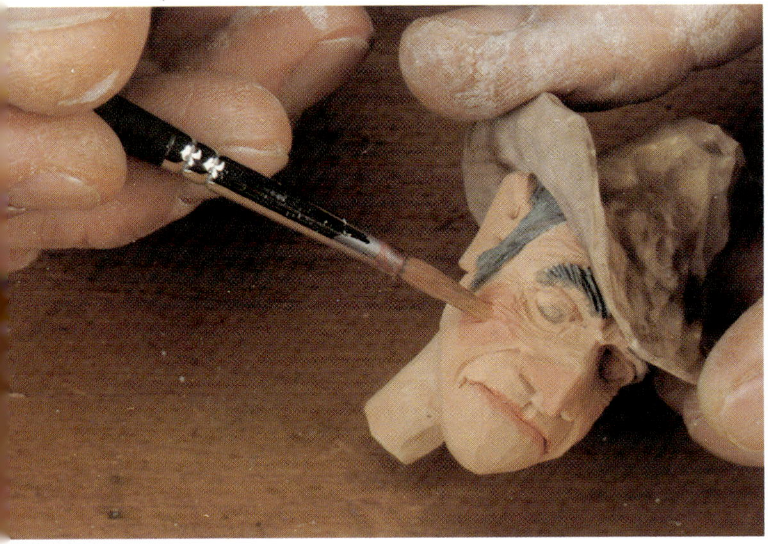

Mix a small amount of your red with flesh tone. Paint the cowboy's lips and cheeks.

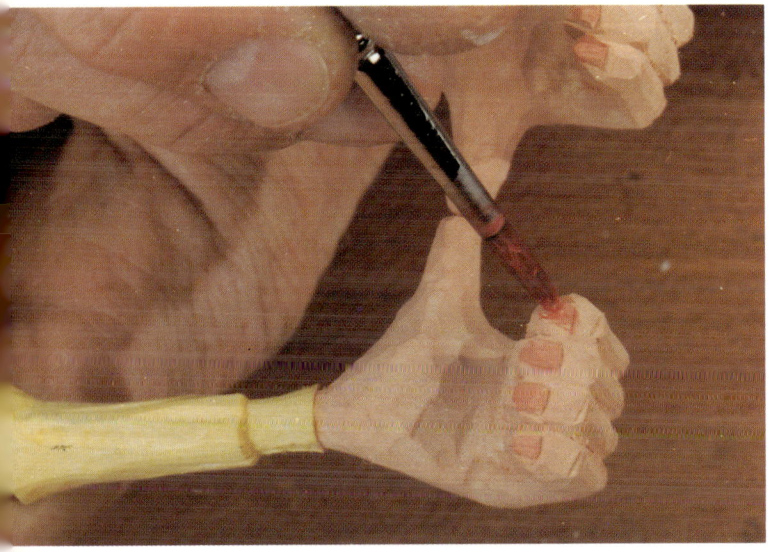

Use this red mix to paint the cowboy's finger nails.

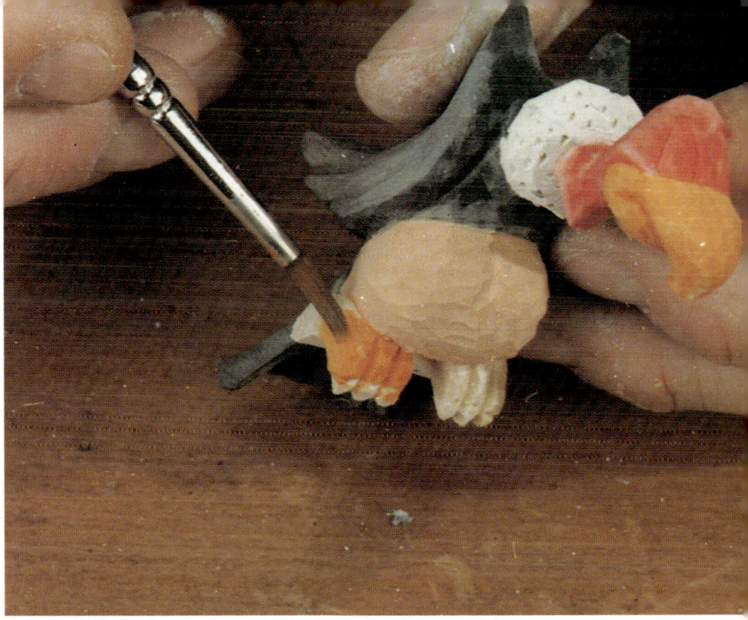

Mix one part Tangerine #2043 with six parts water. Paint the buzzard's beak and feet.

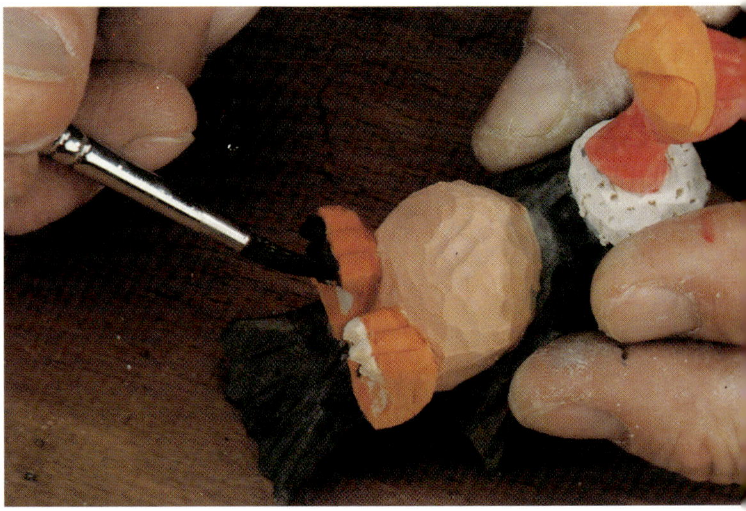

Use black to paint the claws.

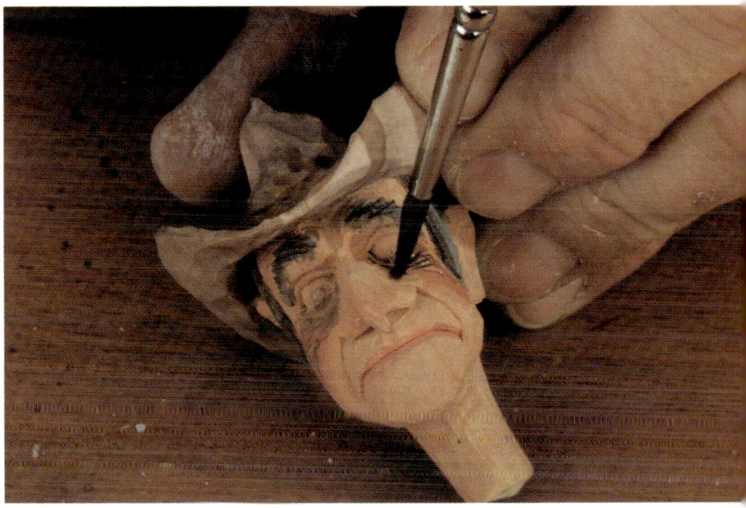

With clear water, wet the underside of the eyes. Load your paint brush with black and lightly touch this wet area. The black paint will spread through the wrinkles, producing an interesting effect.

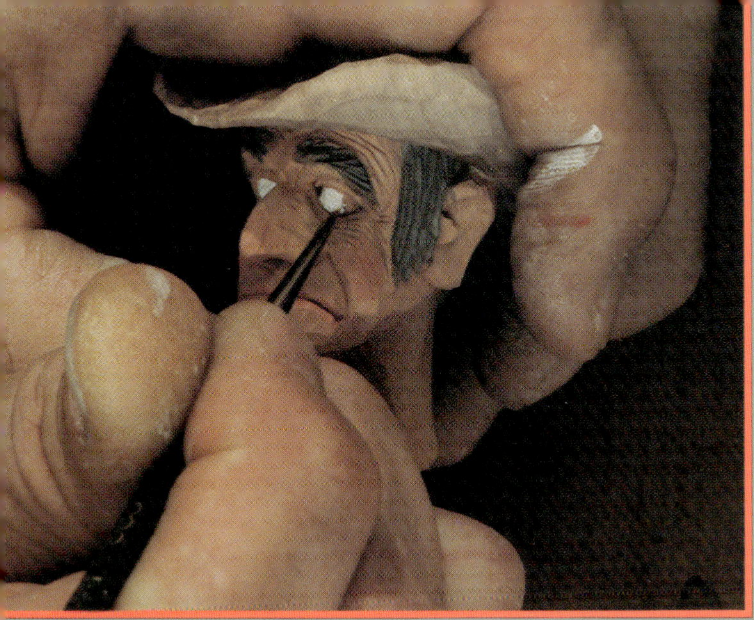

Using undiluted white and a #000 brush, paint the cowboy's eyeballs.

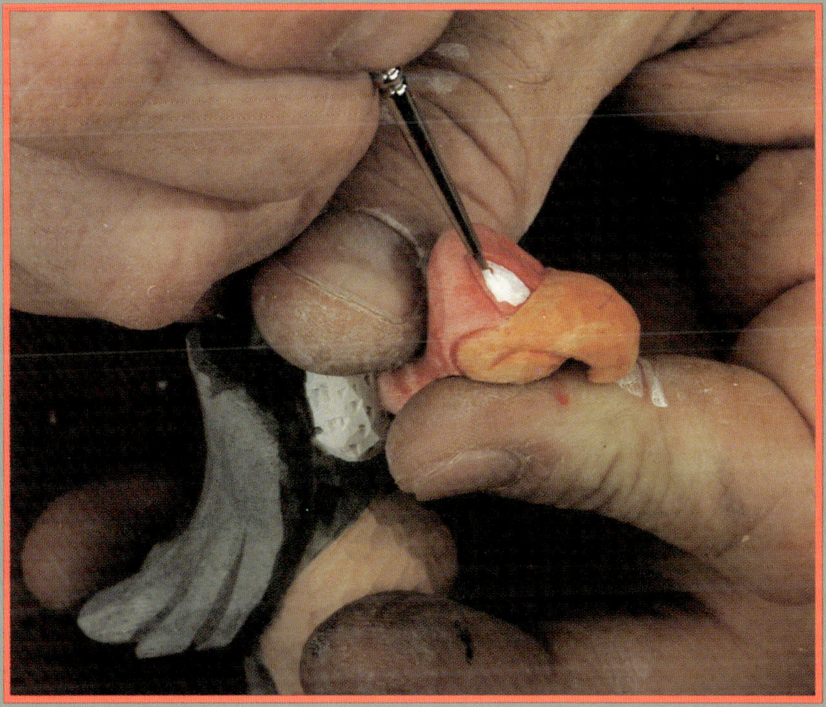

Use undiluted white to paint the eyeballs of the buzzard ...

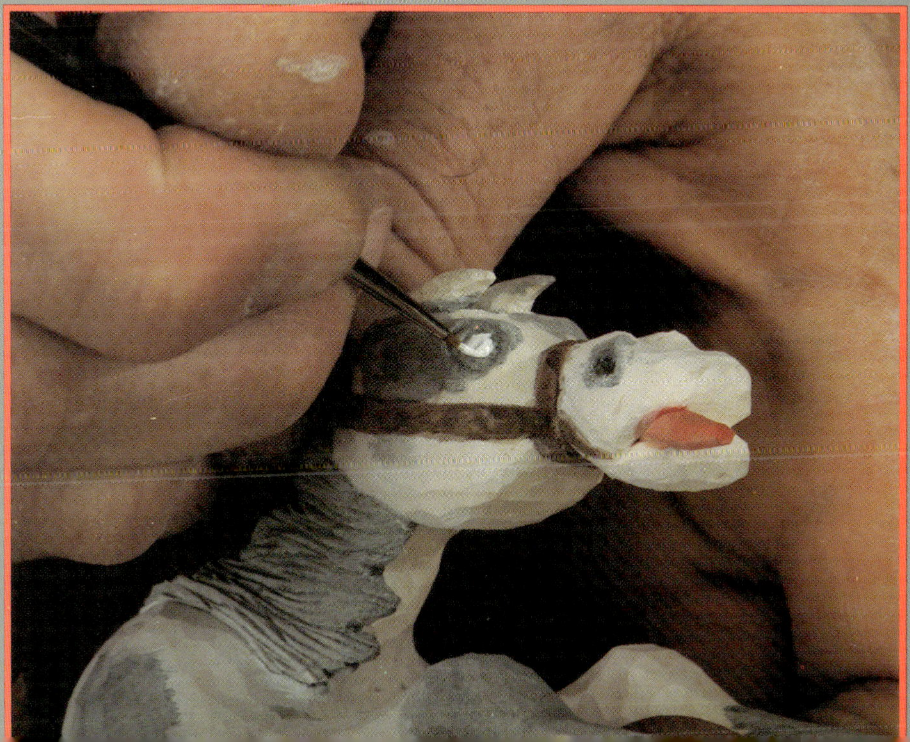

... and the horse as well.

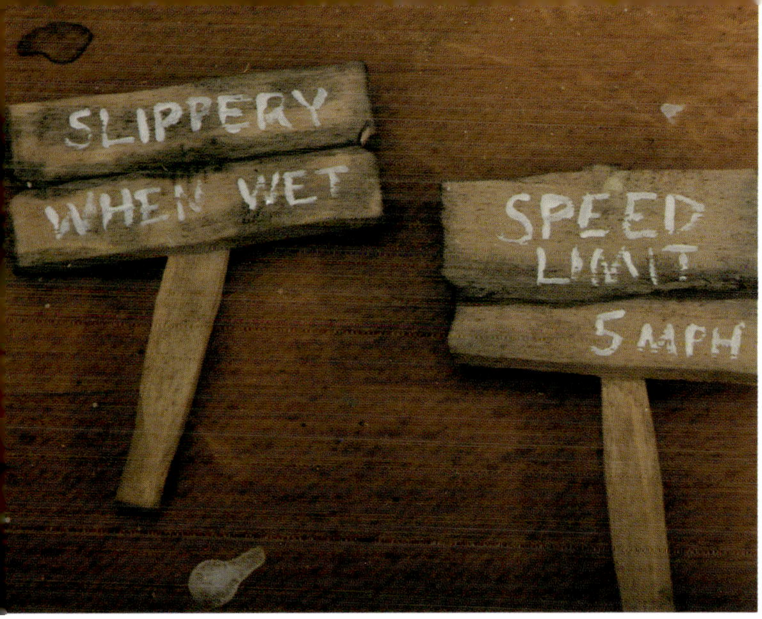

While we're into the undiluted white and using the small brush, let's paint our signs. We want these to look home-made and hand-painted. Don't take a lot of pains with them.

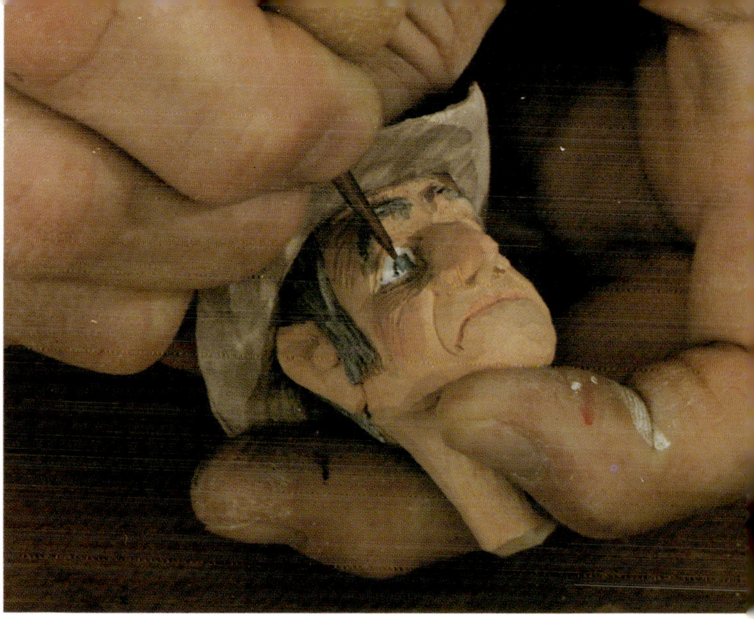

Using a fine point ink pen, draw the iris onto each eyeball. Use undiluted Blue Haze #2122 to paint each iris. Do not cover up the black line.

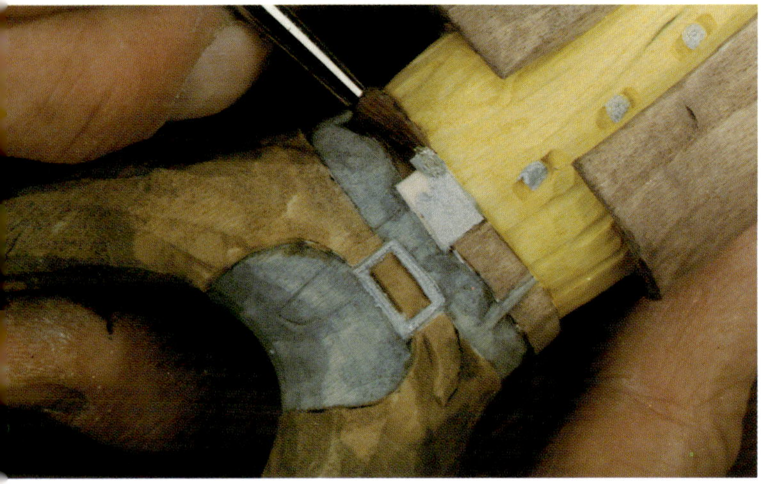

Use undiluted Silver #6003 to paint the buttons, buckles ...

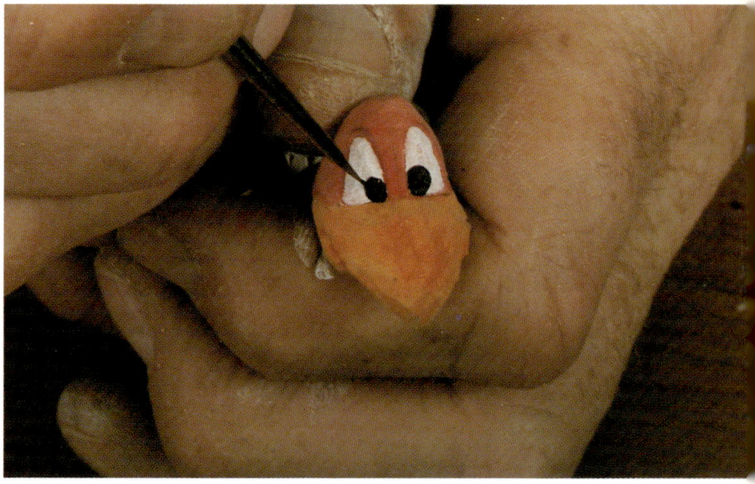

Use undiluted black to paint the pupils of the buzzard's eyes.

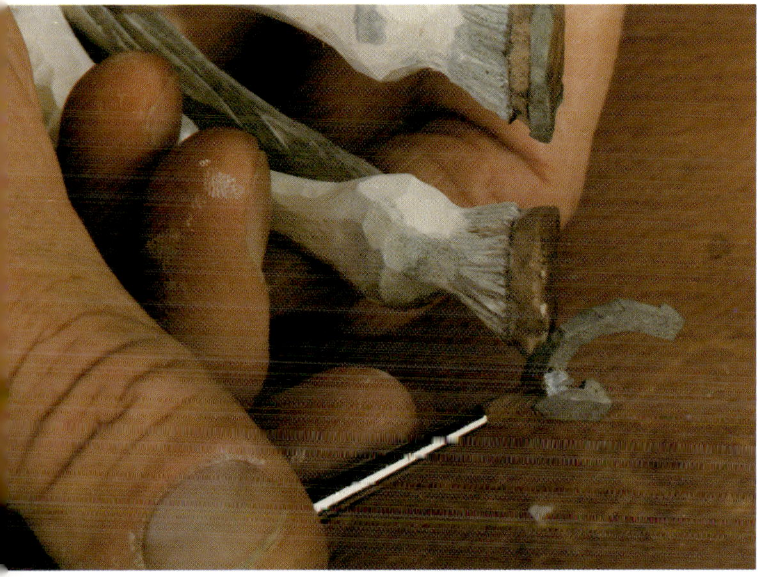

... and the nail attaching the loose horse shoe to the hoof.

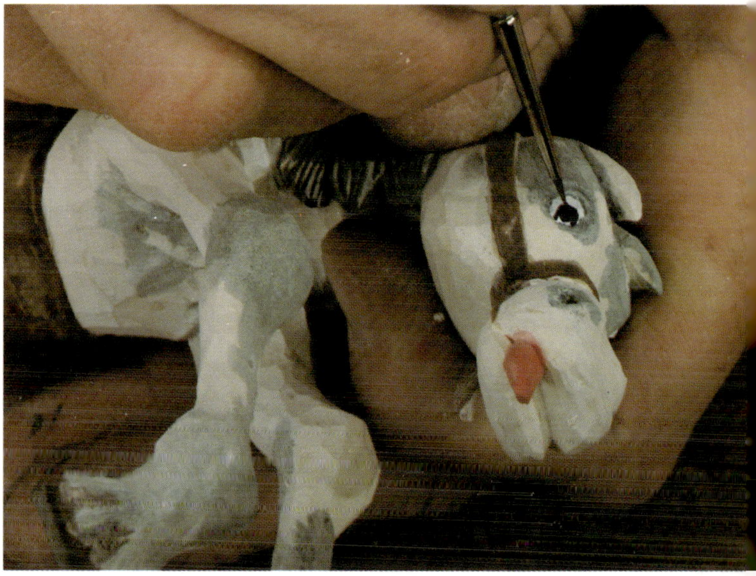

Use undiluted black to paint the horse's pupils.

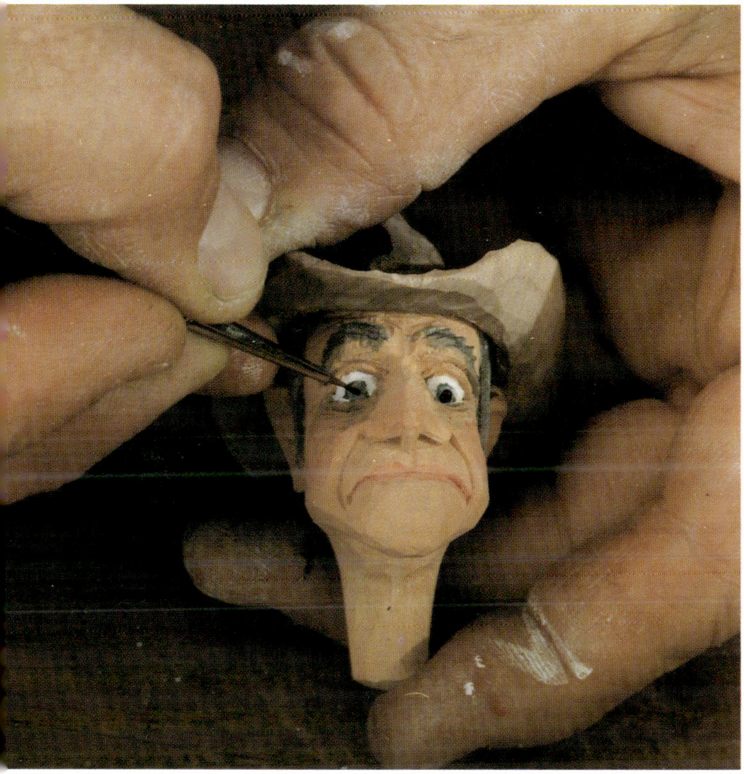

Using undiluted black paint a large pupil in the center of each iris of the cowboy's eyes. Fright increases pupil size.

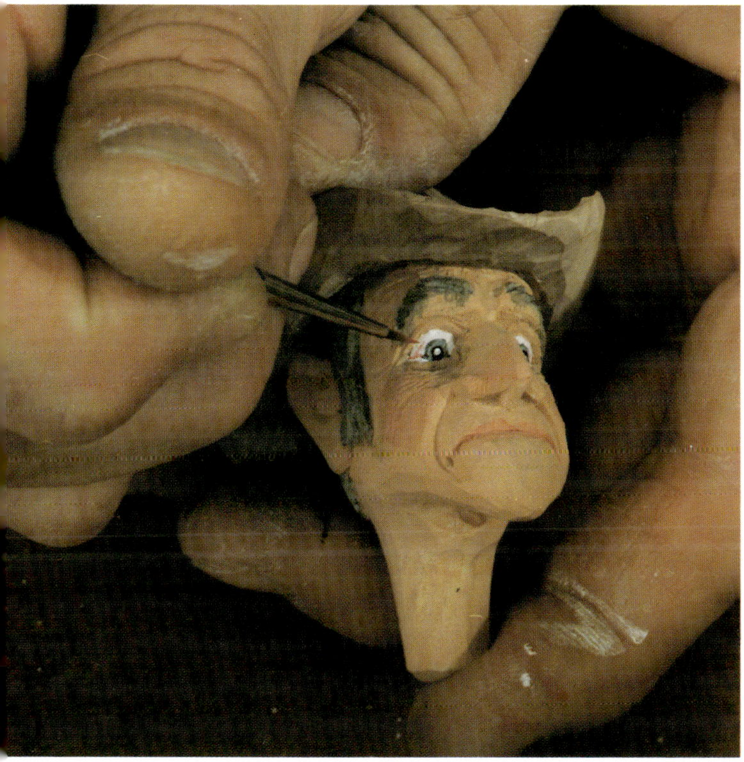

Using undiluted white, place a small dot on each pupil of the cowboy's eyes to simulate the reflection of light. Use undiluted red and dry brush some streaks on the white portion of cowboy's eyes. This gives him one more excuse for falling off the trail.

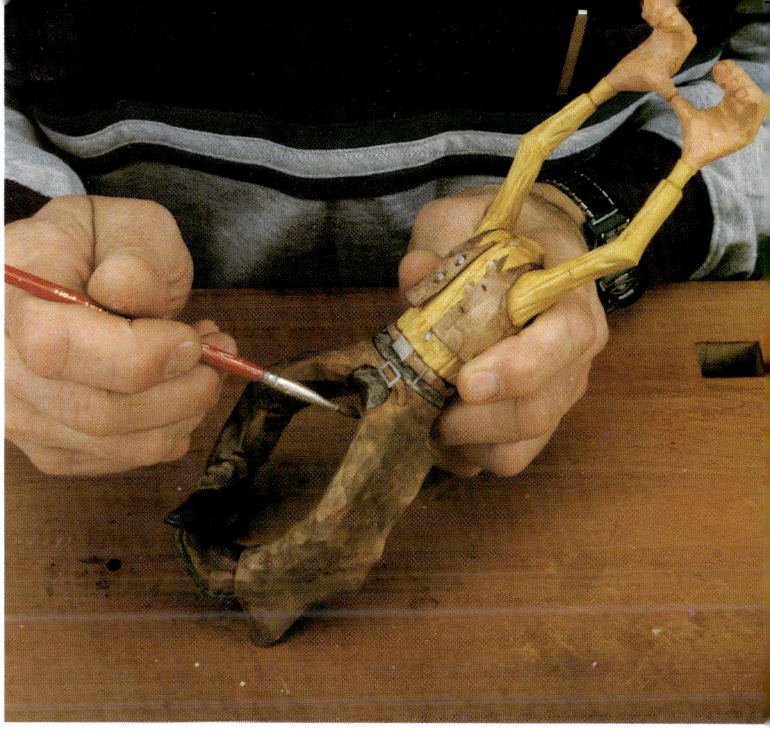

I use a mixture of 10 parts boiled linseed oil to 1 part dark walnut Minwax stain as a sealer and antiquing finish. Use an old, worn out brush and apply this mix liberally to all of the carvings. Wipe the excess solution from the carving. The rag or paper towel used to wipe this solution should be disposed of immediately in an airtight container because this solution has a tendency to spontaneously combust. The final finish that we will apply to this carving is a water base clear matt varnish. The particular brand that I am using presently is Right-Step. Apply this varnish sparingly so as not to create a shine.

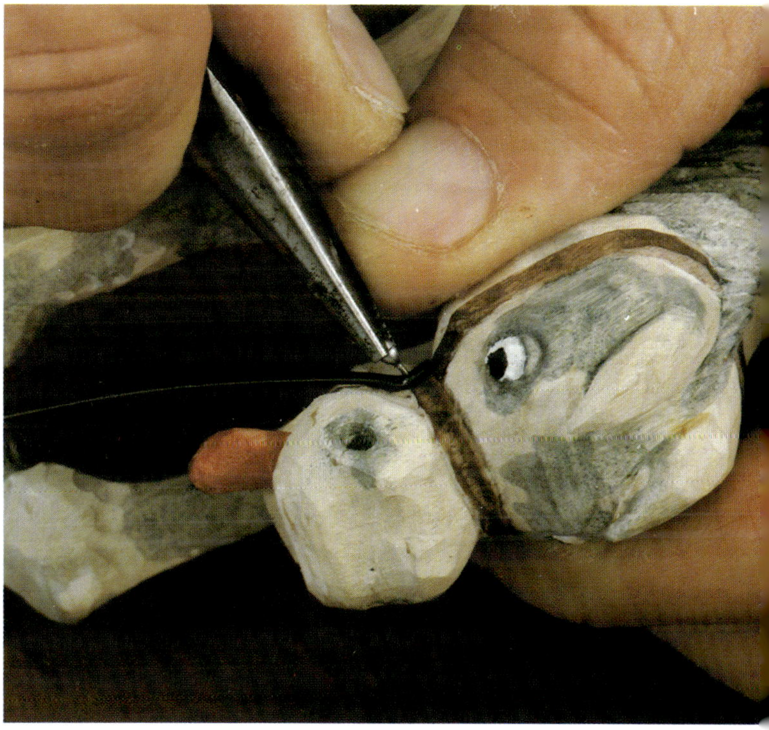

Punch a very small diameter pilot hole along the bridle. This is to receive a straight pin that has been run through the end of an 8" long leather strip. Snip off the end of a straight pin, leaving only 1/4" of it's shaft. Into the pilot hole in the bridle, drop a small amount of Super Glue Gel. Drive the 1/4" long section of straight pin into the pilot hole. Repeat this process on the other side of the horse.

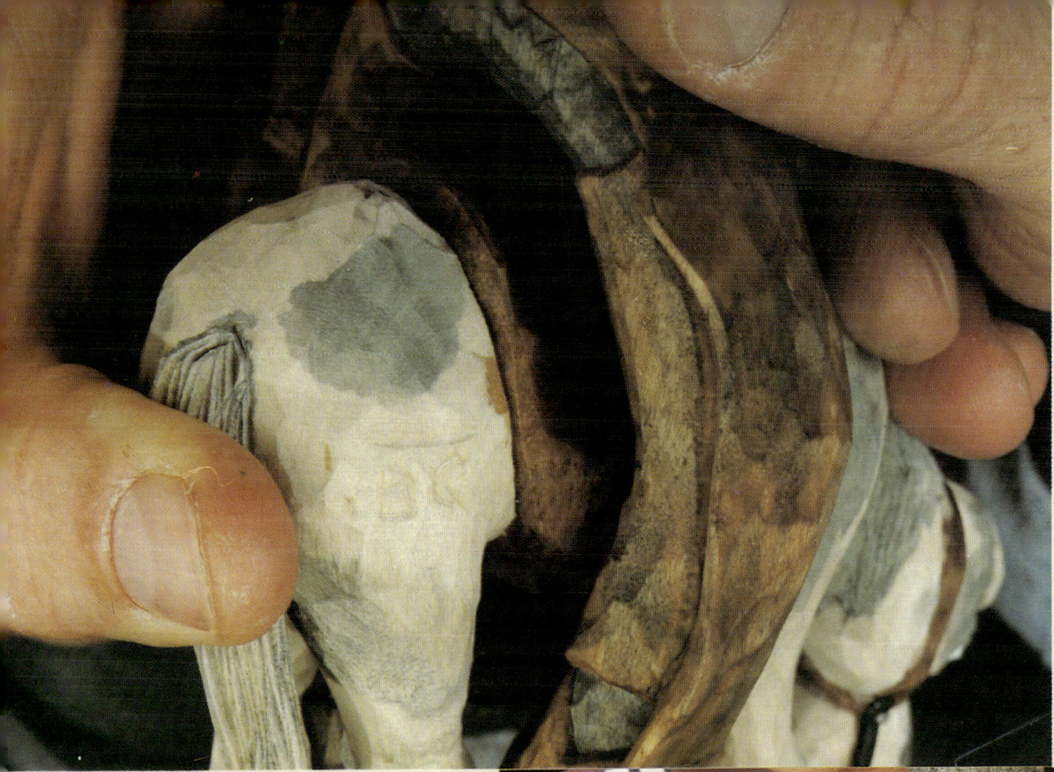

Now fit the two pieces of horse between the cowboy's legs and use Elmer's Glue to seal the two piece of the horse together. Set the horse and cowboy—with his legs wrapped around the horse—aside to dry.

Attach the limb to the cliff base using a 1" drywall screw.

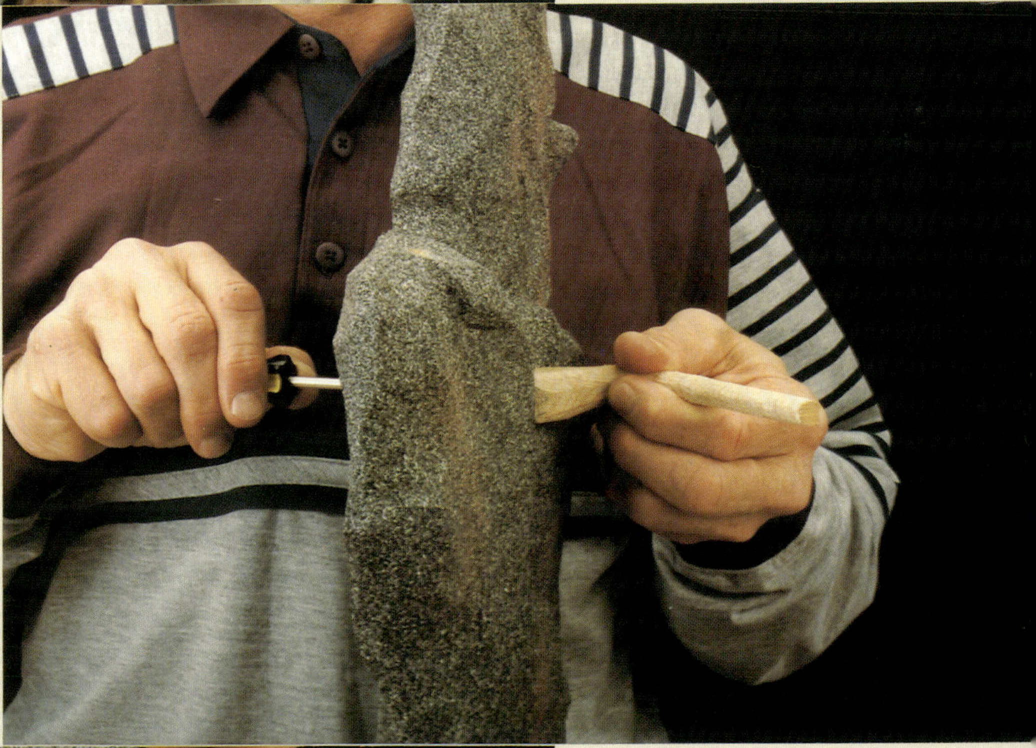

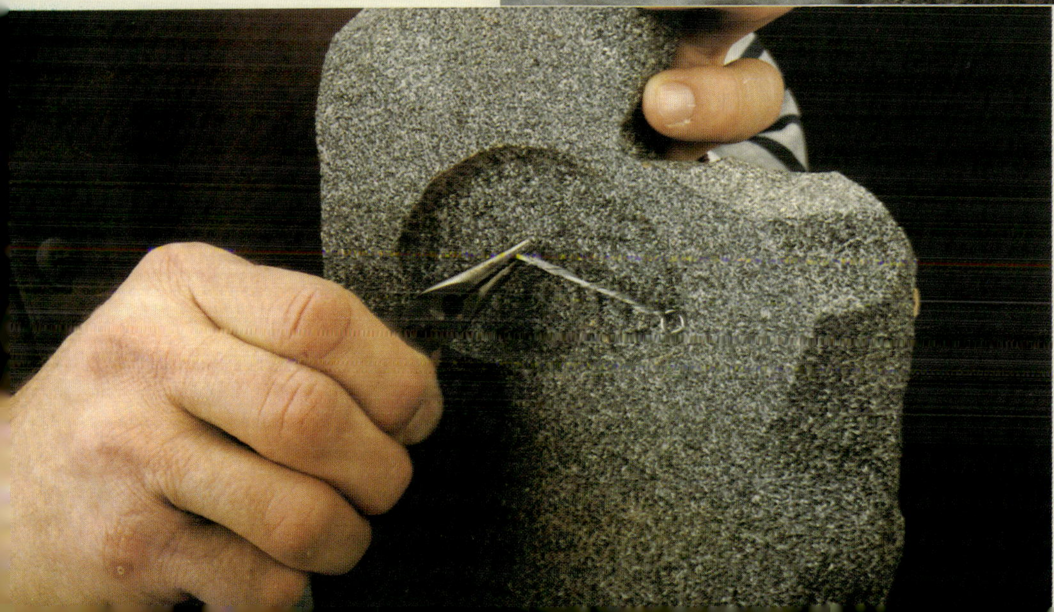

Before we have too many fragile figures attached to the base, let's install our hang wire at the rear.

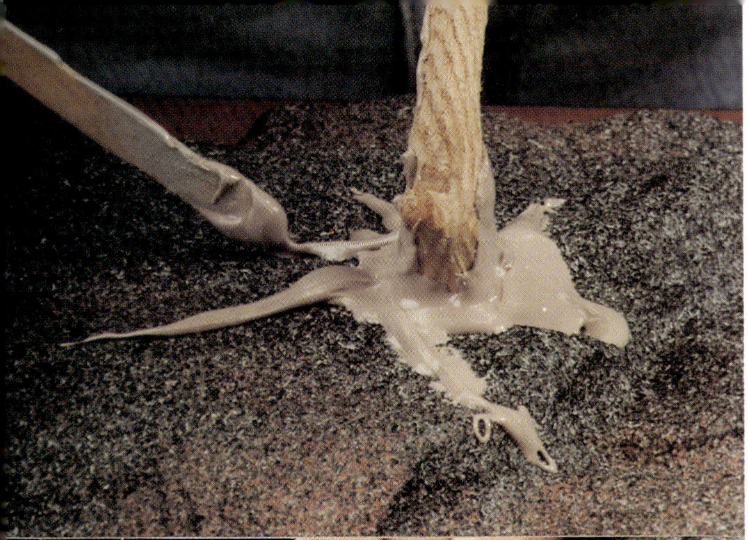

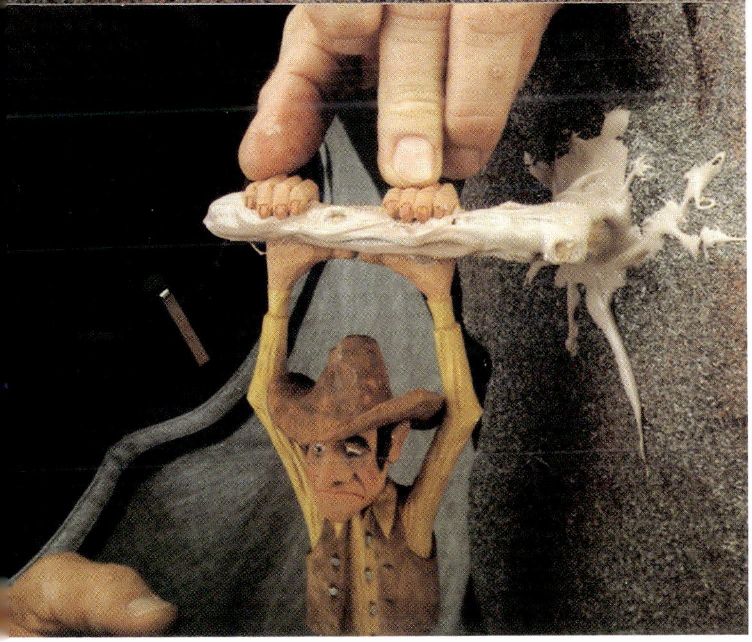

Using Bondo, a two part apoxy filler found at auto stores, fill in around the area where the limb is attached to the base and create a root system on the base itself. Begin to cover the limb with the Bondo but at this point do not go beyond about half way on the limb. We will let this Bondo dry (it will do so within 10 minutes). Once the Bondo has dried, finish covering the rest of the limb with fresh Bondo and attach the cowboy.

Before your Bondo gels, add a small amount to your buzzards feet and set him on his perch.

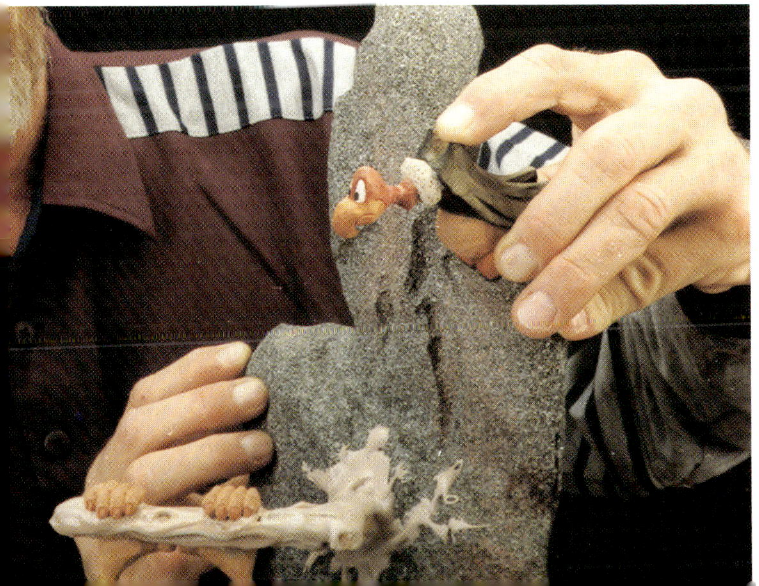

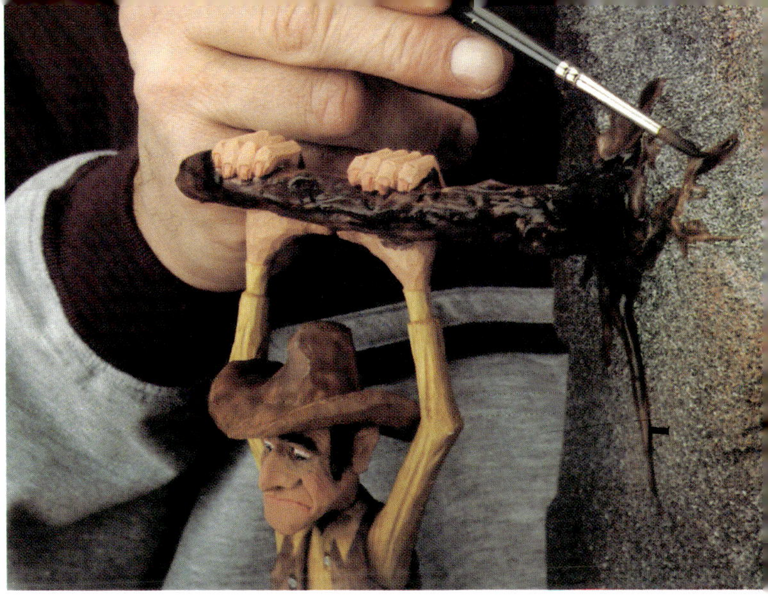

Using undiluted Brown Iron Oxide and undiluted Black, paint the root system. We'll paint the entire root system brown. Before the brown drys we will add some black highlights to add interest and depth to the brown.

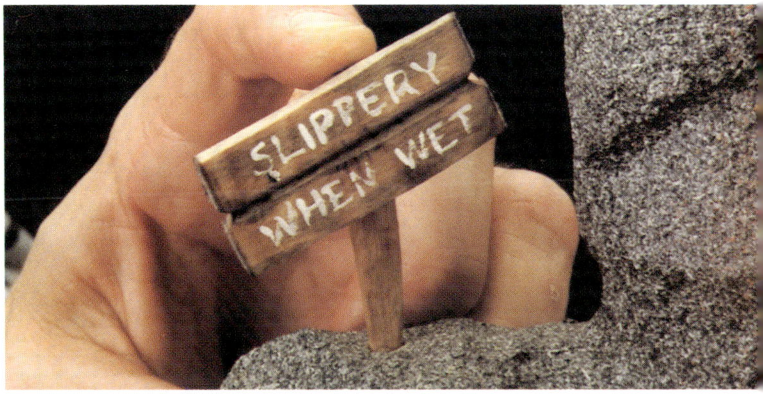

Drill a hole somewhere along the ledge to receive one of our two signs. Glue the sign into the hole...

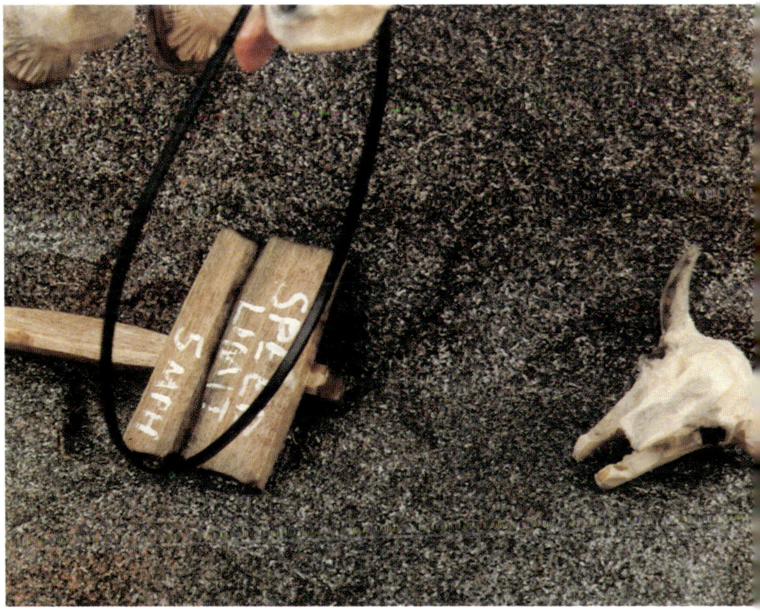

... and the other sign, along with the skull, at the foot of the mountain.

Final shots of the completed cowboy, the cliff, and his predicament.

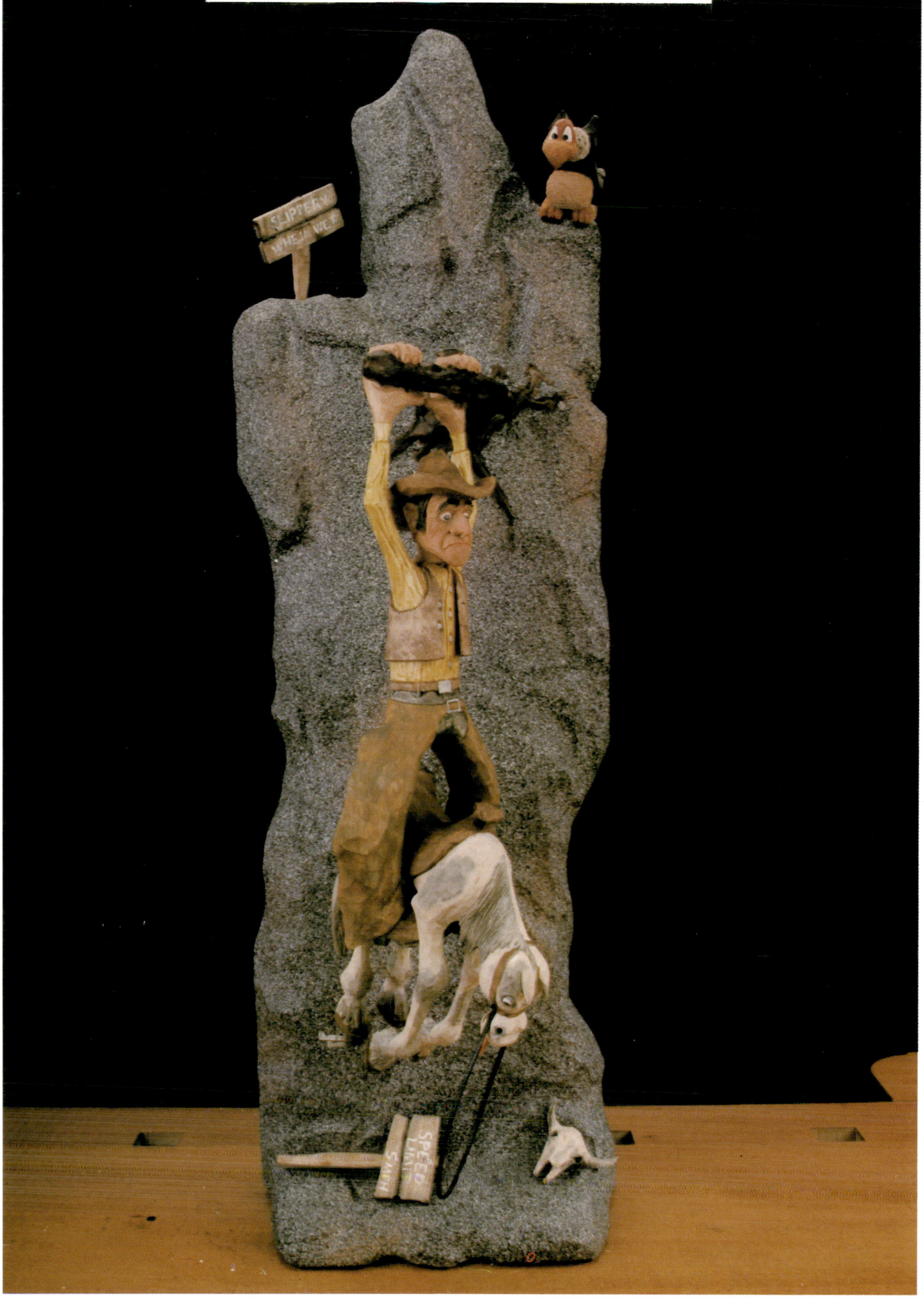

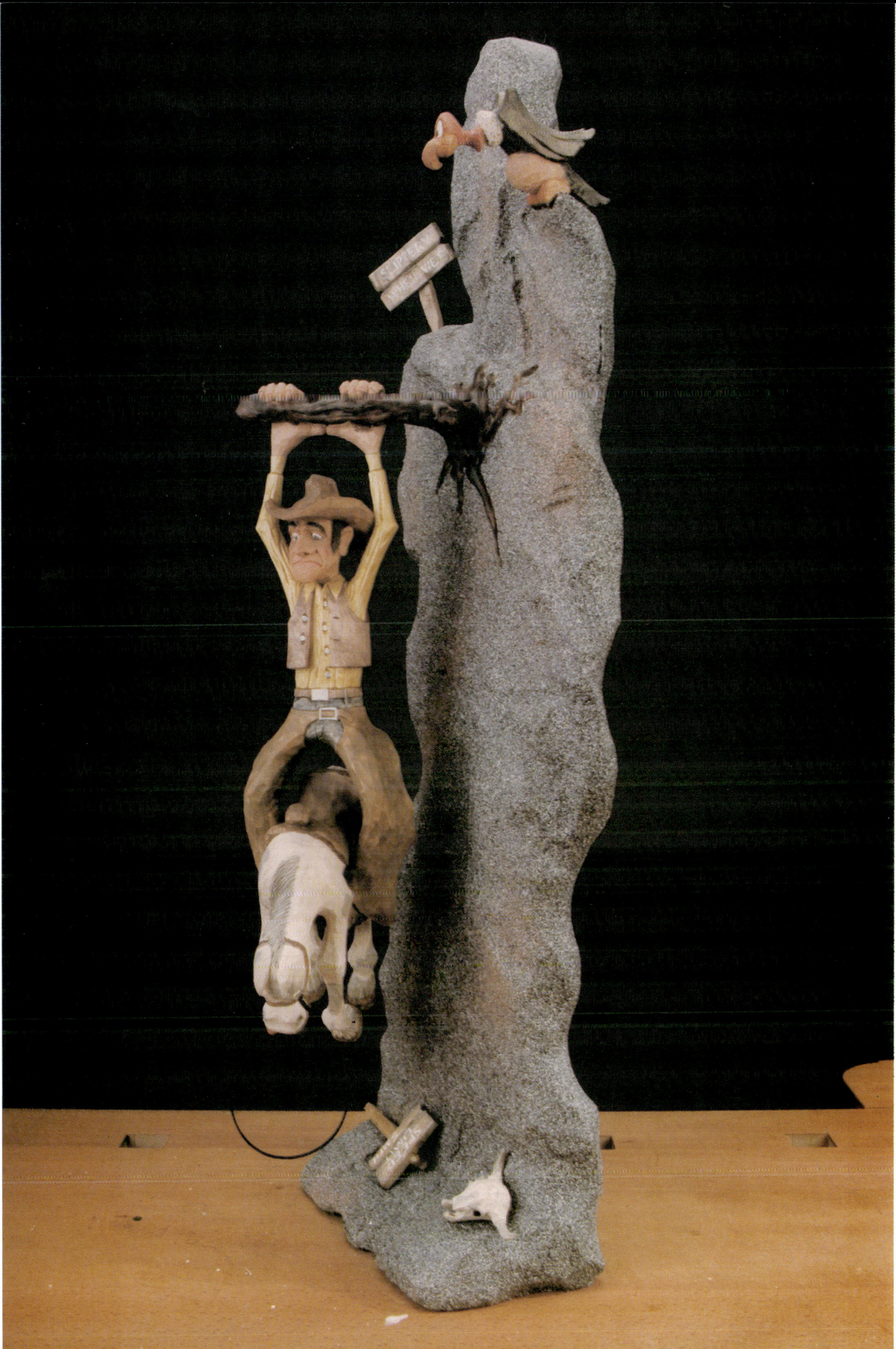

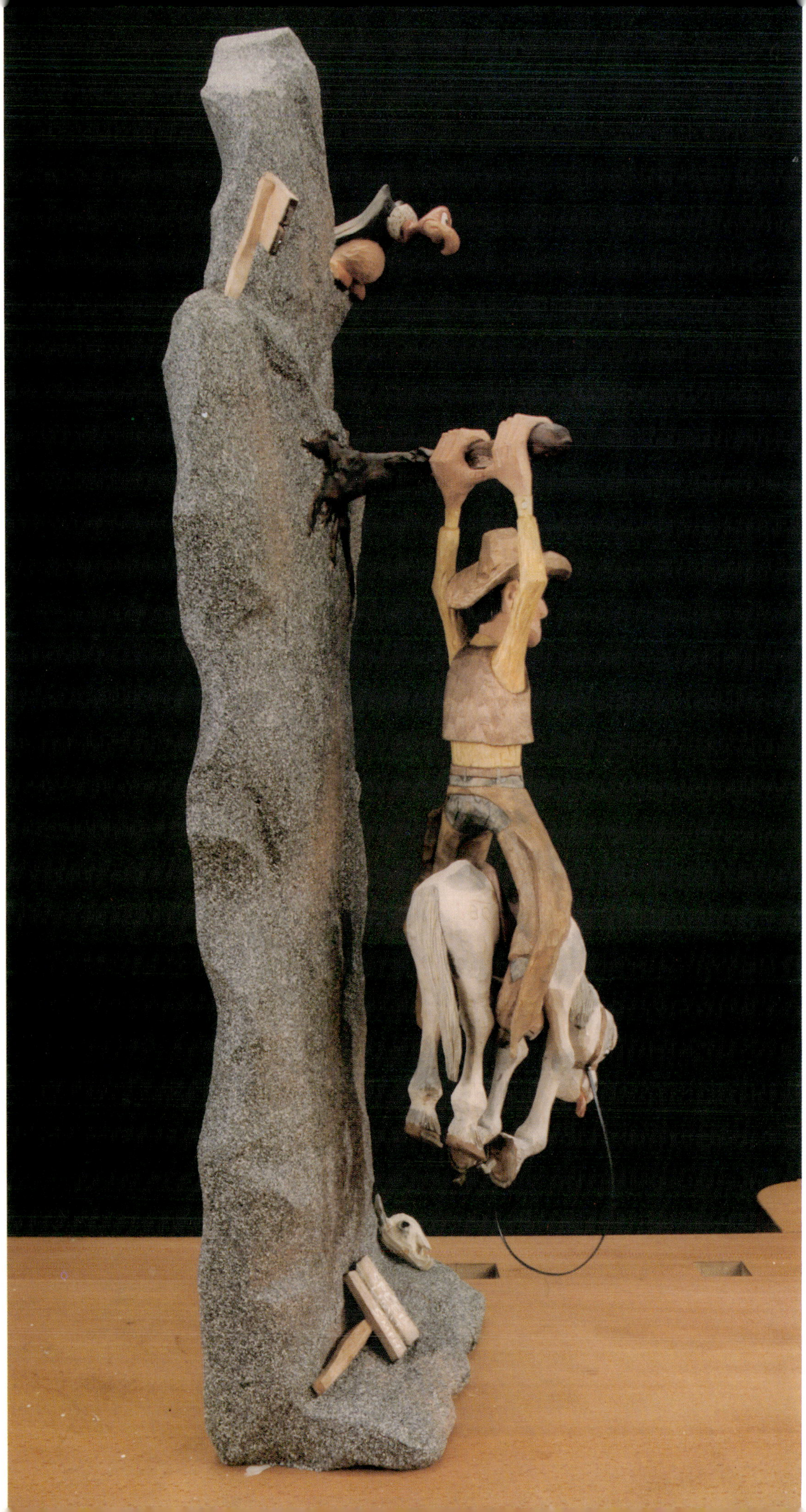

The Gallery

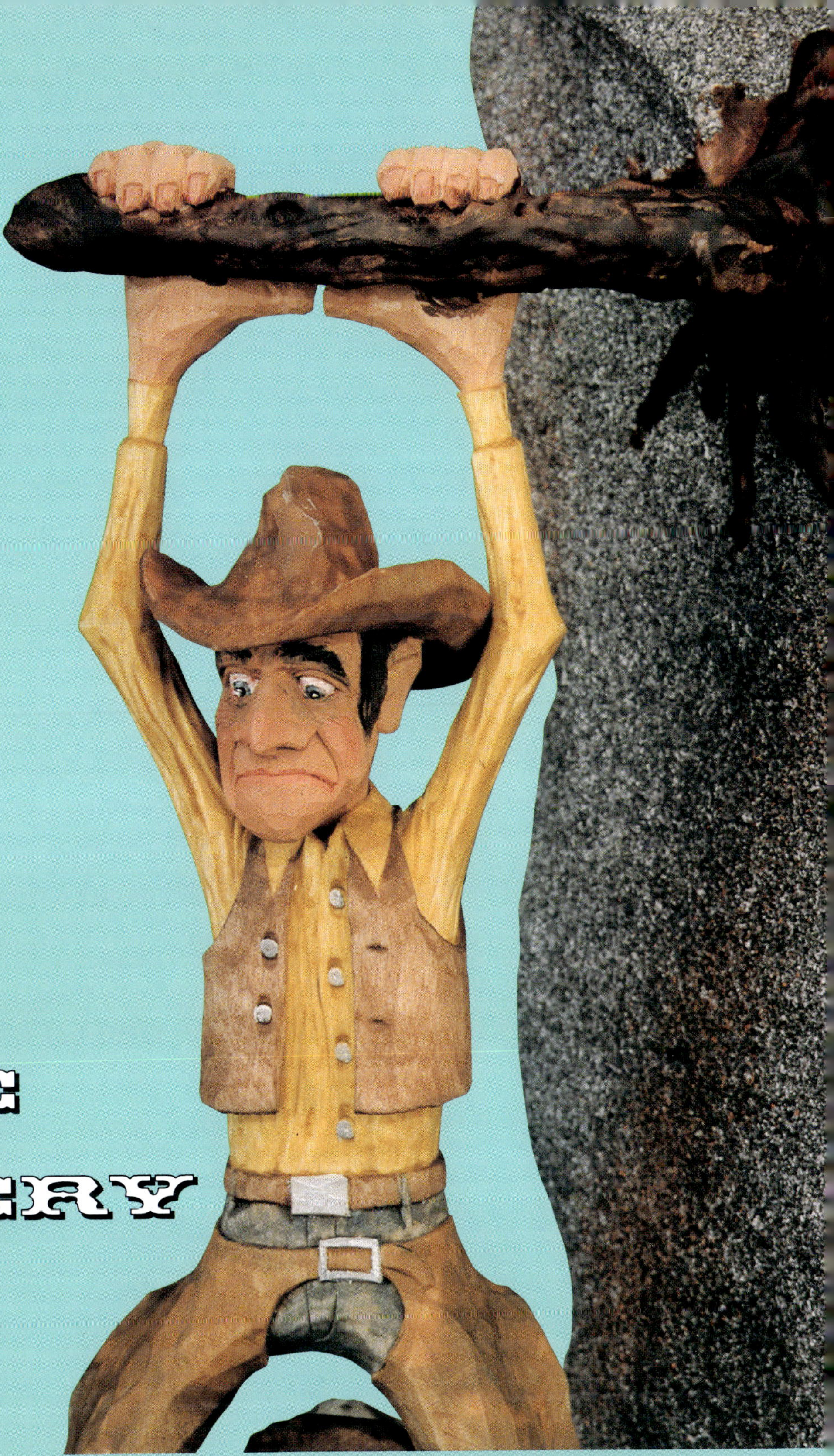

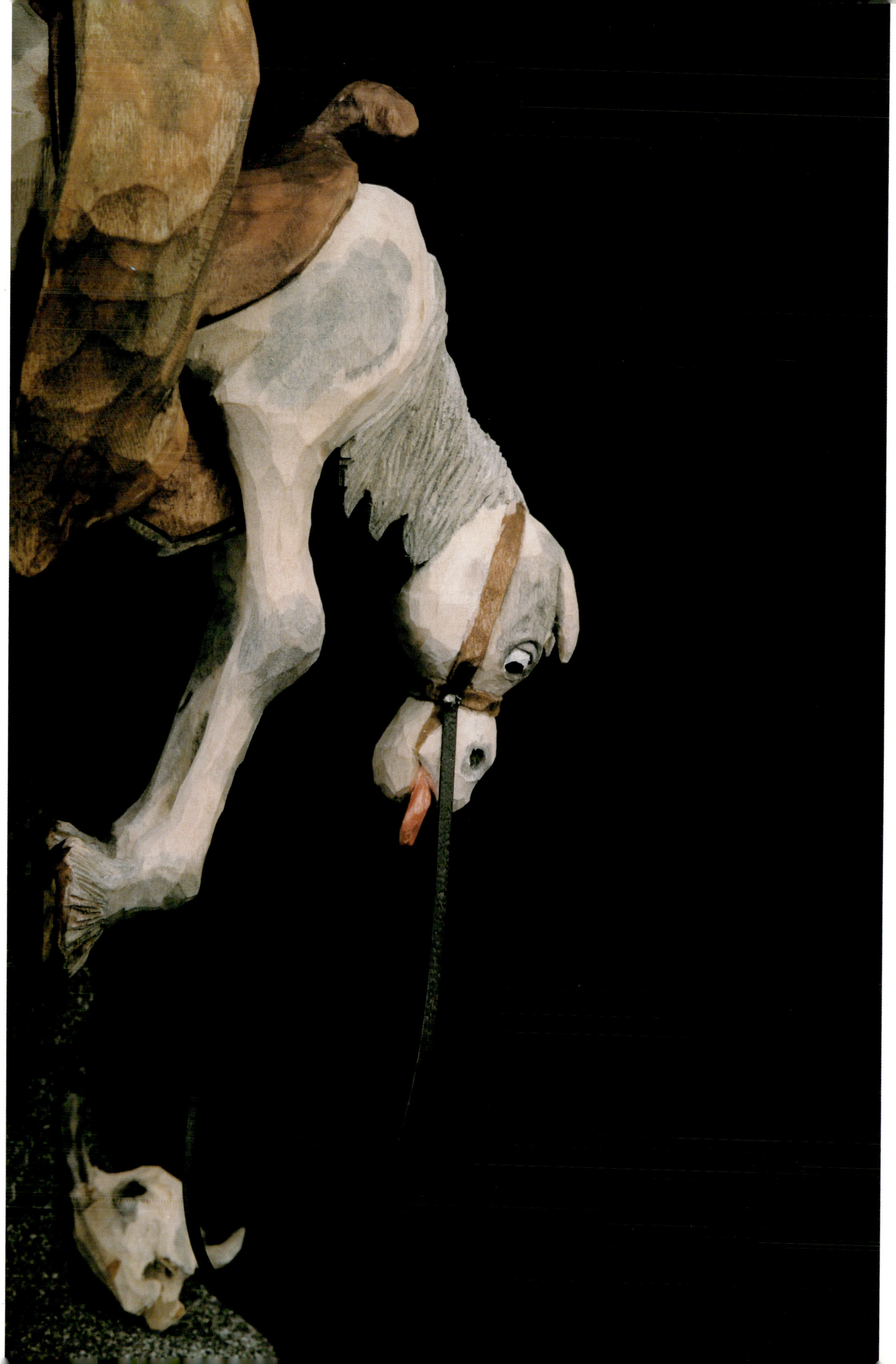

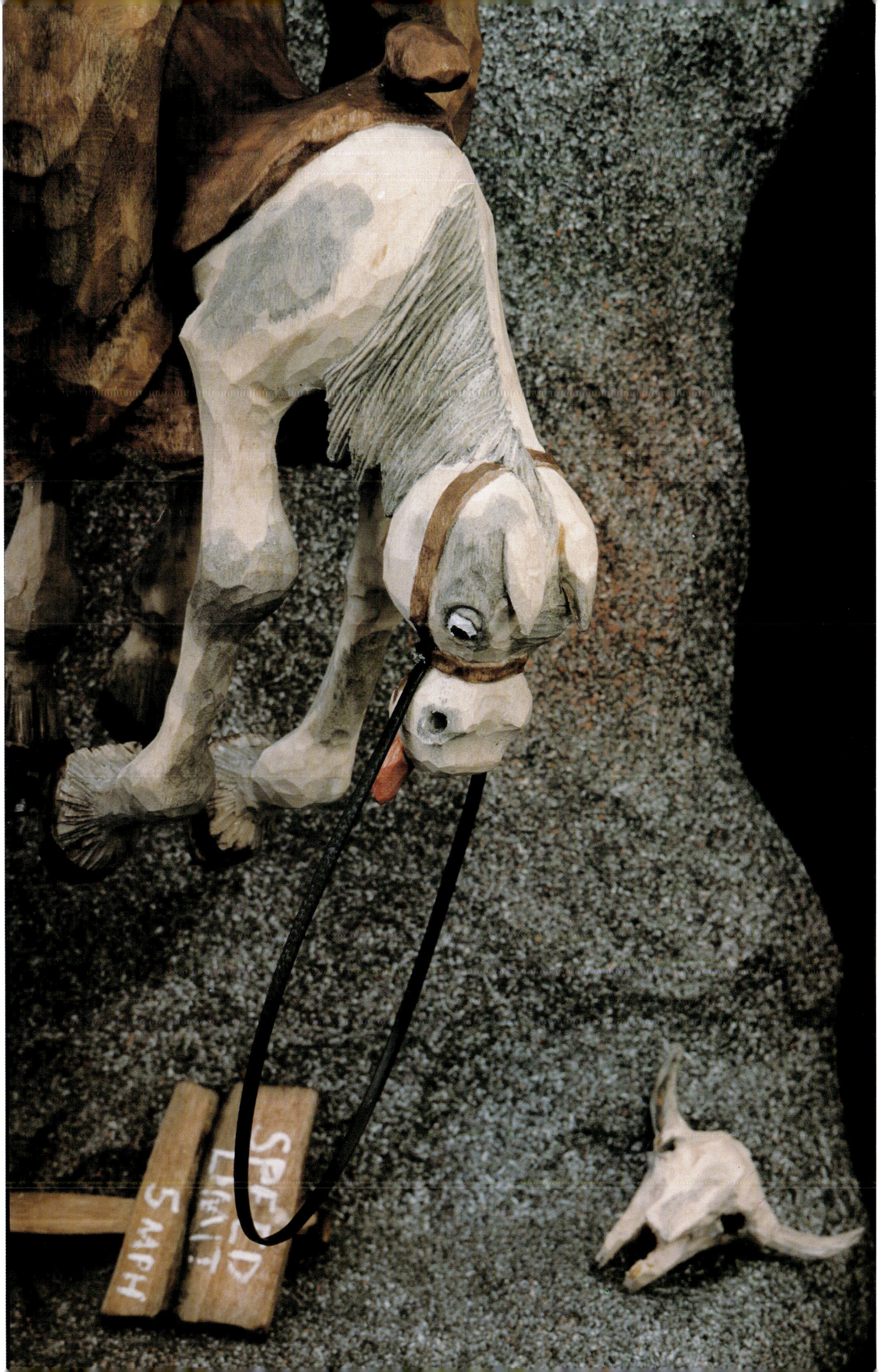
LIMIT
5 MPH

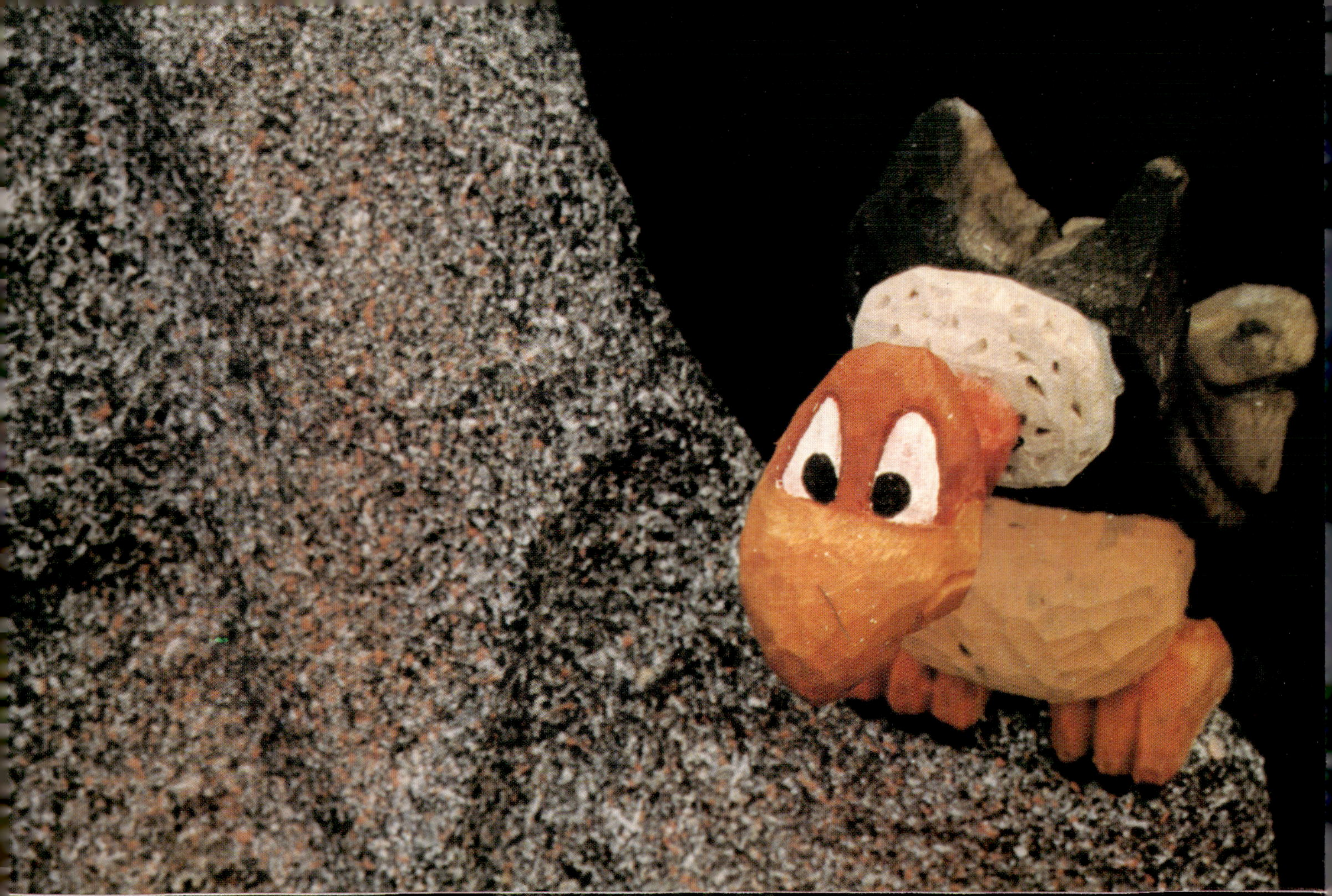

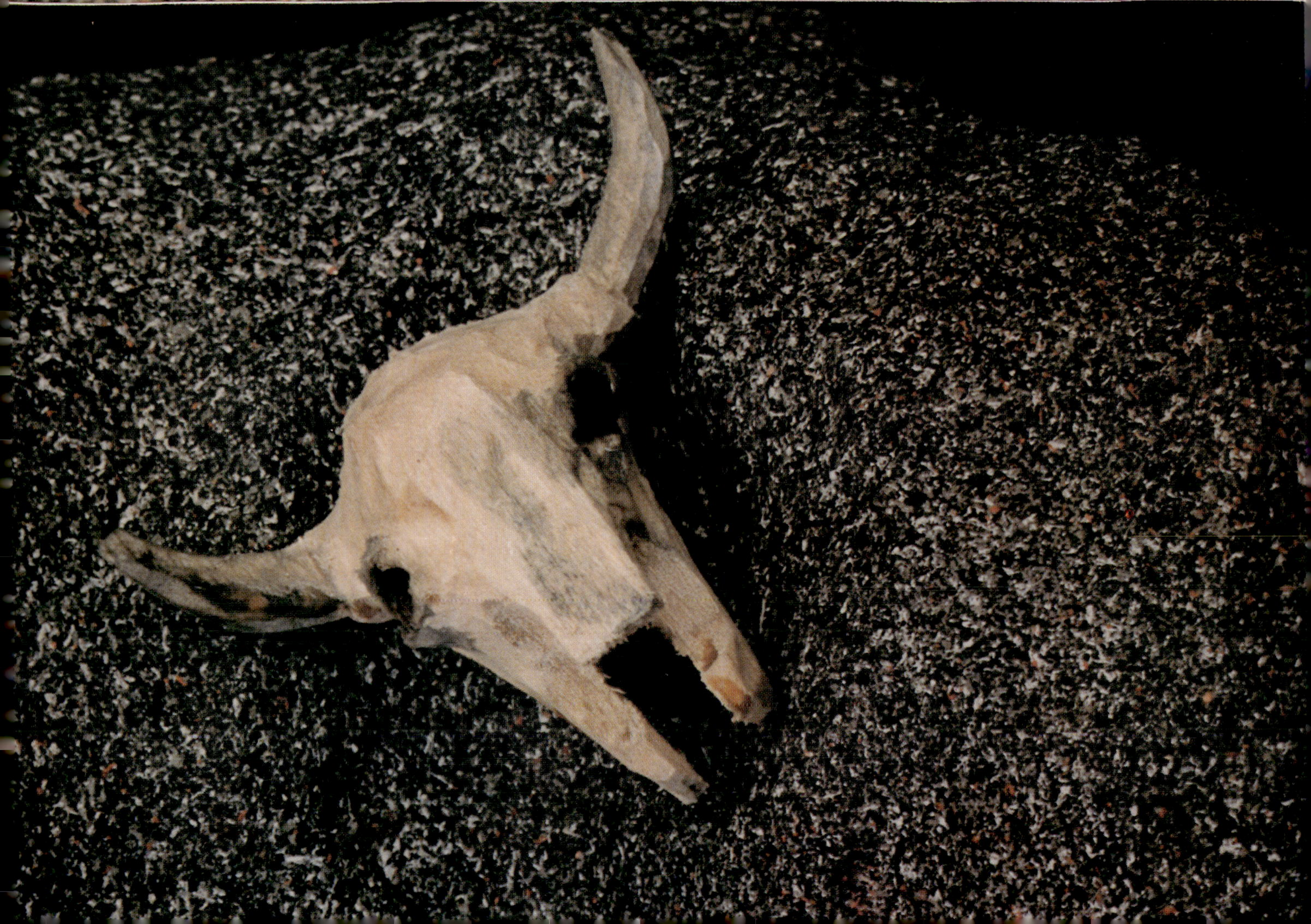

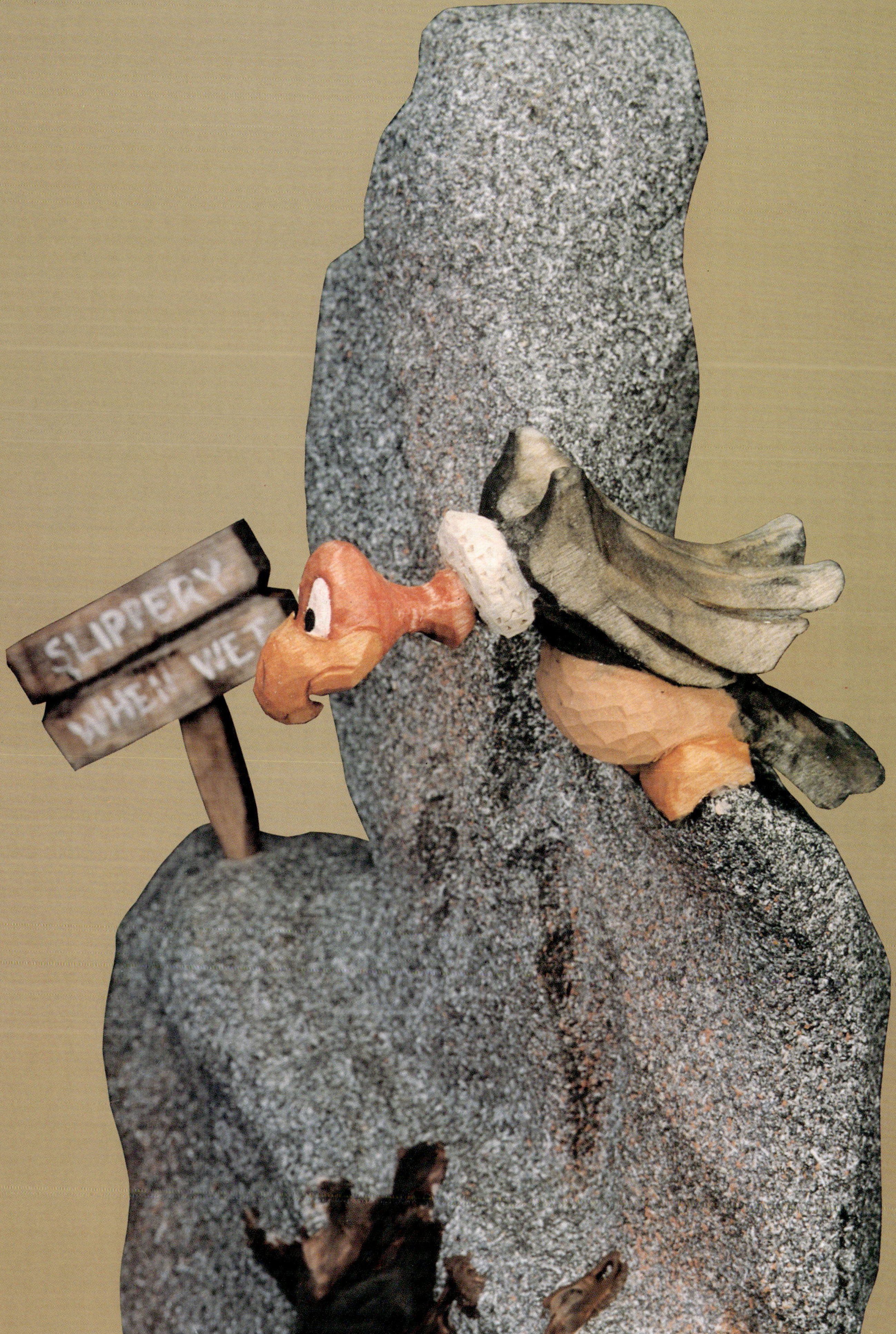
SLIPPERY
WHEN WET

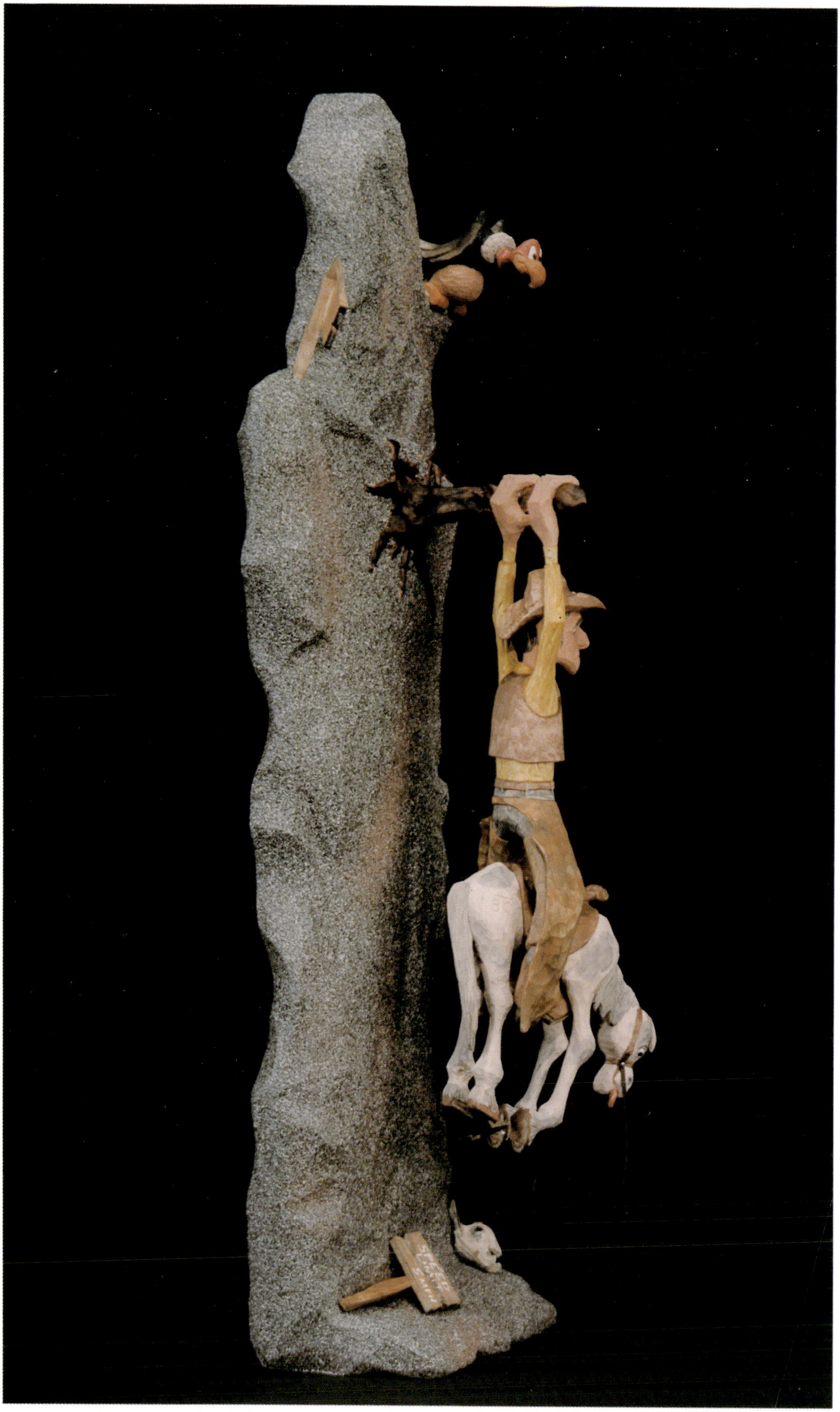

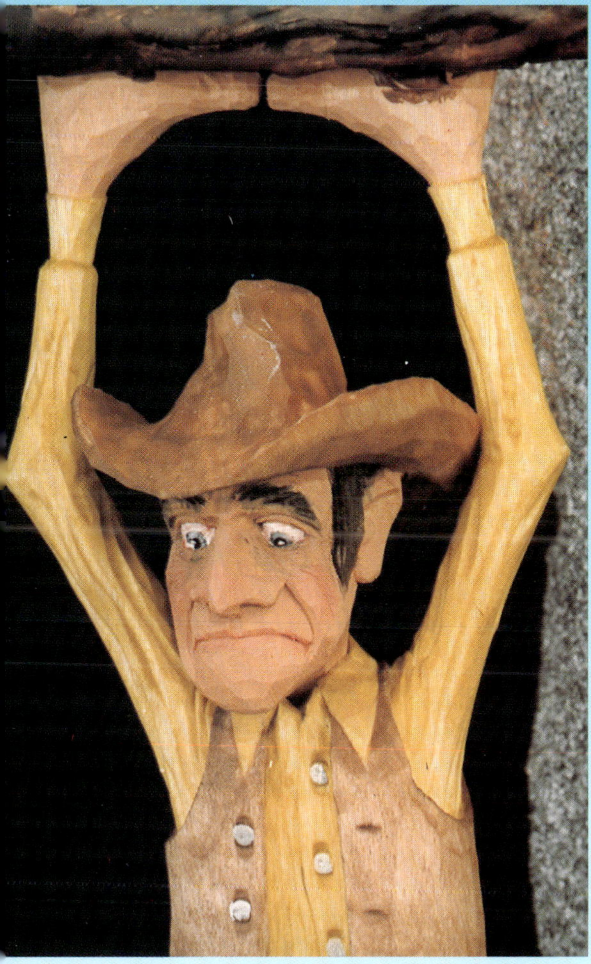

Hangin' In There

with

Cleve Taylor

Text written with and photography by Jeffrey B. Snyder

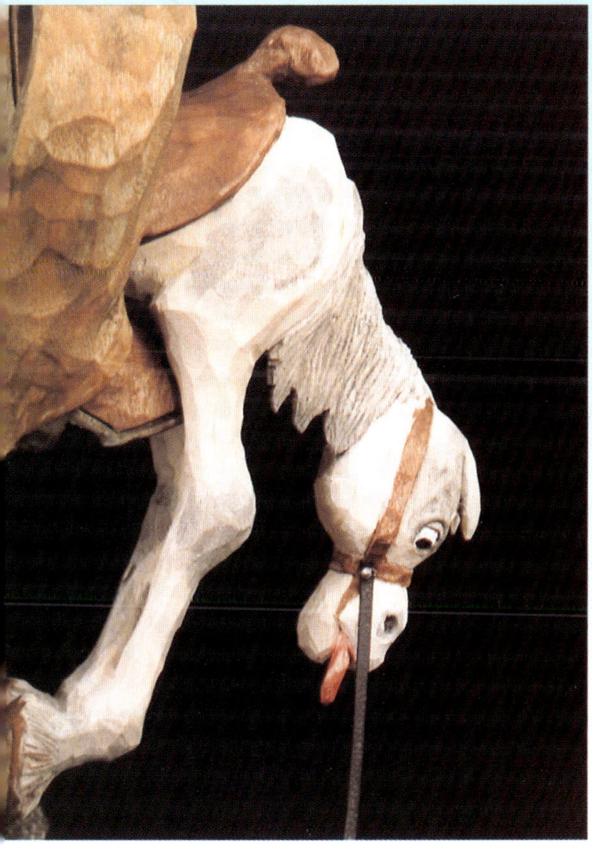

Creative Cowboy Carving

Schiffer Publishing Ltd

77 Lower Valley Road, Atglen, PA 19310

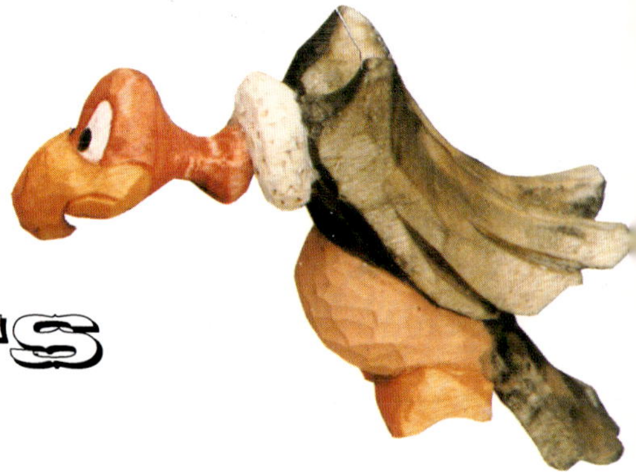

CONTENTS

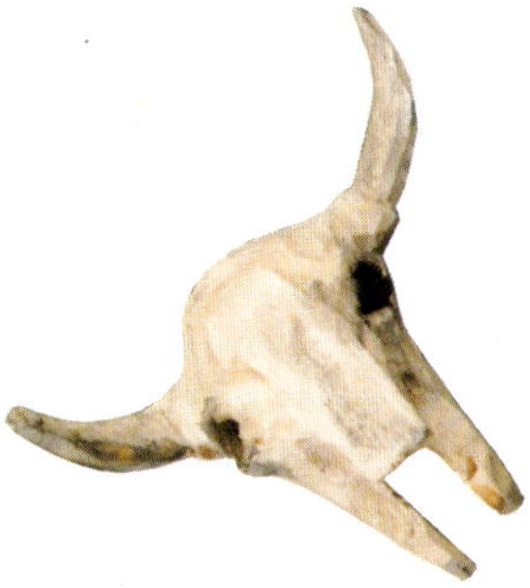

Library of Congress Cataloging-in-Publication Data

Taylor, Cleve.
Hangin' in there : creative cowboy carving / with Cleve Taylor ; text written with and photography by Jeffrey B. Snyder.
p. cm.
ISBN 0-88740-841-9 (paper)
1. Wood-carving -- patterns. 2. Wood-carved figurines. 3. Cowboys in art. I. Snyder , Jeffrey B. II. Title.
TT199.7.T39 1995
731.4' 62--dc20 95-9044
CIP

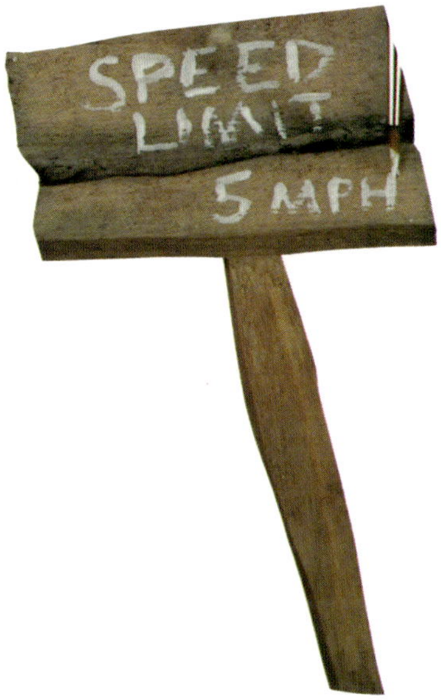

ISBN: 0-88740-841-9

Book Design by Mary Jane (MJ) Hannigan

Printed in China

Published by Schiffer Publishing Ltd.
77 Lower Valley Road
Atglen, PA 19310
Please write for a free catalog.
This book may be purchased from the publisher.
Please include $2.95 postage.
Try your bookstore first.

We are interested in hearing from authors with book ideas on related topics.